OUTLAWS

TONY THOMPSON is widely regarded as one of Britain's top true-crime writers. He has twice been nominated for the prestigious Crime Writer's Association Gold Dagger for Non-Fiction, winning the coveted title for his book *The Infiltrators*. He is the former crime correspondent for the *Observer* and appears regularly on both television and radio as an expert on matters of crime. He lives in London.

OUTLAWS

ONE MAN'S RISE THROUGH
THE SAVAGE WORLD OF RENEGADE BIKERS,
HELL'S ANGELS AND GLOBAL CRIME

TONY THOMPSON

PENGUIN BOOKS

PENGUIN BOOKS
Published by the Penguin Group
Penguin Group (USA) Inc., 375 Hudson Street,
New York, New York 10014, USA

USA | Canada | UK | Ireland | Australia
New Zealand | India | South Africa | China
Penguin Books Ltd, Registered Offices: 80 Strand, London WC2R 0RL, England
For more information about the Penguin Group visit penguin.com

First published in Great Britain by Hodder & Stoughton 2011
Published in Penguin Books 2013

LIBRARY OF CONGRESS CATALOGING-IN-PUBLICATION DATA
Thompson, Tony, 1965–
Outlaws : one man's rise through the savage world of renegade bikers, Hell's
Angels, and global crime / Tony Thompson.
pages   cm
Includes index.
ISBN 978-0-14-242260-1
1. Motorcycle gangs—Great Britain.   2. Motorcycle clubs—Great Britain.
3. Criminals—Great Britain.   4. Gang members—Great Britain.   I. Title.
HV6439.G7T564 2013
364.106′60941—dc23   2013005526

Printed in the United States of America
10 9 8 7 6 5 4 3 2 1

Set in Chronicle Text G4

Designed by Sabrina Bowers

PEARSON

For Harriet

God Forgives, Outlaws Don't
—OUTLAWS MC MOTTO

A one percenter is the one of a hundred of us who has given up on society and the politician's one-way law. This is why we look repulsive. We are saying we don't want to be like you or look like you, so stay out of our face.

Look at your brother standing next to you and ask yourself if you would give him half of what you have in your pocket or half of what you have to eat. If a citizen hits your brother will you be on him without asking him why? There is no why. Your brother isn't always right but he is always your brother! It's one in all in. If you don't think this way then walk away because you are a citizen and don't belong with us.

We are Outlaws and members will follow the Outlaws way or get out. All members are your brothers and your family. You will not steal your brother's possessions, money, woman, class or his humor. If you do, your brother will do you.

—OUTLAWS MC CREED

CONTENTS

PREFACE

In early April 2009, Daniel "Snake Dog" Boone broke the code of silence he had honored since his late teens and agreed to talk to me about his life in an outlaw motorcycle club.

To most people, such clubs are nothing more than an innocent throwback to the sixties, populated by paunchy men with scruffy beards and battered leather jackets, who love to ride their motorcycles and enjoy a good party. The code of silence says different, and members are left in little doubt about the penalties for breaching it. "Three can keep a secret if two are dead," is a common saying among the Hell's Angels, while their rivals, the Outlaws, simply state: "Snitches are a dying breed."

Eager to keep the general public in the dark about what really goes on, the major international clubs—the Angels, the Outlaws and the Bandidos—spend an extraordinary amount of time and energy cultivating a positive public image. They deliver toys to children at Christmas, raise money for worthy charities, and are the driving force behind several mainstream biker rallies. The clubs also file regular lawsuits, citing alleged incidents of police persecution and harassment that they claim are simply due to their desire to live a nonconformist lifestyle. Such harassment is, they insist, wholly undeserved.

Boone knew better. In the course of twenty-three years, he had seen the small back-patch club he had joined in his late teens evolve into something utterly unrecognizable. Slowly but surely, his club turned into a gang—becoming part of an international biker brand steeped in criminality, that put him on the front line of a vicious global conflict that has cost thousands of lives in dozens of countries.

I had written about the criminal activities of motorcycle clubs many times over the years and had come to believe that I knew a fair amount about them. As Boone began to relate his story, it struck me that, in reality, I knew almost nothing. The sheer scale of his operations, the astonishing level of complexity of the networks involved, the depths of depravity and the backdrop of extraordinary, casual violence around which his life revolved simply took my breath away.

I knew the bikers had started out as idealistic rebels, gotten involved in low-level drug dealing and prostitution and then expanded into mainstream criminality. I also knew that the pursuit of profit had ultimately led the clubs to wage war on one another, first in America then on new battlefronts in Canada, Australia, Scandinavia, Germany, Ireland, Spain and Turkey not to mention much of central Europe. What I was unaware of was just how those wars had affected the bikers themselves and fundamentally changed the very nature of what it meant to ride around with a patch on your back.

In his early days with the club, Boone had loved to ride his motorcycle purely for the hell of it, heading off whenever and wherever the mood took him. By the time he came to leave, it was simply too dangerous for him to ride anywhere unless he was part of a much larger group of bikers escorted by several security cars at the front and rear.

Under orders to remain armed at all times—his black 9 mm semi-automatic pistol was rarely out of reach—Boone increasingly felt as though he were living in a military compound. Even if he was just popping out for cigarettes, he could never leave his fortified clubhouse without checking the CCTV cameras to make sure there was no ambush waiting or that his vehicle hadn't been booby-trapped.

Depending on the alert status issued by the club's high command, there were times when he was unable to contact his family for days or even weeks at a time. Regardless of the security situation, he was forbidden to speak to them about any of his club activities or duties, all of which had to take preference over family birthdays, anniversaries and other special occasions. Virtually every aspect of Boone's life was governed by a code of conduct and a series of rules, the most crucial of which were printed in a compact booklet that commanded as much respect as the Holy Bible. Aside from a few minor variations, every club in the world operates under a similar set of rules.

For a long time, it was a life Boone would not have traded for anything. He snorted his way through a mountain of drugs and sank endless gallons of beer. He indulged in threesomes and foursomes and gang bangs by the score. He was shot, stabbed twice and involved in more fights than he could remember. He evaded car bombs, snipers and samurai sword-wielding would-be assassins and somehow lived to tell the tale.

What I liked most about that tale was that, throughout his time with the club, Boone seemed to have an extraordinary knack for being in the right place at the right time. Whether he was inadvertently setting off the brutal Great Nordic Biker War during a visit to Denmark, under siege in Canada, visiting the site of Australia's most notorious biker massacre or nearly being shot at point-blank range in a Florida clubhouse after unwittingly insulting the club's psychotic international president, Boone had truly seen it all.

Over the years, he personally traded vast quantities of narcotics, stole and fenced hundreds of motorcycles, bought and sold guns, set up elaborate frauds and regularly participated in armed "hunting" expeditions that went out looking for members of enemy biker gangs to maim or kill.

It is important to note that Boone is a member of a group that exists in violent and bitter opposition to the Hell's Angels. As such, his story comes with a certain degree of bias. This should not in any way be taken to be any kind of endorsement or preference for one MC over another. Had Boone been a Hell's Angel, his bias toward opposing clubs would be equally strong. As with any conflict, both sides fervently believe in the nobility of their cause, the superiority of their moral code and their absolute right to terminate the existence of the enemy. Seeing all this through the eyes of one side of the biker wars makes it easier to gain an understanding of the opposing view and understand why such conflicts endure.

While not all members of biker clubs are involved in criminal activity, those that are exert massive influence over the trade in cocaine, cannabis and methamphetamine, right from manufacture and importation down to street-level sales. Having infiltrated major ports around the world, they are able to ease the passage of guns, drugs and other contraband into Europe and North America. They also dabble in extortion, prostitution, protection and fraud. In recent years, bikers in Australia have expanded their repertoire to include the illegal trade in exotic animals. According to the FBI, motorcycle gangs collect one billion dollars in illegal income every year.

Bikers operate on a global scale most gangsters can only dream about. The Gambino family, once headed by "Dapper Don" John Gotti and one of five New York-based syndicates that control organized crime in the city and beyond, has at most two hundred members. At the time of writing, the Hell's Angels have around thirty-six hundred members spread throughout thirty countries on six continents. Together, the Outlaws and the Bandidos have a further four thousand members in at least sixteen countries.

It is a formidable international criminal network that continues to grow and evolve. Some of the very newest clubs, like Australia's Notorious and the German chapters of the Mongols, have now dispensed with the motorcycles altogether and are simply gangsters in leather jackets.

In the course of researching this book, I made an official approach to the Outlaws MC hoping to interview a respected former member in order to clarify some of the finer points of the club's early UK history. The request was categorically denied. The club's business, I was told, is no one's business except for members of the club itself.

Boone saw things differently. He still feels enormous loyalty to his club and his many, many tattoos attest to the fact that it will always be a huge part of his life, yet he is willing to risk death threats from his former comrades to reveal the inner workings of this hidden, secretive world. "There's a war going on and it's getting worse," he told me. "People don't have a clue why we do what we do, why people get hurt, why people get killed. To truly understand you have to be there, you have live through it, or at least hear it from someone that did. That's why I'm talking."

Boone's story starts in a small town in the heart of the English countryside but it could have started anywhere in the world. United by their love of biking, fighting and brotherhood and their desire to live as outsiders, it tells how young men evolve from social misfits to organized criminals and then ultimately to cold-blooded killers. This is the story of how bikers are born and made, and how and why they die.

—Tony Thompson
London, 2012

ACKNOWLEDGMENTS

Huge thanks to Boone for sharing his story with me and to the many other MC members, both past and present, who gave assistance despite, in some cases, being told not to do so. Thanks also to the dynamic duo of Caroline Dawnay and Olivia Hunt at United Agents, Dan Mandel at Sanford J. Greenburger, and to my wonderful editor, Kevin Doughten at Viking Penguin.

AUTHOR'S NOTE

This is a true story. However, in order to protect sources, many of whom remain active members of the one-percenter world, some names and identifying details have been changed.

PATCH RULES

Bikers can be found riding en masse in every city in every country across all four corners of the planet. Often they are drawn together because they are fans of a particular make or model of machine, or because they live in a certain area, but more often than not they bond simply through the sheer joy of riding. Many such clubs identify themselves with "patches" or "colors" sewn onto their jackets, but what untrained eyes see as random choices over positions and designs are actually the result of delicate and lengthy negotiations within the complex world of international biker politics.

The majority of organized bikers belong to MCCs (motor cycle clubs) and wear their patches on the front or side of their jackets. Joining such a club is easy and requires little in the way of ongoing commitment. Patches are available for purchase by anyone who turns up to a rally or meeting and the main goal of the club is to enhance the social life of its members.

At the other end of the scale are the MCs (motorcycle clubs). The absence of that one letter makes a world of difference. MC patches cannot be bought, only earned, a process that can take many years and is by no means guaranteed.

MC members wear a three-part, back patch, sometimes sewn directly onto a jacket but usually emblazoned on a leather or denim vest. The club name appears at the top on a curved bar known as a "rocker." The club colors are in the center, whereas a bottom rocker will name the territory. Probationary members—known as prospects—wear only the bottom rocker as a mark of their reduced status.

The major MCs also sport a diamond-shaped "1%" patch on the front of their colors. This originates from the 1947 drag race meeting attended by thousands of bikers in the small town of Hollister, California—a wild street party that supposedly descended into a massive, drunken riot (although there was a fair amount of disorder, it would later be alleged that pictures of inebriated bikers had been staged and events heavily exaggerated by the press). When outraged motorcycle enthusiasts defended themselves and their reputations to the press, they insisted that 99 percent of bikers were well-behaved citizens, it was just that last "one percent" who were nothing more than "outlaws." The term caught on and MC gangs have called themselves "one percenters" ever since.

It is impossible to overstate the importance of a set of patches to an MC member. They are his most prized possession and the loss of them under almost any circumstances is an unbearable disgrace. Patches are absolutely sacred and it is no exaggeration to say that MC members consider them worth fighting for and, if necessary, dying for.

With painfully few exceptions—such as when two new clubs emerge from an unclaimed area at roughly the same time—no new MC will ever wear a bottom rocker laying claim to an occupied area, unless they are prepared to declare outright war on the current incumbents. (When the Mongols MC launched in the early 1970s, their members wore a "California" bottom rocker, much to the annoyance of the Hell's Angels, who not only dominated the west coast state but also considered it sacred: the gang had been founded there in the aftermath of World War II. The Angels warned the Mongols to remove the rocker. The Mongols, composed mostly of Hispanic Vietnam veterans who had been refused entry to their local HA chapters on account of their ethnicity, stood their ground and, aside from the occasional truce, the two clubs have been at war ever since.)

The one-percenter gangs not only control their own territory but also oversee the activities of all other MCC and MC biker clubs within their area. Nothing happens without their say-so and any potential challenge to their superiority, no matter how small, is dealt with harshly. If you have any doubts that this is indeed the case, I suggest you try the following experiment: gather together a group of male friends (women are not generally allowed to join back-patch clubs), equip yourselves with Harley-Davidson motorcycles and choose a club logo. Stitch your colors and a square MC patch to the back of a leather jacket with the name of your club above and the name of your county or state below.

Hold elections to appoint a president, vice president, secretary, treasurer and sergeant at arms (responsible for club discipline) and then go out riding as a group and get yourselves seen by as many people as possible. Within days, possibly within hours, you and your friends will be intercepted by the massed ranks of whichever MC is dominant in your area.

If you are lucky and show sufficient reverence—that is, if they feel you can drink and party and fight and fuck with the best of them—they will invite you to a meeting at their clubhouse, explain the error of your ways and request that you stop wearing your patches.

Far more likely, however, is that you and your friends will be stomped and beaten and chain whipped to a pulp and your patches and cycle will be taken from you. Your fingers or ankles will be broken to make riding impossible and you will be told in no uncertain terms that your little club no longer exists. Period. The seized patches will be burned or hung upside down behind the clubhouse bar and the motorcycle will be stripped down for spares or resold. And if you even consider going to the police, you'll just make an enemy of every other MC in the world and instantly prove that you didn't have what it takes to make it in the scene anyway.

This scenario becomes even more certain if the dominant club in your area is one of the big three international gangs or if your patches feature a "protected" color combination: red on white for the Angels, black on white for the Outlaws, red on yellow for the Bandidos. Coming too close to the logo designs of one of the big gangs would bring even more trouble—all three are trademarked and protected by international copyright law.

The issue of showing appropriate respect to an MC applies even when it is crystal clear that there is no threat. In August 2010, a sixty-three-year-old motorcycle-riding preacher from Altoona, Pennsylvania, was beaten and robbed by members of the Animals MC after failing to seek permission to wear a back patch that featured a red cross on a white background along with the words "Shield of Faith Ministries."

Many equally nonthreatening motorcycle groups, among them the American Postal Workers Riding Club, Bikers for Christ and even the Crippled Old Biker Brothers—a support society for those who have suffered serious accidents—share published protocols that advise their members on how to deal with back-patch clubs: "If someone from an MC requests that you remove your vest/patch, don't argue. The best reply is "No problem," and politely take it off and let your club officer know what MC it was so they can deal with any potential problems. You normally will only get asked once."

Such rules exist because an MC has to be seen to be the dominant club in the area it controls and the best way to do this is to ensure that no other club ever wears their colors without permission. When clubs fail to follow this rule, wars start and all too quickly escalate out of control.

THE END

April 2, 2006, Connecticut, USA

By the time he saw the gun it was already too late.

Hell's Angel Paul Carrol was midway between Boston and New York, cruising south down I-95 with two dozen members of the world's most notorious biker gang, black leather emblazoned with the winged death's head logo, chrome gleaming from their growling, customized Harleys.

Drivers moved aside to let the bikers pass or slowed down to have a good long gape. As the pack approached exit 42 near West Haven, a green SUV with Florida plates that had been coming up fast on the outside lane suddenly decelerated to match its speed with that of club president Roger "Bear" Mariani who, in keeping with club protocol, was riding at the front of the group. Carrol could only watch in horror as a semi-automatic pistol appeared in the nearside window and jerked twice as it fired two shots. Carrol saw a bullet strike Bear in the arm and the car then sped off into the distance.

Tough guys are a dime a dozen in the biker world but Bear undoubtedly stood out from the crowd. A Vietnam veteran, he had not only been awarded the Purple Heart on *two* separate occasions but had also won a Bronze Star for heroism. At the age of sixty-one, he'd lost none of his youthful vigor. Pulling over to the side of the freeway, he set his heavy cycle on its side stand and only then revealed that the second bullet had actually hit him square in the chest. He collapsed and bled to death on the spot in a matter of minutes.

Carrol was so traumatized by what he had seen that when the emergency services arrived, he forgot all about the code of silence that prohibits members of the Angels from discussing anything to do with the club with "citizens"—non-club members. With tears welling in his eyes at the sight of his fallen friend, he told the paramedics that the four men in the SUV had all been wearing jackets that identified them as members of the Outlaws Motorcycle Club—the Angels' longest-standing rivals.

By 2006, the Hell's Angels and the Outlaws had been in a bitter and increasingly violent feud with one another for more than thirty years and both sides had suffered hundreds of casualties. Mariani's death had been the direct result of a series of edicts issued by Jack Rosga, the newly appointed national president of the Outlaws, for members of his club to seek out and murder Hell's Angels as revenge for attacks against members of his club. It was a call that echoed around the world.

On August 12, 2007, London Hell's Angel Gerry Tobin was shot dead in broad daylight as he rode down the M40 freeway at around ninety miles an hour. In circumstances that were almost identical to the attack on Mariani, two shots were fired from a green car. The first bullet smashed through the metal mudguard at the back of Tobin's Harley-Davidson and skirted through his rear wheel; the second skimmed the base of the biker's helmet and lodged in his skull, killing him instantly.

His assassins were quickly identified as members of the Outlaws and within a few days, all seven members of a small English chapter of the club had been charged with his murder. As prosecutor Timothy Raggatt told the jury during the subsequent trial, "This was a man who was targeted not because of who he was, but because of what he was." His killers had not been after Tobin himself but rather a Hell's Angel. Any Angel would do and he just happened to be the first one they saw that day.

So far as the general public were concerned, this was the first time the global conflict between the Outlaws and the Hell's Angels had reached the UK. The reality was very different. The seeds for Gerry Tobin's death had been sown some twenty-one years earlier, and Daniel Boone had been there right at the start.

PART ONE

GENESIS

1

MAYHEM IN THE MIDLANDS

May 14, 1986

𝕯aniel "Snake Dog" Boone had been a full member of the Warwickshire-based Pagans MC for a little less than a month when he got his first opportunity to kill for his club.

It had taken more than a year and a half of fierce dedication and determination for the softly spoken twenty-one-year-old to earn the right to wear the club patch on his back, and the experience had affected him deeply on many levels. Boone had been drinking beer and riding motorcycles long before it was legal for him to do either so it came as no surprise to anyone when, after leaving school and working a series of menial jobs, he started hanging out in biker bars and making friends with members of the local MCCs. Although he enjoyed the social side enormously, he always felt there was something missing. For Boone, motorcycles were never just a hobby, they were a way of life and he wanted to be with others who shared that same level of passion. He found them in the MC scene.

An MC is a band of brothers like no other. During his eighteen months as a prospect, Boone had spent more time with club members than with his friends or family or even his girlfriend. The Pagans lived in each other's pockets, rode, fought, and fucked side by side. When Boone finally got his full patch, it was as though all his birthdays had arrived at once. The bonds between him and his fellow club members were deep, powerful and utterly intoxicating. The love, loyalty and respect they all felt for one another meant that each and every one of them would be willing to do anything for the good of the club. Even take a life.

Brandishing a sawed-off 12-gauge shotgun, Boone joined a five-strong, early morning raiding party as it smashed its way into the home of a leading figure from a rival MC that was threatening to destroy the Pagans. The men stormed up the cluttered staircase and made their way to the master bedroom where they found their prey sound asleep, alongside his girlfriend.

The terrified woman was dragged off the mattress, thrown into a corner of the room, gagged and then covered with the quilt so she would not have to witness the events that were to follow. While three of the team immobilized their target against the headboard, Boone forced the barrel of the gun deep into the man's mouth and began to squeeze the trigger.

The trouble had started a week or so earlier when the club had learned that a man living on the edge of its territory had become a prospect for their despised rivals, the Leicestershire-based Ratae MC. Maintaining absolute control over territory is the first order of business for all MC clubs, but also one of the greatest challenges. Each weekend and as often as possible during the week, the Pagans would gather together and try to get around as much of their turf as possible, partly to remind people that they were in charge but also to give potential recruits the opportunity to approach them.

A favored watering hole was a lively Irish bar called O'Malleys in Rugby, a few miles from the Leicestershire border. But with so much other ground to cover—more than 750 square miles—and none of their 30 or so members living close to Rugby, it simply wasn't practical for the Pagans to drink there more than once in a blue moon.

The Ratae, who had already expanded to the north and east by forging close links with bikers in other counties, were quick to sense an opportunity and started hanging out in the bar themselves.

It was while the Ratae were drinking in O'Malleys that they happened across a local biker who expressed an interest in becoming part of the MC scene. After letting him hang around with them for a while and checking into his background, the gang offered him the chance to become a prospect, an invitation he eagerly accepted.

Once Boone and the rest of the Pagans learned of this their objection was a simple one: if the man wanted to join the Ratae, he would have to move to Leicestershire. As a resident of Warwickshire with an interest in MCs, he should have approached the Pagans in the first instance (though he had now blown his chances of ever being accepted by them). His counterargument was equally simple: he never saw the Pagans in his area, but the Ratae were there regularly so he assumed the town belonged to them.

In truth, the prospect was being used as a pawn. The Ratae knew full well that O'Malleys was outside their turf and wanted to see how far the Warwickshire gang were willing to go to defend it. Anyone could make a threat, but did the Pagans have the balls to follow through? So far as Boone and the rest of the Pagans were concerned, their credibility was on the line, as was their place as the dominant MC in Warwickshire. The Ratae had left them no choice: they would have to take it to the next level.

Becoming a fully patched member of an MC is a lengthy and involved process that is the same for clubs all over the world. It is made deliberately difficult and unpalatable, partly to weed out the unsuitable and ensure full commitment to the lifestyle, but also to prevent undercover law enforcement officials from gaining access to a club in all but the most extreme circumstances.

The road to a full patch begins as an official "hangaround" (a prospective member who "hangs around" in order to become familiar to the club). To attain this status a biker might typically have met several members of a club through drinking at their regular bar, attending rallies or even being a guest of another hangaround at the clubhouse.

Compared to what follows, the hangaround stage is something of a honeymoon period. The club has no real claim on the potential recruit and cannot call on him to take part in anything more than the most rudimentary activities. Likewise, while the hangaround is able to attend certain club events and literally hang around in the clubhouse in order to get to know all the members of a chapter (and vice versa), they have no official association with the club.

It is at this stage that clubs are particularly on the lookout for those attempting to join with a specific agenda in mind. There have been countless cases of bikers who have been bullied or harassed in some way and decided to get their own back by trying to join an MC. They figure that once they are in they can take advantage of the "one in, all in" rule to drag an entire chapter into what is essentially a personal conflict. Such antics are deeply frowned upon: the rule is that if something develops while you are in the club, you will receive full backup. But anything that happens before you join is baggage that you must leave behind.

Some hangarounds have no intention of taking things further, others are eager to become more deeply involved. In both cases the only rule they have to abide by is that you can only be a hangaround with one club at a time. It is the first hint at the level of loyalty and commitment that is required to make it into an MC.

The hangaround stage typically lasts anywhere from a few weeks to a few months. Sometimes it becomes obvious to those in the club that someone isn't made of the right stuff to progress. At other times, the bikers themselves, having gotten a better view of what is actually involved, change their minds and withdraw.

To reach the next stage of membership—prospect—requires the sponsorship of a full-patch holder who remains responsible for the newcomer until he receives a full patch of his own. Bringing high-quality recruits to the attention of the club can enhance the status of a member, but if anything goes wrong—for example, the member turns out to be an undercover police officer—then the sponsor is likely to be severely punished. For this reason, prospects are usually subjected to stringent background checks to ensure they are exactly who they say they are. To become an official prospect for the Mongols, for example, a candidate is required to fill in a three-page application form and provide his Social Security number, access to education and employment records, telephone numbers for relatives, hard copies of tax receipts for five years and, of course, a valid driver's license.

Occasionally there are prospects who rub some existing members the wrong way, but this rarely happens. The truly obnoxious recruits tend to fall at the first hurdle of the hangaround stage. Those who make the cut to prospect usually adapt in order to fit in with the club, often ending up as quite different people by the time they gain their full patch. This blending in with the brotherhood is one of the things that makes the bond between members of an MC so strong.

Most clubs distinguish prospects by only letting them wear the bottom rocker of their colors along with an MC patch, others have special "probationary member" jackets for prospects to wear. Prospects have no identity other than their lowly rank and having a separate dress code makes them all the more easy to identify. A patch holder rarely refers to a prospect by name. Instead it is "Get me a beer, prospect," or "Prospect, drive my old lady home."

As a prospect you are basically a slave and to all intents and purposes you become the property of your club. Whenever a full-patch member tells you to do something, it is an order that you have to obey without question. There is not much a full-patch member can't tell a prospect to do, so prospects find themselves getting involved in everything from stealing cycles and moving drugs to cleaning toilets at the clubhouse and polishing endless amounts of chrome. Some members have their prospects doing push-ups in the gutter simply to dominate them, others force them to take part in crazy stunts, like walking across hot coals during club parties.

For every ten prospects who sign up, on average around three will make the cut. Like most MCs, the Pagans always believed the credo that the patch does not make the man, rather the man has to make the patch. "You take a good man and bring him into the club in order to make the club better, Snake Dog," the club president, Caz, had told Boone. "It doesn't work the other way around. You can't become a prospect and then become a member and then become a better man. That's not what we're looking for at all."

Even in the case of a born natural, there is practically no way to avoid the prospect stage. Those who have been full-patch members of other clubs and left in "good standing" are still required to prospect for whatever new club they want to join, though in such cases they may end up getting their patches relatively quickly. One Pagan, Rabbi, had received his own patch in less than six months having been a full member of an MC called The Filthy Few a short time before. Boone had to wait a year and a half for his.

For a prospect to become a full member, the whole chapter has to be 100 percent in favor. Depending on the reasons put forward, a single dissenting vote may either mean the prospect is out of the club completely or simply has to continue his life of servitude for a few more weeks or months until another vote comes around.

In any MC, the moment a prospect receives his full set of patches is a high point of his biking life and something he will never forget, despite the fact that there is little in the way of an actual ceremony involved. After getting his, Boone spent the rest of the evening and most of the next day just riding around Warwickshire, flying his patches left, right and center, wanting to be seen by as many people as possible. The feeling of pride and satisfaction was so intense it almost made him giddy. All the sacrifices and hard work he had put in over the preceding eighteen months had finally paid off and he had won the ultimate prize. He knew there and then that his life going forward would never be the same.

As a full member, the club becomes your second skin. Each member is permanently on call. If other members are in trouble or need assistance, you are there for them. And between the weekly meetings known as "church" and group events known as "runs," you invariably have something going on that includes club members. Rarely a day goes by when you do not see one of your club mates for some reason or other.

The club is your extended family. The men become your brothers and their wives and girlfriends become your sisters. Their children will be friends with your own children. Some of the younger, single members share houses together. In every MC, if you cut one member, they all bleed.

Hence when, in the late spring of 1986, the Pagans heard that a Ratae prospect was regularly drinking at O'Malleys while brazenly wearing his patches, it was bound to lead to trouble. The more the prospect flew his colors within the Pagans' territory, the weaker their claim on the area. A series of increasingly threatening warnings failed to have any effect, so a decision was made to visit the new recruit in person and take his patches by force.

As it turned out, little actual force was needed. When the group of Pagans arrived at the prospect's door the following day, he offered no resistance. He knew exactly why they were there and exactly what they wanted. He handed over his patches without a single punch being thrown.

The Pagans returned to their clubhouse and waited for the Ratae to make their next move. Tradition dictated that their sergeant at arms would contact his opposite number in the Pagans and arrange a meeting. As separate MCs in separate areas, the proceedings would take place in an atmosphere of mutual respect. Ground rules would be laid out: typically the Ratae would agree not to have any members in Warwickshire and the Pagans would agree not to expand into Ratae territory.

But the men from Leicester had other ideas. Two nights after the prospect's patches were taken, a team of Ratae burst into the Warwickshire home where a popular Pagan named Rocky lived with his wife. After pounding the couple into submission with fists, heavy boots and baseball bats, the Ratae dragged Rocky over to a corner of the room and forced him to watch while his wife was repeatedly and horribly brutalized right in front of him. He was then struck on the head several times with a ball-peen hammer so hard that part of his skull fractured and caved in. His attackers then fled into the night, leaving him for dead.

The attack had taken place in the early hours of the morning and most of the Pagans did not learn about it until much later in the day. They rushed to the George Eliot Hospital and learned that Rocky was in a critical condition, possibly suffering brain damage, and slipping in and out of a coma. His wife was also in the hospital being treated for various injuries of her own. Boone was particularly affected by the attack. Although he felt close to all the Pagans, Rocky, a five-year veteran of the club, had been his personal sponsor and the bond between the two of them had been particularly strong. In the waiting room, the corridors and the parking lot, all the talk between Boone and the other Pagans centered on one topic: revenge.

The vicious attack made it obvious to the Pagans that the situation wasn't going to resolve itself without more blood being spilled. There had been plenty of incidents of interclub conflict in the preceding years but this was something far more serious. Instead of the usual drunken Saturday-night fight, they were truly at war. Fully aware of the level of violence the Ratae had already employed, no one could escape the fact that there was every possibility that some of them might lose their lives, or find themselves being forced to take the lives of others.

Club president Caz called an emergency meeting that same evening to discuss their options and one of the members, a tall, heavyset man who had been around for longer than anyone could recall, stood up and said that he was going to leave. "Listen guys, I can't guarantee that I'm going to be there for you. I haven't got the stomach for this. It's just not for me."

He took off his patches and carefully placed them on the center of the table in front of him and then walked out of the room. No one ever saw him again. Caz quickly got back to the matter at hand.

A car had been spotted leaving the scene of the attack and, thanks to an associate working at the Department of Motor Vehicles, the Pagans were able to match the license plate to an address. Early the following morning five full-patch members—Boone, Rabbi, Link, Dozer and Tank—met up at the clubhouse, armed themselves with a variety of weapons and headed out into enemy territory.

The small, semidetached house was just a few miles into Leicestershire. After double-checking that they had the right target—the car used to trace the address was parked in the driveway—the men hovered about, unsure of the best way to get into the building, until Rabbi, tall and ruggedly handsome with a winning smile, simply kicked open the front door and led the charge upstairs.

The barrel of the gun was so deep inside the mouth of the Ratae that it was making the man gag. All Boone had to do was keep squeezing the trigger and it would all be over. But something was holding him back.

Murder had been in his heart throughout the journey to the man's house. His rage about what had happened to his friend and fellow Pagan was driving him on: more than anything in the world he wanted the man dead and gone. But at the same time, Rocky was still alive. Only just, but still alive. And that was getting in the way. Taking a life in return for having put someone in a coma just didn't seem to be the right thing to do. Boone didn't want to be the one to push things to the next level because of the potential repercussions.

He pulled the shotgun from the man's mouth and used the butt of it to club his victim across the side of the head. Then, without any words being exchanged between them, Boone and the other Pagans repositioned the man on the floor beside his bed with his left arm stretched out, palm downward, in front of him.

Calmly and methodically, deaf to the screams of agony that echoed around them, Boone and the others used a heavy claw hammer to break each and every bone in the Ratae's hand. They finished him off by plunging a hunting knife through the back of his palm, pinning him to the floorboards while they made good their escape.

During the journey back, Boone was bitterly disappointed and more than a little frustrated about what had taken place. He'd been given a golden opportunity to kill one of the enemy to avenge the attack on his friend and he had failed to follow through. He just couldn't be sure if he had done the right thing.

There was precious little time to dwell on such issues as the Ratae were certain to respond with escalating force. Back in their clubhouse, a two-storied property in Leamington Spa, the Pagans began to prepare fortifications, boarding up the windows, sealing the door frames and sinking sharpened metal spikes throughout the back garden that would impale anyone who attempted to jump the wall. The work went on until the early afternoon and once it was complete, there was nothing to do but sit back and wait for the Ratae to make their next move.

2

BIKER'S DOZEN

The first mainstream motorcycles went on sale in the United States during the early 1900s and the first motorcycle-riding associations formed soon afterward. These were somewhat formal affairs—essentially gentlemen's clubs on two wheels—with ties and long coats being considered an essential part of proper riding attire.

As motorcycles became ever faster and more affordable, driven in part by intense competition between the early manufacturers— Indian and Harley-Davidson in America, Royal Enfield and Triumph in the UK—racing clubs sprang up on both sides of the Atlantic. Interest briefly dwindled due to World War I but by 1924 the newly formed American Motorcyclist Association had more than ten thousand members and was organizing regular race meetings all over the country. A significant proportion of the clubs that existed at this time were family oriented but, in the aftermath of World War II as thousands of Army surplus motorcycles were sold off on the cheap, a considerably more rowdy "fighting and drinking" clique emerged, as evidenced by the 1947 "riot" at Hollister that ultimately gave birth to the one-percenter patch.

The Hell's Angels themselves were founded in the San Bernadino/Fontana area of California in 1948. The popular myth says they were former bomber pilots looking for a way to replace the thrill of combat, but in reality most of the members were far too young to have served in the military. (Although the Hell's Angel name had been used by many squadrons during the war, it had been around long before and had first been popularized by the 1930 Howard Hughes film of the same name. Veterans *were* prominent in biker clubs, but then at this point in history, one-fifth of all U.S. males were veterans.)

Many of the founding members of the Angels had previously been members of clubs like the Boozefighters and the Pissed-Off Bastards of Bloomington and were just that—boozed-up, pissed-off kids looking for trouble and a way to recreate the kind of camaraderie they had been unable to experience firsthand. They drank to excess, raced one another on public highways at breakneck speed and beat the crap out of anyone who got in their way. They wore leather bomber jackets, then added Luftwaffe symbols and Iron Crosses, purely for shock value, and generally gave society at large the finger.

Hollywood cashed in on the growing public concern with the 1953 release of *The Wild One* starring Marlon Brando and loosely based on the Hollister incident. The highly controversial film (it was banned in the UK for being too inflammatory) left the public in no doubt that biker gangs were nothing but vicious troublemakers.

In the years that followed, the Angels expanded in California and soon had more than three hundred members but remained virtually unknown outside the state until the summer of 1964 when two underage girls claimed they had been raped by four members of the club while at a beach party near Monterey. The Angels raised money to hire lawyers by selling vast quantities of meth—their first foray into large-scale dealing. The charges were eventually dropped, but the case received blanket news coverage and established the gang as the ultimate all-American bogeymen. Everyone wanted to know more about their violent world and once again, Hollywood moved fast with leading actors of the day quickly signed up for biker roles. In 1966, Roger Corman released *The Wild Angels* starring Peter Fonda with the tagline: "Their credo is violence, their God is hate." The next year John Cassavetes starred in *Devil's Angels* (tagline: "Their God is violence . . . Lust is the law they live by!") followed a few months later by Jack Nicholson taking the lead in *Hell's Angels On Wheels* (tagline: "The violence . . . The hate . . . Exactly as it happens!") alongside actual club members who appeared in the film as extras.

Around the same time, a young journalist by the name of Hunter S. Thompson released his first book, *Hell's Angels: A Strange and Terrible Saga of the Outlaw Motorcycle Gangs*, an expanded version of an article he had written about the Monterey rape case two years earlier. The book sold well and, along with the films, not only ensured the Hell's Angels were by far the best known of all the biker clubs but inspired a plethora of copycats making free and easy use of the Angel name all over the world.

Much of this publicity had been personally orchestrated by Ralph "Sonny" Barger, president of the Oakland chapter of the Hell's Angels. He negotiated a healthy fee for the entire chapter to star in yet another film, *Hell's Angels '69*, and negotiated five hundred dollars' worth of beer for the Angels to act as security guards at a Rolling Stones concert at Altamont Speedway outside San Francisco, an event during which one of the Angels stabbed to death a fan who had tried to rush the stage.

Barger had joined the club in 1957, almost a decade after it had been founded, but had the foresight and marketing skills to see the full potential of the club. Charismatic, intelligent and willing to lead by example, Barger brought the California chapters together, hammering out bylaws, codes of conduct and harmonizing patches, colors and tattoos. Under his guidance, Oakland soon took over as the administrative HQ of the Angels, and Barger became the de facto leader of the entire organization.

The Ratae MC started life in the late 1960s when a group of young bikers from Leicester, a town in the English Midlands, happened across a copy of the Hunter S. Thompson cult classic, recently published in the UK. Seduced by the rebellious "fuck the world" attitude and lifestyle chronicled in the book, they formed a club with the sole intention of re-creating everything they had read about, right there in their hometown.

The Leicester youths called themselves the Hell's Angels Motorcycle Club Ratae (the latter being the original Roman name for the city) but did so just as, realizing the power of their brand, Barger quickly incorporated the Hell's Angels and restricted use of the name. From that point on, any clubs wishing to join the organization had to apply direct to Oakland. The London Angels received their charter—the first to be granted in Europe—in July 1969 and set about trying to unite other clubs in the UK under a single "All England" banner. The Ratae opted out, preferring instead to drop the "Hell's Angels" part of their name and remain independent, like thousands of other small clubs throughout the United States and Europe.

Despite being relatively small, the Ratae succeeded in making a name for themselves throughout the county. They embraced any behavior that was likely to cause offense, got banned from most of the pubs in town and were regularly vilified in the pages of their local newspaper. More than anything, they loved to fight. They fought with other bikers but also with skinheads, mods, punks and even the police.

In 1971, the Ratae achieved a new level of notoriety of their own after starting a riot at a Who concert. The gang had gatecrashed the gig at Leicester University and immediately began, in the words of guitarist Pete Townshend, "idiot dancing over everyone," forcing the band to stop playing in the middle of "Pinball Wizard." When Townshend admonished the bikers, one of the Ratae joined him on stage and blindsided him with a bottle of Newcastle Brown Ale, leaving a head wound that required eight stitches.

A few years later, the Ratae found themselves at war with an MC called the Coventry Slaves. A series of tit-for-tat clashes escalated, until both gangs gathered their forces to settle the dispute once and for all. In the fight that followed, one of the Ratae stabbed the president of the Slaves, and the two sides ended up in a massive Mexican standoff with dozens of guns trained on one another. Eventually both gangs decided to stand down but as they were leaving, a gasoline bomb was thrown and one of the Ratae was set ablaze. The president of the club, Scout, ordered that rather than trying to douse the flames, the burning man should be thrown out of the back of the now-speeding vehicle to prevent the fire from spreading. Such a request didn't seem to completely fit in with the spirit of brotherhood that most MCs claim to have at their core, but Scout ruled his club with an iron fist and no one ever questioned his orders. The human fireball was quickly ejected.

Using Hunter S. Thompson's book as their bible, Ratae members insisted on following every depraved ritual and tradition they could find. They awarded one another "wing" patches for public acts of oral sex—white for a white girl, black for a black girl and red for a girl who was on her period. They also followed the supposedly official initiation ceremony during which a bucket of dung and urine is collected and then tipped over the head of the new member. The mixture is worked into their jeans and patches and thereafter, the items, dubbed "originals," can never be washed. They have to be worn until they are literally falling apart and are then worn over other clothes to further extend their life. Although the ceremony is detailed in *Hell's Angels*, such practices were never as widespread as the journalist was led to believe and by the 1970s most bikers had significantly cleaned up their act. Right from the start, the Warwickshire Pagans were cut from a different cloth. First coming together in 1978, they saw themselves as part of a new wave of biking culture, while groups like the Ratae were something of a filthy throwback. No one in the Pagans had any wish to be defiled or degraded. When they saw the Ratae wearing their filthy jackets, they thought they looked stupid. With two completely opposed ideologies, it was clear the two clubs were never going to get along.

The Pagans chose blue and white as their colors and announced from the start that they had no alliances. They had no desire to be Hell's Angels or part of any other larger club. Their commitment was to motorcycle riding and partying and to being themselves, which meant being ready to honor and protect their club's colors at any cost. To be a member of the Pagans was to live the life of a hedonist twenty-four hours a day.

Warwickshire had been more or less open territory when the club started up, but there were still plenty of opportunities for fighting. Any side patch or MCC deemed to be too big for their boots would be taken out of the picture and any club daring to wear the Pagan colors would have hell to pay. By the mideighties, membership of the Pagans had grown to around twenty-five, many of whom, like Boone, hailed from upmarket, well-to-do towns in the county like Stratford-Upon-Avon, birthplace of William Shakespeare. Their ages ranged from late teens to early thirties. Some were unemployed, others unskilled while a handful held pretty good jobs. What bonded them together was brotherhood and biking, that and the fact that above all else, they loved to fight and to fuck.

While Scout ruled by fear, Caz, the Pagans' president, was a softly spoken natural-born leader who won the trust and loyalty of those around him by always being firm but fair. Heavily bearded with thick sideburns and a small potbelly, he was utterly fearless and the rest of the Pagans would have followed him to the end of the earth. Their neutral stance meant that the Pagans could party with anyone. The Hell's Angels one week, the Cycle Tramps from Birmingham the next, the Scorpio from Cornwall whenever they were in town. They had even partied with the Ratae. Boone had been a lowly prospect at the time and not privy to what had been going on at the higher levels of the organization, but he recalled a tense evening with the deep animosity between the two sides smoldering away all night. He felt like a school kid being told to play nice with the kids from across the street while their parents did their best to make small talk.

The experience was not to be repeated. The next time Boone heard anyone mention the Ratae was when their prospect turned up inside the club's territory.

After the Pagans had battered one of his men, leaving him with a shattered hand, Scout's vision for the future was crystal clear: it was going to be an absolute bloodbath. He wanted far more than just simple revenge: he had decided that the Pagans should be taken out completely. The Ratae were going to wipe their rivals off the face of the earth and assume control of Warwickshire in one fell swoop.

Bikers from all corners of the Ratae empire, including gangs from counties to the north and east, were drafted in to join the attack and by the time the convoy of cars and vans and cycles reached the outskirts of Coventry, there were more than eighty of them. Once in the city center they immediately sought out members of the Slaves, the same gang they had previously clashed with.

The Slaves were no friend of the Ratae, but they didn't exactly see eye to eye with the Pagans either. The Warwickshire gang significantly outnumbered and outgunned the Slaves and the two clubs had existed in a state of cold war for some years. But the Slaves had a healthy fear of Scout in particular and the rest of the Ratae in general and now they saw a chance to build bridges with the Ratae and potentially rid themselves of an enemy in one fell swoop. So when Scout and his armada rolled into town the Coventry boys did not hesitate to explain exactly how to get to the Pagans' George Street clubhouse.

The arrival of the massive convoy had not gone unnoticed by Coventry police, who initially believed that the Ratae had come to town to war with the Slaves. By the time officers arrived at the meeting between the two, the Ratae were just leaving. Seeing that no one was hurt, that nothing was broken and that no crimes appeared to have been committed, the Coventry force simply escorted the bikers to the edge of their jurisdiction and then let them carry on, assuming they were heading home to Leicestershire.

The Pagans themselves were under no such illusion: within minutes of the Ratae leaving Coventry, a tip had been phoned into George Street from a friend of the club who was aware of the events of the preceding days, had seen the numerous shotguns the Ratae were wielding and was deeply concerned about where it all might lead.

Once news of the approaching convoy had been received, little discussion was needed. With only thirteen on duty at the clubhouse, the Pagans knew they were horribly outnumbered. A few urgent phone calls were made to those members who lived farther away telling them to drop everything and rush to Leamington; but even if everyone managed to get there in time, they would still number only thirty at most. The Pagans rarely backed away from a fight, even when the odds were against them, but it was clear that this particular battle was not going to end well. Discretion was, they decided, the better part of valor: they would abandon the clubhouse and wait to fight another day.

The group of thirteen headed to Boone's place, crossing the river into the northeast of the town, and settled down with a few beers. But as they were sitting there, snickering to one another about how disappointed the Ratae would be to find the place deserted, they suddenly realized that the Pagans they had called in to back them up were still on their way. Back then, cell phones were just a gleam in the eye of telecom engineers. Once someone was en route somewhere, there was simply no way to get in touch with them. If the other Pagans arrived at the same time as the Ratae, they would be slaughtered.

"Shit," said Caz. "We can't abandon them. We have to go back." No one was happy about the order but they all quickly agreed they had no choice. *It's one in, all in.* They made their way back across the river and made their way to George Street and whatever fate awaited them.

The clubhouse fortifications had been designed to give them a measure of protection but with such a large number of attackers on their way, it seemed unlikely they would hold for long. Tank, the shortest and thinnest of the Pagans and all the meaner because of it, recalled seeing an old black-and-white film about a siege in which the defenders deliberately left an obvious weak spot so that the attackers would focus all their attention there, allowing the defenders to pick them off more easily. The Pagans decided to do the same, removing the metal grid they had placed over a low-level panel in the door, though none of them were sure if the Ratae would be dumb enough to fall for it.

In many ways they had no choice. As it was a row house,

you could only attack the clubhouse from the front or the back. The gate to the back garden had been secured, making it impossible to open. The rest of the rear was protected by an eight-foot-high wall, topped with shards of broken glass. If anyone managed to get over it, they would have to jump down into the garden where dozens of sharpened three-foot-long metal spikes waited to impale them. The front of the house, especially with that one vulnerable spot, would seem like a far better option.

The thirteen Pagans had just about finished making the adjustments to the fortifications and defenses when Dozer, a lanky Scotsman, suddenly realized there was someone else they had to worry about. "Fuck! We've forgotten about Maz Harris," he gasped.

As a writer for most of the major biker magazines and founding member of the Kent chapter of the Hell's Angels, Dr. Ian "Maz" Harris was already a legendary figure in the motorcycling world. Tall and gangly, he had obtained his PhD from the University of Warwick for a thesis entitled "Myth and Reality in Motorcycle Subculture" and had since become the official Angels public relations man, presenting a far more articulate, intelligent and media-friendly face than previously possible. He had also become the envy of most of the MC scene by being appointed an official tester of Harley-Davidson in the UK. But most important, Maz was also a regular in the Colonnade pub, three doors down from the Pagans' clubhouse.

"What's this got to do with Maz?" asked Boone. "They're after us, not him."

"Yeah, but if it spills over and he gets caught up in it and hurt, then we'll have the Red and White on our backs as well. Someone needs to get over there and tell him to piss off."

Tank drew the short straw and found himself heading to the pub to pass on the news, desperately hoping the enemy didn't turn up before he could get back. He arrived to find

Maz sitting in his usual seat at the bar sipping at a pint, his long dark hair tied up into a ponytail. Tank rushed over to him, almost breathless with excitement. "Listen, mate, you'd better get the hell out of here," he told him. "There are eighty fucking Ratae, armed to the teeth and on their way over so I suggest you make yourself discreet."

Maz simply shook his head like a disappointed father listening to a lie. "Listen, Sonny, you're only young. You don't know what you're on about because it's all new to you. I've been around for a while so you should listen to what I'm about to tell you. Here's the thing: if the Ratae are in Coventry brandishing weapons and whatnot, I can tell you now they've got no intention of coming here. No intention at all. It's all a show. They're doing it to scare you. They're doing it so you get in touch with them and stop all this trouble. That's all. It's all a tempest in a teacup. You've nothing to worry about. You should calm down."

Tank couldn't quite believe what he was hearing: it was as if he was speaking to someone from another planet. Tank may have been young but the events of the past few days had left no doubt in his mind that the Ratae were deadly serious and not the type to put on a pointless show of force. But it didn't really matter what Maz thought. They had covered themselves with the Angels by telling him what was going on. If he didn't feel the need to act on the information and ended up getting hurt, he'd only have himself to blame.

Back at the house, Boone sat nervously at the base of the stairs and slipped out of his patches. He unzipped and took off his leather jacket so he was wearing only his T-shirt. He put his patches back on and zipped his jacket over the top of them. Dozer, who had been sitting on the beer-stained sofa at the side of the room, was looking on, his face slowly morphing into a confused frown.

"What you doing, bro?"

"They're not getting my fucking patches," said Boone.

Dozer shook his head slowly. "Really? I'm dying with mine on."

The words hit Boone like a kick in the gut. So much had happened so quickly that there had been precious little time to take stock. Now for the first time the full reality of the situation they were facing, of what was about to happen, began to dawn on him. This was serious. This was totally fucking serious.

"What do you mean dying?"

"Come on, Dog. You don't actually think we're getting out of this alive do you?"

"Shit. Fuck. You're right. I don't think we are."

"Exactly."

Boone was surprised to see how steady his hands had become as he unzipped his jacket for the second time, removed his patches, replaced his jacket and restored his patches to their rightful place over the top of his clothes. He then turned to Dozer, a sudden wave of absolute calm washing over him.

"I'm with you. I'm dying with mine on as well."

3

SIEGE

Stationed downstairs at the front of the house, his view of the street obscured by the barricades and boarded-up windows, Boone could only hear, not see, the arrival of the Ratae raiding party. Tires screeched as the first vehicles appeared. Dozens of heavy boots stomped up and down the pavement outside; iron crowbars and baseball bats clattered and clanged against the metal grids as the attackers probed for weaknesses. Above it all was Scout's voice, manically barking orders like an insane general at the head of an invading army.

Inside the house, each Pagan had chosen his battle station. Boone, armed with a heavy pickaxe handle, was on one side of the door panel that had deliberately been left vulnerable. Opposite him stood the formidable figure of Link, grasping the sawed-off shotgun—the only firearm in the house—so tightly that all the blood had drained out of his knuckles. His pale blue eyes were narrow with concentration and were perfectly framed by his unkempt mane of dark hair and full beard. Two more Pagans were at the back of the property and four more in the center of the living room as a floating backup. The remainder were spread throughout the second floor, guarding the top of the stairs and manning the windows that overlooked the street. But if all went according to plan, it was Link and Boone who would bear the brunt of the first wave of attack.

As luck would have it, the plan worked like a dream. The Ratae took the bait. After a brief period of eerie silence, a flurry of kicks and clouts battered the unprotected door panel and it quickly gave way. Half a dozen hands appeared and frantically tore at the edges of the hole to make it larger; a split second later a head poked its way through. The head turned slowly upward, just in time to see the barrel of the shotgun swing up to meet it. Link fired at point-blank range. The face vanished leaving a cloud of red mist and a scream of agony in its wake.

Link immediately dropped to one knee, reloaded, poked the gun through the hole in the door and let rip with a second shot. This time a jet of white-hot flame shot out of the top of the gun and the whole weapon fell apart in his hand. He reeled back, clutching at his scorched flesh as the head and shoulders of a second Ratae came through the hole. Boone swung down on the head of the invader with his pickaxe handle, using all his strength. The man's body went limp, blocking the gap for those behind.

Out in the street, they could still hear Scout screaming at the top of his lungs. "Get in there! Fucking get in there!" seemingly oblivious to the fact that at least two of his men had already been badly hurt. Such was his power that the members of his club would rather risk injury or death during the attack than face his wrath by retreating.

The Ratae now turned their attention to the large bay window to the right of the front door, frantically trying to pry off the barricades. Link and Boone fought them off as best they could, using their weapons like battering rams to smash into the faces and bodies of anyone who got too close. The other Pagans in the living room joined in but they knew it was impossible to stop them all.

With all their attention focused on the window, Boone and the others did not see the body blocking the doorway being pulled free. Almost immediately, several Ratae began kicking and throwing their weight against the frame again and again until it split and splintered open. Dozens of enemy came streaming through into the building. The first few were taken out by furious hits from bats and bars but more and more followed, clambering over the bodies of their fallen comrades and the Pagans soon found themselves in imminent danger of being overrun.

Everything and anything became a weapon in the desperate battle to hold their ground. Chairs, crash helmets, fire extinguishers, table legs, even stereo speakers were all thrown and swung and crashed against the invaders but it was no good; the sheer weight of numbers meant there was nothing they could do. Abandoning their outer posts, the Pagans made a hasty retreat upstairs to their own private Alamo.

The Ratae followed close behind and it was only now that an element of sheer foolishness in their plan of attack became clear. The narrow staircase on the left side of the living room was wide enough for only one person to ascend at a time, but the landing that overlooked it allowed up to half a dozen Pagans to simultaneously attack anyone making their way up.

The first Ratae managed to use sheer momentum to barge his way past those at the top and did not stop until he found himself in the bathroom at the top of the stairway. Inside and surrounded by Pagans, he realized he was in deep shit and took desperate measures to escape, turning around and making a perfect swan dive headfirst back down the stairs.

A second wave of Ratae made a charge, led by a man with a shotgun of his own. Link was desperately looking for a weapon and eventually grabbed the first thing at hand—an old manual typewriter—heaving it down the stairs toward the mob surging up at him. The lead Ratae ducked, but not far enough. The metal bottom edge of the machine caught him just behind the forehead and sliced off a neat strip of skin and hair all the way to his crown. The scalped man fell back, eyes wide, screaming in agony. Another headed toward Boone, who hacked at him with a samurai sword before kicking him back down the stairs.

Other Pagans closed in around the landing, raining down blows on the fresh waves of Ratae with unmitigated ferocity, driving them back time and again. It didn't matter how many of them there were: the narrow staircase gave the Pagans a supreme tactical advantage. Like the three hundred Spartans defending the pass at Thermopylae, the superior numbers of the enemy made little difference. There was no way the Ratae were ever going to be able to break through.

Recognizing the impasse, Scout pulled his men back to regroup. Boone and some of the others moved to the front bedroom, overlooking the street. From the windows they could see a sea of Ratae heaving about on the road in front of them, loading shotguns and preparing gasoline bombs.

The Pagans had Molotov cocktails of their own already prepared, along with weighty chunks of stone and brick with which they could pelt the enemy. Rabbi lit the fuses of two of the bombs, then handed them to Boone before lighting two more for himself. Boone stepped forward but then did nothing, caught in a moment of bizarre illogicality. He couldn't work out what to do. If he threw the bomb, it would explode inside the room as the windows were closed. He couldn't open the windows because both his hands were full. At the same time, he couldn't smash the windows because this was the clubhouse and he'd be pulled up at the next meeting and forced to explain himself. He'd have to pay for the damage and might even be busted back down to prospect.

He felt as though he was standing there forever, but in reality it was only a fraction of a second before the answer suddenly came to him. *Just smash the fucking window, you fucking idiot.* Boone kicked out the glass and threw down the first bottle, sending some of the Ratae scattering. Up until that point the attackers had not paid much attention to the upstairs windows at the front of the building, but that was about to change.

As Boone and Rabbi rained liquid fire down into the street, the attackers replied with gasoline bombs of their own. Little wonder that confused eyewitnesses would later report that the Ratae were throwing bombs and that the Pagans were catching them and throwing them back.

In truth, the Ratae's bombs were having a devastating effect. All around Boone and the others, furniture began to burst into flames. The enemy then began using their shotguns to fire up at the windows. Boone saw one Ratae take careful aim and sidestepped to safety just in time. But Rabbi was too slow. Boone watched as the blast tore through the open window, passed directly through the middle of Rabbi's body and ripped a massive hole in the plaster of the wall directly behind him. Rabbi had been shot. He was a dead man. He had to be a dead man.

Rabbi stood motionless in the window frame for a second,

his lower jaw hanging slackly. He slowly turned to Boone and then shrugged. Boone stared at the spot where he had seen the shotgun pellets pass through the body of his friend: there was nothing there. There wasn't a mark on him. It made no sense. Boone had been so certain that Rabbi had just been shot in the middle of the chest—the mark was still there in the wall behind him—but now he could only assume that somehow he had been mistaken.

There was no time to dwell: two more bombs landed in the room and the fire intensified, flashing over the ceiling and threatening to engulf all those inside. The wooden shelves, chest of drawers and even the state-of-the-art stereo were now all ablaze. Boone and the others made a run for the door and once they were all safely through, he slammed it shut to prevent the fire spreading into the hallway. As he gripped the handle, he could feel it pulling away from him as the diminishing oxygen levels in the room created a suction effect. Boone held on even more tightly, well aware that if the door were to spring open now it would create a backdraft that would send a fireball raging through the entire property and kill them all.

But the suction quickly became more powerful and Boone found himself having to hold on with both hands. It was only when the handle started to turn back and forth that he realized what was happening on the other side. He let go of the door and it sprang open and out came a Pagan named Sparky, a wild-haired man mountain, who had somehow been left behind when everyone else had made their hasty exit.

Fires were burning everywhere now and the whole of the upstairs of the house was filled with thick, acrid smoke. The Pagans had no choice but to go to the one place the flames had yet to reach—the downstairs living room. As they cautiously descended they were brought up short by a deafening explosion that echoed around them. It sounded like a massive gunshot but no one could see where it had come from and no one seemed to have been hit. It would only be much later that they would realize the sound had been caused by the intense heat of the fire cracking the entire side wall of the house.

The Pagans gasped when they reached the base of the stairs. It wasn't just that the room looked as though a tropical storm had torn through it, it was the fact that there was not a single member of the Ratae anywhere. It seemed too good to be true. The Pagans carefully checked around all the corners and alcoves, expecting an ambush to be launched at any moment, but it soon became obvious that their attackers had fled. The battle had lasted a couple of minutes at most and ended almost as quickly as it had started.

A siren sounded in the street outside as a solitary patrol car arrived on the scene, hardly a proportionate response. The attack on the clubhouse just happened to coincide with a major diplomatic event in the Warwickshire area that had stretched the capabilities of the local police force—the smallest in all of England—to its absolute limit. When dozens of terrified neighbors and passersby began calling the police to report what was going on in George Street, that single car was all that was available.

The two unarmed officers—one young, one middle-aged—who emerged from the vehicle were completely out of their depth: nothing in their experience or training had prepared them for anything like this. The eyewitness reports had described a scene that seemed more suited to Lebanon than sleepy Leamington Spa. As well as the shotguns and the gasoline bombs, there had also been reports of at least one man running into the street with his hair on fire. But as far as the police could make out, the whole area was now deserted. The officers had no real idea of what had taken place, who had been involved or what had happened to any of them.

Unwilling and unable to enter the still-burning building themselves, they gingerly called through the smashed-in

doorway for any inhabitants to come out and make themselves known. The thirteen Pagans remained out of sight behind the stairwell until the police officers moved away to
investigate the back of the building.

At this, Boone and the others saw their chance and slipped
out of the house, splitting up and heading off in different directions. As Boone rounded the first corner, he ran into the
younger of the two police officers coming the other way. Fear
and apprehension were etched into the man's face—he was
clearly having trouble taking it all in.

"Who are you? What's your name?" the officer asked.

"What do you want to know that for? I haven't done anything. I've been down the pub."

"Didn't you just come out of that house?"

"Nah, I was in the pub. Why, what's going on here?"

Overwhelmed and underresourced, the officers gathered
up the scattered Pagans as best they could and took a note of
all their names, not that it would do them much good as
everyone in the gang gave an alias. The bikers were then sent
on their way as the officers waited for the fire department and
backup to arrive.

Thirteen may be unlucky for some but it turned out to be an
extremely lucky number for the Pagans that night. None of
them had been seriously injured though they knew without a
doubt that the same could not be said of the Ratae. The clubhouse had been all but destroyed but at the end of the day that
was just a building. The club was the important thing and the
Pagans had proved themselves.

In retrospect the Ratae never stood much of a chance. It
wasn't just the layout of the building but also the attitude of
the Pagans that put them at a massive disadvantage. They had
all been terrified. Boone would later believe what made them

so dangerous was the fact that none of them believed they were going to come out of it alive. It meant they had nothing to lose. Once they had accepted that fact, they had no fear.

Instead of police backup, the next cars to arrive on the scene brought the late-arriving Pagans from the outskirts of the territory whose eyes and mouths immediately fell wide open with shock. "Jesus Christ! What the fuck happened here?" they gasped in unison.

As more police officers and other emergency workers began to arrive on the scene all the Pagans converged on Boone's house. They sat down, smoking, drinking, and even laughing about what had happened, taking apart each and every moment and trying to work out exactly why things had gone their way.

They all felt a certain exhilaration to have survived it, the same way that soldiers who have been in the middle of intense battles feel when they realize they are somehow still alive.

The Ratae had raised the stakes yet again and the Pagans had no choice but to raise them in return. This time around there would be no mercy, no hesitation. In the space of a few days the violence had escalated out of all control and it was now blatantly obvious that it wouldn't end until someone was dead. For their next move the Pagans were going to head deep into the heart of enemy territory, find a Ratae, and kill him.

4

KILL ZONE

The hours that followed the attack on the George Street clubhouse were filled with a heady mixture of adrenaline, anxiety and anticipation. The thirteen Pagans who had successfully fought off the Ratae repeatedly related their experiences to the fifteen or so other club members who had failed to arrive in time. With no serious injuries on their side and the police so clueless they were unable to press charges on anyone, the Pagans who had missed the house fight were eager to see some action for themselves.

Although the Pagans knew the exact location of the Ratae clubhouse in the center of Leicester, they had no plans to launch a frontal assault of their own. The Ratae themselves had already proved the folly of such a move and if anything, their clubhouse was likely to be even more heavily fortified than George Street.

What the Pagans needed were the addresses of individual Ratae. That way they would retain the element of surprise and be able to pick off the members of the gang one by one. But getting this info wouldn't be easy. In the pre-Internet age few clubs had any kind of public presence. The regular inter-gang hostilities that had erupted since the start of the eighties meant that most members were keen to keep their personal lives as low profile as possible.

When a tip came through about a lone Ratae living in a small house just outside Pagan territory, Boone and the others took off in a multivehicle convoy to confront him in the early hours of the following morning. It was overkill by any standard—it seemed as though every member of the gang wanted to be there. No one wanted to miss out on a golden opportunity to take revenge.

It took less than an hour for the group to make the journey to the small village. Having left their vehicles just outside the perimeter they armed themselves with a couple of shotguns they had managed to scare up along with some pickaxe handles and Bowie knives, vaulted the fence and made their way up to the main entrance. They kicked the door off its hinges and stormed inside, only to find the whole place deserted.

Pumped up with aggression and spoiling for a fight, the disappointment was palpable for many of those there. By the time they returned to Link's house, which was now serving as a temporary Pagan HQ, they were itching for the next opportunity to present itself.

In the meantime the police were pursuing their one and only lead from the clubhouse battle: the piece of scalp with long dark brown hair attached was being kept in a jar at Leamington police station and officers had launched a national manhunt to find out who it had belonged to.

The Pagans watched the developing story with interest but then had a lucky break that put them back on track. The registration number of one of the vehicles that had driven the Ratae away on the night of the attack had been noted and, through the same friendly contact at the Department of Motor Vehicles who had helped them out before, the Pagans managed to obtain an address. This time around the property was a small farm in Brackley, Northamptonshire, and just before dawn on the following morning, the gang began preparing to mobilize again.

By now Boone, Rabbi, Dozer and Tank had been awake for seventy-two hours straight. At first the sheer adrenaline buzz had prevented them from sleeping; then the need to have guards watching over the properties and homes of Pagan officers in case of revenge attacks meant they had not been allowed to rest.

It was Link's birthday so club president Caz presented him with a large bag of premium-quality marijuana and ordered him and the others to relax and enjoy themselves. "We've got more than enough people already. We don't need you on this job," he told them. "You can all stand down."

It seemed like a good idea at first, but Tank and Rabbi were still eager to be part of the attack. They argued the point with Switch, the club's stocky, clean-shaven sergeant at arms and the man in charge of all matters of discipline. He backed his president, ordering the men to head home and get some rest. Still eager to get involved, Rabbi waited until Switch and Caz weren't looking then sneaked into the back of one of the vans that was heading to Brackley.

By the time Boone and the others noticed what he had done, the vehicle had already pulled away. Eager to share in the latest adventure, the three managed to squeeze into one of the last cars leaving for Northampton. If Rabbi was going to see some more action, they wanted their fair share too.

What none of the Pagans realized was that the Ratae knew they were coming and were more than ready for them. The owner of the farm just happened to have attended the same high school as a newly recruited Pagans' prospect called Shandy, and the pair had remained on friendly terms despite having joined rival clubs. Having seen the size of the force that took part in the last raid, Shandy became concerned for his friend's welfare and decided to call ahead and warn him to make himself scarce. Having stormed one empty home earlier in the week, Shandy didn't think the other Pagans would be suspicious if it were to happen again.

But instead of fleeing, the farm owner called the one man he believed would know exactly what to do: Scout. Sensing a chance to seize a tactical advantage, the club president hastily arranged for as many Ratae as possible, all carrying as many guns as they could manage, to travel to the farm and take up defensive positions around the main approach.

Once again, the Pagans parked their vehicles on the edge of the perimeter, armed themselves, vaulted the fences and made their way toward the entrance. And as they did so, the whole sky seemed to open up. All they could hear was gun-fire. All they could see were the flashes from the muzzles of the dozens of shotguns and rifles bearing down on them from the windows and rooftops.

It had all turned to shit. It was a textbook, military-style V-shaped ambush, and the Pagans had walked right into the heart of the killing zone. Rounds were hitting the ground, kicking up dirt in all directions. Fence posts and tree branches burst into fountains of splinters. Clouds of blue-gray dust and smoke drifted in the twilight air. Every kind of explosion echoed around them.

Caz was screaming at the top of his voice: "Get the fuck out of here, get the fuck out!" Shadows flitted this way and that as the Pagans ran for cover, zigzagged, threw themselves to the ground, pulled their friends to safety, screamed and howled at one another, trying to make themselves heard above the barking of the guns.

Boone felt a sharp pain in the back of his thigh, like an in-visible fist had punched him from behind. He fell, pulled him-self up and ran for his life back the way he had come, each step on legs of jelly. He made it back to where the vans had been parked and launched himself into the nearest, a jet-black Toyota model. The noise of the gunshots became quieter. His head was spinning. It was a waking nightmare.

As his eyes adjusted back to the darkness Boone could see someone on the floor beside him, groaning and holding his stomach. At first he feared he had hurt someone when he jumped into the van. Then the sticky blood on the floor began to soak through Boone's jeans and he saw the gaping hole in the center of the man's chest. For a split second the face was unrecognizable, twisted and distorted with agony. Then the familiar features returned. It was Rabbi. And this time there was no mistaking the fact he had been shot.

While Boone and others tried to administer first aid, keeping pressure on the wound to slow the bleeding, Shandy the prospect jumped behind the wheel and began driving to the nearest hospital. Only he had no idea where the nearest hospital was. None of them knew the area at all well and they had no map. They were driving blind and racing against time. The nearest large town was Northampton so they headed for that.

Rabbi had taken the full force of a 12-bore shotgun cartridge in the center of his chest. With a shiver, Boone realized that the hole was in exactly the same place that he had seen a shot pass through his friend two days earlier during the battle at the clubhouse, only this time the shot had entered at a downward rather than upward angle.

The van sped along the country roads. Unknown to those inside, the Pagans actually passed two other hospitals on the way to Northampton. The closer they got to town, the more Rabbi's condition worsened. He began screaming, calling out the names of his three daughters, the youngest just eight months old: "Don't let me die, don't let me die," he wailed. "I have to live for my girls, for my little girls."

Confusion and recriminations flew back and forth inside the van as the Pagans tried to make sense of how it had all gone so horribly wrong. There was only supposed to be one person there, not a whole army. They were supposed to have the element of surprise, not walk into a trap. They had gone there to get revenge for the destruction of the clubhouse, not to get their noses bloodied.

By the time they arrived at the hospital, Boone was convinced that there was no hope for Rabbi. He had simply lost too much blood and his wounds were too severe. His breathing was becoming increasingly shallow and they could no longer find his pulse. Boone had known Rabbi for years and he was also close to his longtime girlfriend, Jackie. He simply couldn't bear to be around if the news was going to be as bad as he feared. While two other Pagans and the prospect entered the hospital to await the official verdict from the doctors, Boone slipped off into the shadows.

Thirty-two-year-old Stephen "Rabbi" Brookes lived a few minutes more but died on the operating table as doctors began working on him. There was nothing they could do. Debates would rage in the weeks that followed about whether Rabbi would have survived if he had been taken to a closer hospital, but it was a pointless discussion.

The Pagans had fucked up big-time. Even if they had known that such a large force was waiting for them at Brackley, they still would not have stood a chance because of the Ratae's overwhelming firepower. The operation had been completely botched from the start. Instead of relying on careful planning, the whole thing had been thrown together simply to satisfy those members who had not yet been in combat. As a result they had paid a heavy price.

Police arrived at Northampton General Hospital soon afterward and arrested the three Pagans milling about in the waiting room. The trio refused to say anything about what they were doing there or how Rabbi had come to be shot. For Northampton police, well aware of how their neighbors in Warwickshire were struggling with their own motorcycle-related inquiry over the attack at the clubhouse, it didn't bode well at all.

In the meantime, back at Brackley, Scout was celebrating his victory and ordering the rest of the Ratae to undertake a massive cleanup operation. Fence posts were sawed off to remove all bullet holes, any parts that could not be removed were simply drilled out in order to remove potential evidence. Teams of Ratae spent hours crawling across the fields on their hands and knees picking up every cartridge casing, every piece of wadding, every piece of shot to ensure that by the time the authorities arrived, there would be nothing for them to find.

Only once the cleanup was complete did the owner of the farm at Brackley head over to his local police station and hand himself in. He had, he explained, been woken one morning earlier in the week by the sound of someone trying to break into his property. In order to scare them off he had taken his .410 shotgun, pointed it through his bedroom window and fired a shot up into the air. This seemed to have done the trick and the potential burglar had run off, but as time had passed he had become increasingly concerned that he might have just possibly, completely accidentally of course, hit someone.

The .410 shotgun was taken away for testing and quickly eliminated as the weapon that had killed Rabbi. When police went to visit the farmhouse, there was nothing to suggest that anyone other than the owner had been there. There was nothing to suggest his account of the events of that evening were anything other than the whole truth.

Police forces across the country began to link up under the umbrella of Operation Biker to investigate the wave of MC wars and at last made a firm connection between the events in George Street and those in Brackley. What shocked them most was the revelation that a large group of heavily armed, well-organized men had been crisscrossing the country for several days and carrying out acts of horrific violence, yet until a man had been killed, they had known virtually nothing about it.

For the first time, the police realized that all those groups of dirty bikers they had tolerated in their territory for so many years were actually far more sophisticated, dangerous, organized and capable than they had ever imagined.

Within days the task force announced that they were look-ing for another body, somewhere between Leamington and Rugby. They had learned that one of the Ratae had put his head through a door or window during the first stage of the assault on the clubhouse and had been shot at point-blank range. The story going around was that the body had been thrown out of a van and was lying in a ditch somewhere along that route.

Three vehicles belonging to the Ratae—a Capri coupe, a Ford van and a Volvo sedan—were searched and found to be carrying an arsenal of weapons including sheath knives, pickaxe handles, sawed-off shotguns and baseball bats. Sev-eral members of the gang were arrested, some after high-speed car chases, and it emerged that some had traveled more than one hundred miles in order to take part in the battle.

Most MC gangs have rules that forbid members from mak-ing statements or cooperating with the police. (They can, however, give evidence in court, just so long as their testi-mony does not incriminate any other club member.) In some cases the rule is actually written down and appears alongside other regulations. In other cases, it is simply something that is understood by one and all. The thinking behind this is that the club is not part of society as a whole and what happens in-side the club concerns only its members.

For the Pagans the rule was introduced in the mideighties following an incident in which another MC, the United Bik-ers, took off in a car loaded with weapons to carry out a hit on their rivals, the Birmingham-based Cycle Tramps. On their way, they had the misfortune to almost run over a police offi-cer on foot patrol. The cop approached the driver to berate him only to have the man immediately reach beneath his seat and produce a shotgun. The officer was instantly alarmed but it lasted only a second, as the man held up the weapon to sur-render it. "You got us dead to rights officer," he said, to the astonishment of the rest of the men in the car. "You caught us red-handed."

Each of the four potential hitmen were imprisoned for three years and biker gangs throughout the area decided to ensure that from that moment on, everyone in the club knew the rule: when confronted by the police, no one says anything.

Among the Ratae, only the farm owner—whose actions were a preemptive strike aimed at diverting attention from the rest of the gang—gave the police a statement. The rest said nothing at all.

The investigating officers knew it didn't make much sense. Rabbi had been hit by a shot fired at a downward angle that suggested the killer had been on one of the rooftops. But with none of the Pagans willing to give their version of the events, the police had no choice but to draw their own conclusions: Rabbi had, they surmised, been among a large group of bikers who launched an attack on the Brackley farmhouse. They had been scared off when the owner fired his own weapon in the air. Somehow in the confusion, Rabbi had been shot by his own men. The only thing the police didn't yet know was exactly who was responsible.

With no one else to investigate, blame fell on the nearest warm bodies: the three Pagans who had been arrested at the hospital. Their adherence to the code of silence meant there was nothing they could do to defend themselves. They were all brought out of their cells, lined up in front of the custody sergeant and formally charged with the murder of Stephen Brookes.

Standing there, they looked at one another, their faces blank and ashen. Spending some time in prison was a risk they had all been prepared to take when they became Pagans in the first place. But if they were convicted of the murder of one of their own—a crime they were wholly innocent of— there was only one sentence they could possibly receive: life.

5

LIFE ON THE LAM

News of the impending murder charges sent many of the remaining Pagans scattering across the country to hide out. Every county had its own MC scene and because its main emphasis was always on brotherhood and partying, the Pagans had met almost all of them at one time or another. Wherever they decided to hide, they could usually count on some friendly bearded biker to help them out. Many were happy to shelter fugitives in their clubhouses, all too aware that it would take only a simple twist of fate for them to find themselves in need of similar assistance.

Boone made his way to London, Link and Caz headed to the southwest coast (though to separate hideouts) while Dozer went north. Only a few chose to face it and remain in Warwickshire. Among these was Tank, who took to covering his naturally fair, short hair with a long dark wig. It not only looked completely natural, it totally changed the shape of his face and rendered him strangely unrecognizable. Although the police had started rounding up anyone connected with the Pagans, he soon became confident enough to walk around town with virtual impunity, secure in the knowledge that no one would work out his true identity.

Just two days later, a police car pulled up alongside him as he was walking home after a pub lunch. His heart sank as the officer in the passenger seat wound down the window, called him over and held up a small photograph.

"Do you know this man?" The photograph was of Tank himself, minus the wig.

"Yeah, I know him," Tank replied wearily.

"How well do you know him?"

"Well, you know, pretty well I guess."

"Great. Do you mind coming down to the station with us. We'd like to ask you a few more questions about him."

"Okay. Why not?"

The game, it seemed, was up. The biker recognized the police officer behind the wheel as one he had crossed swords with on a traffic violation a few months earlier and assumed that the two of them knew exactly who he was and were just being smart asses. He decided to play along.

It was only after he had been taken to the station in the back of the police car without being placed in handcuffs, and then led to a front-of-house interview room rather than the secure custody suite that Tank began to realize that the officers hadn't actually recognized him at all. When they began asking him questions like when had he last seen himself and where did he think he might be hiding at that precise moment, it was all he could do to keep a straight face.

He told the officers any old nonsense, pulling stories and anecdotes out of thin air, until he felt he had been as helpful as any innocent member of the public might be expected to be. He then announced that he had an appointment at the dentist that afternoon and would have to leave. The officers shook his hand, thanked him for his assistance and waved him off. It wasn't until weeks later that the police discovered their blunder. Heads rolled.

Boone briefly considered fleeing to the States. In the months leading up to the battle a couple of club members had begun writing to members of a Pennsylvania-based MC called the Pagan's (the apostrophe in their name was a deliberate ploy to antagonize the Hell's Angels whose own patch neglected to include one). Boone and a few others had talked about arranging a trip to visit their near namesakes, though there were concerns that the Pagan's were more of a gang than a club. Then, at the last minute, a club associate living in an apartment building in south London offered to put Boone up for a few days.

Boone headed to the capital and attempted to keep a low profile, telling only a few close friends where he was hiding out. Since his friend wasn't due home until later that day, Boone headed to a nearby pub and had a couple of drinks to calm his nerves. As he stood by the bar, a large, heavyset man approached and seemed to stumble just as he arrived at the spot next to Boone. The man threw out a hand to steady himself, his open palm grazing down the line of Boone's back as he did so. To most people it might have seemed like a simple accident but Boone immediately knew what was going on: the man was feeling to see if he was wearing patches underneath his jacket.

As Boone looked over, the man turned slightly, showing the back of his own leather jacket. Just the sight of the center logo was enough: a large brown rodent baring its teeth and looking ready to pounce. The man was a member of the Road Rats MC, arguably the oldest, toughest and most ruthless biker club in the country.

The Rats started out as a street gang in the early 1960s before evolving into a full-blown MC. The club established its fierce reputation in October 1970—a year after the London Angels first received their charter. The Rats had been offered the chance to patch over and become Angels themselves but declined. After months of increasing tension and a number of small skirmishes, the two groups met up at Chelsea Bridge in Central London (a popular biker hangout since the 1950s) to decide which MC would have overall control of the capital.

Paul Luttman, the twenty-year-old president of the Road Rats, and Peter Howson, the twenty-one-year-old leader of the Angels, approached each other from opposite sides of the bridge in a scene that would later be described as looking like something out of *High Noon*. When they were six feet apart, Luttman pulled a sawed-off shotgun out of the folds of his jacket and fired. Howson was hit in the stomach by more than 150 pellets, blowing him backward through the air and ripping his guts to shreds.

Pandemonium broke out. The remaining Angels and the Rats flew at one another and dozens more bikers were injured in the vicious fighting that followed. The Angels suffered far worse and to add to their humiliation, two visiting members from the newly appointed Zurich chapter had their patches taken during the melee. The Swiss complained directly to Sonny Barger, who immediately dispatched two of his top men to London to see whether the group's charter should be withdrawn on the grounds that they were unable to control their territory.

The London Angels were allowed to continue only after, under the direction of their visitors from California, they made two valiant attempts to retrieve the patches, which were by then hanging upside down behind the bar of the Road Rats clubhouse. During one attack, one of the Angels was kidnapped and repeatedly kicked in the head, ending up with a fractured skull and permanent hearing loss. The Angels have had a healthy fear of the north London gang ever since.

The Rats cemented their reputation for violence in 1983 at a party in the quiet village of Cookham in the heart of the English countryside, in an incident that made front-page headlines and that Boone remembered reading about all too well. A queue of bikers had formed to have sex (possibly consensual, probably not) with a young brunette who had been partly undressed and then staked out Red Indian style on the ground inside a tent. Fighting broke out when someone started taking pictures of the proceedings. The ensuing battle, chiefly between six members of the Road Rats and twenty-four members of the Satan's Slaves, involved axes, knives, guns and chains.

Two Road Rats were killed quickly—both stabbed in the heart—but the remaining four fought on for another half hour, slashing and beating the Slaves back and eventually forcing around twenty to barricade themselves in a nearby cottage. The Rats had just managed to set the building on fire when members of the local Hell's Angels, who were hosting the event, intervened, wanting to know what was being done for the dead and wounded.

The Pagans had been to parties attended by the Road Rats every now and then but had never really had much to do with them. The Rats were notorious for falling out with pretty much every other club in the country at one time or another and Boone couldn't help feel a little uncomfortable when he realized who had patted him down. Boone was a big man but the Rat towered above him and was almost as wide as Boone was tall. Seeing the rising tension in Boone's eyes, the man raised an open palm to reassure him.

"No need to stress, mate, I know exactly who you are. I just had to check. You're Boone from the Pagans, right? I'm Mick. Just keep your head down. You're fine and your bike is safe."

"What's going on? Am I in trouble?" Boone's first concern was that somehow he was being accused of bringing trouble into the territory of the Rats, something they were unlikely to welcome.

"Nah, mate, you're fine. You just need to keep your head down. You're going about this the right way. Don't talk to too many people, don't tell them where you are. Do you have somewhere to stay?"

"Yeah, I've got a friend with a place near here."

"Good. Once you're inside, don't leave for any reason. Stay indoors the whole time. We know exactly what's happened.

The world and his wife are out looking for you guys at the moment. You need to stay off the radar."

An hour or so later, Boone made his way to the home of the guy who had agreed to put him up. He received a warm welcome from the man himself but his girlfriend was clearly unhappy with the situation. Though she didn't say anything, it was clear from her body language and general demeanor every time she laid eyes on him that she wanted him gone as soon as possible.

Unable to leave the property, the sheer boredom of life as a fugitive set in far quicker than Boone could ever have imagined. Reports were coming in from around the country about various members of the gang being rounded up, and now only a handful was left at large. Boone had no long-term plan and knew full well that the police would not stop looking for him. The hopelessness of the situation soon started to get to him and after only a few days he began to sink into deep depression.

The apartment had a large balcony that provided a panoramic view across London as well as a bird's-eye view of the streets and houses on the other side of the main road. The apartment's owner had an obsession with military equipment and had filled an entire wall with an impressive display of replica swords, pistols and machine guns. Early one morning, while the owner and his girlfriend were arguing in the kitchen about how much longer their fugitive guest would be staying, Boone pulled a long-barreled pistol from the living room wall and went out on the balcony to get some air. He saw a postal worker down below going about his rounds and suddenly the world in front of him turned into an ultrarealistic video game. Boone held the weapon between both hands, lined up the postman in the sights and gently squeezed the trigger.

The report of the gun was as loud as thunder and a jet of

bright yellow flame shot out from the end of the barrel. The postman's body slammed to the ground just behind a parked car as the sound of the blast echoed into the distance. "Holy shit," gasped Boone, "I've fucking killed him."

The owner of the apartment came running out onto the balcony, half-dressed. "That's it. You've got to go. You've got to go right now. What the fuck is going on?"

"Shit! I've killed the fucking postman!"

"You what?"

Boone nodded toward the street and both men gingerly looked over the balcony, just in time to see the terrified postman on his knees, cautiously peering up over the hood of the parked car, trying to work out where the shot had come from.

Boone was overcome with relief. He was convinced he'd made a direct hit but the man had dived for cover like a pro. It was a fairly rough area though—perhaps postal workers received combat training. Boone turned back to his reluctant host. "What the fuck are you doing with a loaded gun on your wall? You're just asking for trouble."

"It's a replica. It's only got blanks in it. They all have."

"You're fucking insane!"

"I'm insane? You're the one who fired it! You've got to go. You've got to get out of here right now."

The postman was back on his feet now and had been joined by a few other bystanders. They were looking upward and pointing in the general direction of the apartment building.

Boone grabbed his things and rushed out of the apartment, his heart pounding like a drum. He hesitated for a few moments, unsure whether he should take the elevator or the stairs and eventually decided on the latter. By the time he reached the bottom, breathing heavily, a small patrol car was just arriving on the scene. He made a run for it but he had no chance. He was soon overpowered, arrested, and on his way back to Warwickshire.

• • •

Link seemed to have fared better. He had headed down to Cornwall to hide out with members of another club, the Scorpio MC. Over the years the Pagans had made good friends with many groups of bikers across the country but none more so than the Scorpios, who were based in the popular tourist town of St. Austell.

The two clubs first got to know each other when Sparky was serving time in prison and found himself sharing a cell with the then Scorpio president, Mark "Snoopy" Dyce. The two men got on well and stayed in touch once they had been released. Invitations to party with each other's clubs were accepted and soon extended to other members. Within the space of a few months, the Scorpio and the Pagans had become like sister clubs, making regular runs to see one another, exchanging motorcycles and tokens and getting completely trashed during weekend-long drink- and drug-fueled benders.

The match seemed almost fated—both clubs had chosen blue on white as the color combination for their patches. Personal friendships blossomed, both between the men and the *old ladies*—the term used to describe girlfriends of bikers—in both groups. They became, in essence, one club: de facto chapters of the same gang, but for the distance between them and the fact that they operated under two different names.

During one trip to Warwickshire, the Scorpios even assisted the Pagans in shutting down a small MC that was threatening the Pagans turf, joining the vicious attack on the smaller club and helping to snatch away the patches of its members.

With the benefit of hindsight though, hiding out with the Scorpios wasn't all it was cracked up to be—in fact, Link would later conclude, he could not have picked a worse place to be or a worse time to be there.

· · ·

As soon as he arrived, Link was taken to see Snoopy, who lived in a small mobile home out on the moors. The Scorpio president could immediately see just how stressed he was and came up with a novel solution to help him relax. He handed Link two pump-action shotguns and a bag of ammo and told him to go out and enjoy himself.

"We're in the middle of nowhere out here, but there are loads of old abandoned cars and fridges and other bits that people have dumped," Snoopy explained. "Go out and de-stress yourself. Just don't shoot anything that has a face."

Link went out with the two guns at his hips and shot every-thing and anything he could see. He had a whale of a time and before he knew it had already gone through half a box of shells. By the time he returned to the trailer, he felt much more relaxed.

For Link and the rest of the Pagans, one of the best things about the Scorpio gang was the widespread availability of top-quality drugs among virtually all its members. All bikers love to party, and drugs that give you a lift and allow you to party harder for longer are firm favorites. Because of this, vir-tually every one-percenter MC has a member or two with the ability to "sort out" anyone who needs a few party favors.

When deals take place among club members, they are done for as close to cost as possible. Although some trading might go on with outsiders, this is usually just a way of subsidizing the cost of drug use within the club. But the Scorpio had taken things to the next level. The Pagans knew the Scorpio were increasingly selling speed and cannabis to people outside the club and doing a brisk business in LSD and cocaine, but none of the Warwickshire gang could ever have imagined the true scale of the operation that the Cornwall gang had put in place.

In less than a year, the Scorpio had managed to corner the

entire market for cannabis, amphetamines and LSD for more than thirty miles in every direction, using strong-arm tactics to drive other suppliers out of business, and earning themselves more than one million pounds in the process. The gang made casual use of extreme violence both to "persuade" those who failed to pay their drug debts and to bully those who dared to purchase their supplies from elsewhere. Potential witnesses were intimidated into keeping quiet. Way beyond occasional party favors, the gang had moved into the drug trade on a transcontinental scale.

Under the guidance of Snoopy and Vice President Gary Mills, gang associates purchased large quantities of amphetamine powder and cannabis resin in Amsterdam, paying for them using money orders from Thomas Cook. Packets of the drug were then concealed in false compartments in a fleet of specially adapted Ford cars and driven through customs.

From a safe house in east London, far from the gang's home territory, the drugs were then divided up in brown paper, labeled "motorcycle parts," and shipped around the country using British Rail's Red Star service. Although the Scorpios were running the entire scheme, the gang employed a number of nonmembers to run the safe house and courier the drugs around—thus distancing themselves from potential prosecution.

The network had been operating successfully for almost eighteen months and would have carried on but for the fact that Snoopy and two other members of the gang, wearing full combat gear and masks, broke into the wrong house while looking for a dealer they believed had ripped them off. The innocent home owner immediately called the police and the local law enforcement officers finally found out what had been going on right under their noses. A task force named Operation Enmesh was launched to target the gang and initially came up against a wall of silence, but help eventually came from a completely unexpected source.

Helen White was the least likely member of the Scorpio entourage. Stunningly attractive, well educated and the daughter of a highly successful businessman, she had trained as a ballet dancer and was expected to have a glittering career before her. But the breakup of her marriage sent her into a tailspin. She became fascinated with the biker scene and began modeling for numerous motorcycle magazines. She picked up a minor drug conviction, allowed her blonde hair to become matted and tousled and finally had an eagle and FTW (fuck the world) tattooed on her left shoulder. Then she fell in love with Snoopy.

Beauty and the beast were not destined to live happily ever after. Helen soon developed a cocaine habit, which Snoopy readily agreed to support, provided she started working as a courier. The pair began living together and she was slowly taken more and more into the gang's confidence, being entrusted with large sums of money and huge quantities of drugs, which she hand delivered around the country.

But as Helen became increasingly disturbed by the gang's violence, and sickened by her own role in the business, she moved out of Snoopy's apartment to live on her own. She had also become fed up with Snoopy himself, who continued to see other women during their relationship.

Quick to exploit a potential weakness, the police arranged to meet with Helen and asked her to play a dangerous game. In return for immunity from prosecution, they wanted her to continue as a courier and feed them information about drug supply lines. She agreed and for the next six months lived a double life. She remained friendly with Snoopy, and sometimes slept with him, but all the while she was making a note of times, dates and dropoff points for shipments, helping detectives to construct a picture of the international network.

During this time, the Scorpios became even more successful. Having cornered the amphetamine market, they expanded, dealing in LSD, shipping in vast amounts of cannabis resin from North Africa, and liaising with Colombian cartel representatives to receive cocaine direct from South America, though like most biker gangs, they refused to deal heroin.

Operation Enmesh began with soft-approach busts to avoid arousing suspicion. It had been scheduled to reach its climax sometime in late June, but then the surveillance team keeping an eye on the bikers saw Link turn up, which threatened to provoke a monstrous headache over jurisdiction. Warwickshire police were hot on Link's heels and threatening to come down to Cornwall to raid the Scorpio clubhouse themselves. Months of work were at risk. The task force had no choice but to bring the operation forward and move in as quickly as possible.

Teams of heavily armed police from five forces carried out a series of coordinated dawn sweeps making more than fifty arrests, some as far away as London and Manchester. Copious amounts of cash and numerous weapons including guns, crossbows, machetes, a spiked ball and chain and Chinese throwing stars were recovered, along with bulletproof vests and cocaine worth one hundred thousand pounds.

Documents seized at the Scorpio clubhouse revealed that the gang had kept accurate records of their success and were every bit as tough and uncompromising with members who stepped out of line as the Angels. Minutes of the meetings showed that one member was subjected to a punishment beating for "drinking too much," while others were fined for being absent or late without having a good excuse. Ever conscious of possible police surveillance, drug deals were never spoken about during meetings but were instead negotiated through a form of sign language, or written on paper, which was eaten or burned at the end of meetings (some clubs use chalkboards).

The gang kept many of its drug stocks in well-hidden stashes: twenty thousand pounds' worth of amphetamines was known to have been buried in nearby woods, but a team of police and army engineers using dogs and metal detectors failed to find it.

Most of the Scorpio ended up in a local jail to await trial while the majority of the Pagans were taken back to Warwickshire. Boone, however, was initially taken to a jail in Birmingham where around fifty members of the Ratae and their supporters were being held.

When the police officers escorting him there had tried to remove his patches, he objected in the strongest possible terms. "You'll have to fight me for them," he said bitterly. "There's no way I'm going to give them to you."

As they approached the prison, Boone tried to hide his fear. He knew full well that this was the place that all the Ratae would have been taken. It was the last place he wanted to be but at the same time his sense of machismo would not let him ask the police for any assistance. He was taken to the reception area to be signed over to the prison guards. At one point he happened to turn around, allowing the prison officer to see the club name on his back patch for the first time.

"Pagans? What the fuck is he doing here?"

"It doesn't matter, mate. Just take him."

"Not in this jail we won't. He'll get fucking killed."

The police officers were desperate to get rid of him but the prison guards were equally adamant about not taking him on. Boone had already decided that if he was booked in this prison, the first thing he would do was to attack the largest Ratae he saw. He knew this would get him more jail time, but it had to be the wisest course of action. He wasn't prepared to die in prison, and if he didn't take the initiative, that would be just what would happen.

One of the guards solved the problem for him: "Sorry about this, lad. Bit of a fuckup. It's not your fault, but there's no way you can come in here."

"That's not a problem," said Boone. "I didn't really want to anyway."

A couple of hours later he was in prison in Warwickshire, alongside virtually all of his club mates. They swapped stories about how they had evaded arrest, how they had been caught and what they had heard about the precise nature of cases against them. But by far the greatest topic of conversation during the months that followed was the revelation about the size of the Scorpio's drug dealing network and the massive profits the gang had been making. The Pagans had dabbled in various forms of criminality over the years—mostly motorcycle theft and some low-level insurance fraud—but nothing on the scale of their colleagues in Cornwall.

For the first time, they could see a whole new world of highly profitable possibilities out there.

6

INSIDE MAN

The Hell's Angels refer to their incarcerated members as the Big House Crew while their arch rivals, the Outlaws, have dubbed theirs the Lounge Lizards; but for the Warwickshire Pagans who suddenly found themselves with more members in jail than out in the free world, no special name was needed for their brothers behind bars: essentially the entire club had been locked up.

By the time the bikers had their first mass court appearance, the police were still struggling to work out exactly what had happened during the events prior to Rabbi's death and the true motive behind the sudden outbreak of violence. While this process was ongoing, Boone and the others found themselves being held under some of the most vague charges ever issued in British legal history: a conspiracy to do things unknown with persons unknown at places unknown sometime between May 1 and May 31, 1986.

The initial murder case was soon dropped due to lack of supporting evidence but more than a dozen Pagans found themselves accused of manslaughter. Tank managed to avoid being connected to Rabbi's death but Boone and in particular Link, who was covered in gunshot residue thanks to the time he had spent shooting up old cars and refrigerators with a couple of shotguns, did not. Unfortunately, the code of silence meant there was nothing any of them could do to defend themselves.

It's a moral dilemma that hard-core MC members face on a regular basis. Once when a group of Hell's Angels roared into a supermarket gas station in Cardiff, a driver at an adjacent pump named Neil Lake stared at the bikers a little too long, prompting one of them to approach him. "Have you got a problem?" the man asked. Before Lake could reply, the Angel struck him hard in the face. That single blow with a heavy gloved hand caused multiple fractures and Lake needed several surgeries and three metal plates inserted into his skull to repair the damage.

The bikers rode off but Lake managed to write down the license plate of the Harley-Davidson his attacker was riding. The machine was quickly traced to a man named Sean Timmins, a long-standing member of the Angels' Wolverhampton chapter. Arrested and charged with the assault, Timmins made no comment until his court case began some months later where he explained to the jury that he had been more than one hundred miles away at the time of the attack and that another Angel had copied his license plate number.

"I went nuts when he told me," said Timmins. "I know his

name but it's against Hell's Angels rules to tell you it, even if it means me going to jail. I would be kicked out of the club. We don't blab on each other and that's a fact. If that means being held in contempt of this court so be it. I know I'm in a serious position but I can't tell you who it is—I would rather go to jail. I've been arrested for something I haven't done. I made a 'no comment' interview to the police because in the Hell's Angels we don't make statements—the rules of the club prevent it. Even if you are in jeopardy, these are the rules of the club."

Timmins was cleared of the assault and left court a free man. Others were not so lucky. The most extreme example of suffering the consequences of following this rule involved John Megson, the vice president of a small but well-respected English MC called the Druids.

Megson went on to become a legendary figure in the one-percenter community after being wrongly accused of stabbing a man to death at a campsite party. Megson refused to give evidence at his trial and, despite knowing which of his club mates was truly responsible, continued to keep his mouth shut even when he was given a mandatory life sentence with a minimum term of fifteen years.

While he was in prison his father, Shaun, repeatedly pleaded with him to tell the truth but Megson insisted he had to stick to the code of silence, an edict the Druids had actually included as part of their written constitution: "Rule 9: No statements to be made to any police." Week in, week out, Shaun tried to wear his son down but Megson would not budge. But then the Druids, who had initially been visiting Megson on a regular basis, began to drift away. He found himself wondering if the bond of brotherhood he believed was at the heart of the club was actually nothing more than fancy window dressing. His doubts grew further when he learned that, during his trial, the remaining Druids had sold his motorcycle and spent the proceeds on a massive drinking binge.

"If they had kept visiting him I wouldn't have stood a

chance," Shaun said later. "One day I thought, fuck it; he was going to tell me one way or another. I decided to tell him that if he didn't give me the name, I would stop visiting him just like they had done. He would be on his own."

The pair sat in the visiting room of Wakefield prison and stared at each other in silence for some time. Megson insisted he still could not say anything so Shaun suggested he write it down. The only piece of paper at hand was a wrapper from a chocolate bar. The moment Megson finished writing his father snatched the note away. It read: "Colin 'Animal' Mc-Combie."

But even then, Megson refused to make any kind of official statement and continued to serve his sentence. He was ultimately saved by the former girlfriend of another club member, who was shocked to see how little the remaining Druids were doing for Megson and came forward to name the real killer. The Druids did their best to "persuade" the woman to change her mind, forcing her to move home and seek shelter among the Henchmen MC, a notorious biker gang in north Wales. She remained there under Henchmen protection until she gave evidence at a retrial, after which Megson was finally released. He had served five years.

Eager to ensure none of their own members turned against the club, the remaining Pagans did their level best to guarantee that everyone in custody received as much support as possible. Monies were taken out of the club's funds to pay bills and help families put food on the table. Arrangements were made for child care so that wives and girlfriends could be driven up for regular visits; freelance workers were recruited so that small businesses being run by club members were able to keep going.

In the one-percenter MC world it is generally accepted that you need a minimum of six full-patch members to form or maintain a chapter. Below this number it is considered to be impossible to control territory and avoid losing it to another

group. At first there were just seven full-patch Pagans left
free but, fearing more troubles to come, the numbers fell once
more until the club consisted of just one full member and two
prospects. Had the Warwickshire gang been a mere chapter
of a larger organization, it would have been dissolved. As an
independent MC, the Pagans were just about able to wing it.

What helped enormously was that the club had managed
to maintain good relations with most of the gangs in the surrounding areas. To the west in Birmingham were the Cycle
Tramps and a little farther out the Wolverhampton chapter
of the Hell's Angels. Bordering the Pagans territory to the
northwest were the Eagles MC. To the north were the Road
Tramps with whom the Pagans had regularly partied and to
the northeast were the Pariah MC, a relatively new gang that
had also fallen out with the Ratae. To the southwest was a
small gang called the Wolf Outlaws.

When it came to Rabbi's funeral the Cycle Tramps literally
put themselves in the firing line of the Ratae by agreeing to
be pallbearers and help out with security during the service
and procession. Friends and associates of the club chipped
in as best they could and a local MCC, the Road Rejects, was
picked clean of all those who had any potential to make it into
the Pagans by signing them up as prospects.

The club didn't ease up on giving out actual patches—if
anything it became even harder to get into, and it was an open
secret that many of those who were being allowed onto the
fringes of the gang would not normally have made the cut.
But bolstering the number of prospects and hangarounds at
least gave the impression of strength of numbers while the
remaining members were on remand pending trial.

The first few weeks inside were relatively easy. Boone had
never been behind bars before and, having never had much
time for figures of authority, he initially struggled in such a

controlled environment but was helped by the fact that so many of his club mates were with him at the time.

The prison wing was horribly overcrowded so not only did everyone have to share their cells but the prisoners who were still awaiting trial were being mixed in with those who had actually been convicted. Boone and Link spent a few weeks bunking together before Link was moved and Boone got a new cell mate, Dean "Trotter" Taylor, an MC member with whom he shared a common enemy.

Trotter belonged to the Coventry Slaves MC and had also ended up inside as a result of a clash with the Ratae. Along with a few of his club mates, Trotter had traveled to Leicester with several sawed-off shotguns to attempt to retrieve some patches that had been taken from a club member during a fight. Trotter had been sentenced to three years for aggravated burglary. He was a bit of a nut but a fun nut who would regularly have the whole wing laughing.

Although the Pagans partly blamed the Slaves for giving away their location to the Ratae prior to the attack on the George Street clubhouse, Trotter had been on remand at the time so hadn't been involved. He and Boone soon bonded, especially when they talked about Trotter's beloved and pristine Triumph Bonneville 750 motorcycle, a machine almost identical to the one Richard Gere had ridden in the hit film *An Officer and a Gentleman*.

Boone and Trotter would spend hours discussing the curious world of the one percenter, trying but usually failing to come up with a comprehensive answer as to why anyone would risk so much for the sake of a patch, why under certain circumstances otherwise ordinary family men were prepared to kill and maim one another.

The closest they came was the realization that it wasn't really to do with the patch or even the actual club at all. Like soldiers in any war, they fought not for their country or even for freedom; they fought for each other. The men in an MC chapter knew each other better than they knew their wives and girlfriends. Getting into a club took so long and so much effort and the elation of getting a patch was so intense that it was impossible to avoid its becoming some kind of spiritual experience. The dedication and loyalty of full members knew no bounds. The spilling of blood in the middle of desperate battle made them as close as any blood tie could have done. It was all about the fact that, whatever struggle they were going through, that struggle was always shared.

There was no doubt in Boone's mind that some of the Pagans would see prison as a turning point, a bridge too far, and leave the club as soon as they got an opportunity, despite the best efforts of those around them to persuade them otherwise. But Boone could also see that there would be others, like himself, who felt the death of Rabbi had brought them closer together. And at that moment he knew that the Pagans would be a part of his life until the day he died.

The authorities soon realized that having so many bikers belonging to one gang all in the same prison was something of a ticking time bomb and constituted a serious threat to the safety of the staff. The guards became particularly concerned about the steady stream of burly, tattooed visitors who on more than one occasion were suspected of planning to break one of the inmates out.

Trotter was released after a couple of months and Boone was on his own for a few days before having a new cell mate assigned to him. He didn't pay too much attention to this newcomer—he was too preoccupied with himself and a forthcoming court appearance. They had talked briefly about the reasons each was being held in custody and while Boone didn't pay much attention, something about the story the man was telling didn't make much sense.

Then, a couple of days later, the news story came on the

radio about a man who had been arrested for abusing children. Boone spoke his mind: "They shouldn't arrest him, they should take him outside and fucking shoot him," he said. His cell mate shook his head. "You say that now, but you'd let him shag your kids for a million pounds."

And then it suddenly clicked why the story Boone had been told hadn't made much sense at all. Boone was sharing his cell with a pedophile. "You're a fucking sex case, you are." The pair stood frozen to the spot for a split second then the cell mate dived for the panic bell. He just managed to hit it when Boone was on him, laying into him with punches and kicks. The attack lasted only a few seconds before the door flew open and a team of prison guards, batons at the ready, stormed in.

Boone curled up into a ball, waiting for the guards to start pounding him, but nothing happened. He peered out from behind his forearms and saw them dragging the pedophile out of the cell.

"What the fuck is going on?" asked Boone.

"You fucker. I lost 200 quid on you," said the nearest guard. "I bet you'd figure him out on the first night. You let me down there. Let me down big-time."

Repeatedly denied bail on the ground that he had fled once and was likely to do so again, Boone spent almost a year on remand, finally being released under a host of restrictions, just in time to read the first reports from the other big biker case of the year.

In April 1987, the ten members and associates of the Scorpio MC who had been arrested in the Operation Enmesh drug bust, stood trial. After just two days, the proceedings had to be abandoned after an "evil-looking" woman told four of the jurors that their faces would be remembered and they would regret any guilty verdicts. A police investigation failed to track the woman down and the judge felt he had no option but to order a retrial.

The second time around the case proceeded without interruption and all the defendants were convicted. Mark "Snoopy" Dyce was given nine years for conspiracy to supply drugs as well as aggravated burglary. The story was reported widely and made the front page of the *Sunday Times* though, in keeping with the popular misconceptions of the time, the press universally referred to the gang as "Hell's Angels."

The first Operation Biker trial began just as the Scorpio hearings were coming to an end. Because there were so many defendants—at least sixty in total—the cases were split up into six different trials.

In June, twenty-five members of the Ratae were jailed for their part in the violence, both the attack on the George Street clubhouse and the numerous clashes that had led up to it. The longest sentence was handed out to Scout himself, who was given ten years for conspiracy to cause grievous bodily harm and carrying offensive weapons.

A week later, a further twelve bikers—a mixture of Pagans and Ratae—were sent to prison and the trial involving the remaining members of the Pagans also came to an end with all but one found guilty and given sentences ranging from six months to five years. Seven Pagans were also convicted of the manslaughter of Rabbi with the longest term of nine years being handed down to Sparky. Although they had nothing to do with the death of their friend, their adherence to the code of silence meant they were unable to say a single word in their own defense.

Although the two cases represented a massive victory for law enforcement, they made precious little progress when it came to throwing any light on the MC world. The Scorpio had been pursued because they had been causing havoc and selling drugs throughout Cornwall. The fact that they were a biker gang was seen as nothing more than a coincidence, particularly as the club was active in such an isolated area. No one thought to wonder if similar activities were going on with other MCs elsewhere in the country and in the world.

As for the battles between the Pagans and the Ratae, the police were the first to admit that, had it not been for Rabbi's death, they would never have found out about the incidents that led up to it. Despite having prosecuted the case, they were still in the dark about what had been behind it all.

The case meant the end for the Ratae, who simply fell apart once Scout was out of the picture. The Pagans, on the other hand, despite having just one full member on the outside, used their prospects, hangarounds and the good will of neighboring clubs to ride out the storm, looking forward to the day they would all be back together again.

PART TWO

SIZE MATTERS

7

MONEY, MONEY, MONEY

otorcycle clubs throughout the United States had long hosted rallies and festivals as a way of earning extra income and by the mideighties the idea was starting to take hold in the UK. Some clubs, the Road Rats in particular, refused to go down such a route, fearing it would force them to present a false public relations image for the sake of profit.

The Hell's Angels had no such qualms. Since 1979 they had staged a Custom Bike Show in Kent that from humble beginnings had grown rapidly to become one of the largest festivals of its kind. The Angels also occasionally hosted a Crazy Daze weekend. Both events earned tens of thousands of pounds for the club, a significant proportion of which was passed on to local charities.

Eager to get in on the act, the Wolf Outlaws approached the owners of a nearby former Royal Air Force base and requested permission to stage an event of their own. They hoped to cash in by offering attendees a unique opportunity to ride their motorcycles, either alone or racing against another rider, down the main runway that was as straight as an arrow and almost a mile long.

The only obstacle in the way of their plans was that the base was in Pagan territory, so the Wolf Outlaws approached their friends and neighbors to get permission to hold the event there. At that time, with all the Operation Biker court cases at an end, the ranks of the Pagans were so decimated that they were barely able to exert control over their territory and couldn't have objected even if they had wanted to. Knowing that the Wolf Outlaws would happily let them cohost the event in the future, the Pagans gave permission for the show to go ahead on what was effectively their turf.

The first festival at the former air base took place in August 1987 and, although relatively small and not particularly well organized, it was a massive success. Among the many attendees were dozens of members of the Kent chapter of the Hell's Angels. They were hugely impressed with what they saw, so impressed in fact that they decided to completely take over the event and run it themselves the following year.

The Wolf Outlaws were far too small to take on the Angels and with most of the Pagans still behind bars, the Warwickshire club was in no position to challenge them either. By the time the Pagans were back to any kind of strength, the show was firmly linked to the Hell's Angels and had been renamed the Bulldog Bash.

Over the course of the next two decades the Bash would go on to become one of the biggest and most lucrative biker events in Europe, attracting up to fifty thousand visitors from all over the world and earning millions of pounds in profits for its hosts. The Wolf Outlaws and the Pagans were understandably peeved about the lost business opportunity, not to mention the annual invasion into their territory. And as the years went by and the festival became ever more successful, that seed of resentment grew and grew until it ultimately reached the point where it would cost the Hell's Angels the life of one of their own.

The first Pagans to emerge from prison—those who had received time off for good behavior or had spent the longest on remand—were back on the road during the early spring of 1988. (In the United States, prisoners typically serve 85 percent of their sentence before being eligible for release. In the UK you become eligible for parole after serving between one-half and two-thirds of your sentence.) In their absence the club had limped along with a single full member and a couple of prospects and should by all rights have been shut down, but as soon as there were six full patches around, the Pagans were finally able to behave like a real MC again. With more than a dozen members still behind bars, the main priority for all those who had regained their freedom was to get their hands on as much cash as possible.

All MCs require a constant flow of income in order to meet the costs of running the club, and the Pagans were typical in terms of how they went about achieving this. A small but steady stream of cash came from membership dues, which averaged around twenty-five pounds per month for each biker, but which those in prison were exempt from having to pay.

More cash came in the form of fines that the Pagan officers imposed on members who breached rules such as missing a mandatory run, turning up late for church—the weekly club meeting—having their motorcycle off the road during riding season or losing a set of patches. Fines typically ran from five pounds up to several hundred pounds at a time and would often produce more monthly income than all the member- ship dues combined. The amount of the fine varied according to the offense but also in line with whatever the particular member was thought to be able to afford. The richer you were, the more you paid.

Much of this money—known as "central funds"—was then invested into legitimate enterprises, often involving the pur- chase of secondhand cars and motorcycles that, thanks to the high levels of mechanical expertise among the membership, could be bought on the cheap, fixed up and sold at a signifi- cant profit. The Pagans even opened up their own custom shop, building dream machines to order for members of the public, many of whom were so delighted with their purchases that they wrote the firm letters of commendation.

If a member came up with a good business or moneymaking idea, he could bring it up at church and apply for a loan from central funds to help him pursue it. Many MC members set themselves up as mobile mechanics, driving around to assist other motorists using vehicles and tools paid for by their clubs. If the business became successful, a percentage of the profits would be returned to the club. If it failed, the member would still have to pay back the original amount plus interest so the club was always in a win-win situation.

Rather like terrorist cells, this organizational structure is one of the reasons the police all over the world find it so difficult to clamp down on the clubs. If a member happened to come across an opportunity to invest in, say, a major drug shipment, he might do so using central funds. Thereafter, even if he is caught red-handed, it is almost impossible to tie his crime directly to the club. If he succeeds, the club profits from the drug trade while retaining plausible deniability about the details of that business.

This is particularly true of the larger clubs, when contacts made between members from different countries can help facilitate the movement of drugs, weapons and other contraband across international borders.

No one-percenter MC has ever denied someone membership because he has a criminal record. That said, there are many members, some of them senior, who do not have so much as an outstanding parking ticket in their names. If you join the mafia, you know you are going to be breaking the law on a regular basis, but it is possible to be a law-abiding biker. You must, of course, be tolerant of those around you breaking the law and understand that you risk being tarred with the same brush, but unlike a drug cartel or mafia clan, criminality is not a condition of membership.

This kind of setup means that, even if a particular club or chapter is wealthy as a whole, the levels of affluence among the individual members can still vary widely. The membership of the Pagans included its fair share of working Joes but also a sprinkling of management types and the odd company director. There was a paramedic, a restaurant owner, the floorman of a chroming business, a few mechanics, the director of an engineering company with more than forty employees, a gamekeeper who worked on an estate owned by Prince Charles, a scene builder for the Royal Shakespeare Company and a man who trained police dogs for a living.

In times of special need, everyone in the club would be asked to make a contribution to central funds, often as much as several thousand pounds at a time. This money would be used to build up the kitty until it contained enough to pay for a large purchase such as a truck or even a clubhouse.

Most new MCs begin by renting the houses they use as a base, usually in the least desirable part of town where prices are at their lowest. Once the clubs become established, they invariably prefer to own. This means that any modifications or fortifications necessary to ensure the survival of the club can be carried out without having to worry about the wishes of the landlord.

As well as being a refuge and social center, the clubhouse is a key source of income. The heavy-drinking, party-hard lifestyle favored by bikers means clubs can make a lot of money from running an unlicensed bar. Alcohol is bought in bulk at discount rates and then resold to members for prices that are lower than those on the outside but still high enough to make a tidy profit. Some clubs would extend this principle to other commodities, purchasing bulk quantities of motorcycle spare parts and accessories to sell to members. The larger the club, the more money such schemes would generate.

Money taken behind the bar could also come from outside the club. Most weekends, the doors of the Pagans clubhouse— and those of many other MCs—would be opened to nonmembers for wild, all-night drinking parties that would ultimately push profits even higher. Only one or two actual members might be in attendance, but the visitors would get the dubious thrill of entering the domain of a semisecret organization and the club coffers would swell dramatically.

The battle at George Street meant that the Pagans no longer had access to that source of income. It wasn't just that the property had been reduced to a burned-out shell, it was also the fact that the locals, once accepting, had turned against the gang and no longer wanted them anywhere near their town. In fact, it was impossible for any Pagan to ride through Leamington without being pulled over by the police and subjected to a lengthy, ultimately pointless search. It was harassment pure and simple and it worked like a charm.

A new clubhouse was soon located on Tudor Road in Nuneaton but having lost money from the sale of the property on George Street, which had only limited insurance coverage, the Pagans were in urgent need of even more funds. It was during times like this that the Pagans, while still acting as individuals, would collectively get involved in low-level criminality.

Several Pagans had experienced the misfortune of losing their wallet on a plane or train or ferry. While stuffed with enough ID to ensure it would be handed in to staff and returned to its vacationing owner, it had by then been emptied of cash. With most travel insurance policies covering up to 500 pounds, central funds would receive a welcome boost at least once a year.

Boone had already pulled the wallet scam twice in the past three years so when the postprison drive started he turned back to another mainstay of MC funding—motorcycle theft. There was one general rule: you could not steal a motorcycle that was parked outside the clubhouse or outside the home of a member. Cycles that had been built by the Pagans' own custom shop were also off limits. The shop was run as a fully legitimate enterprise and it was important for the gang to retain full integrity in its dealings with the public.

At first, stolen motorcycles would simply be resold. As the business developed, they would be chopped up into parts and then sold in this way. These spare parts would also find their way into the Pagans' own stores for use by members. (Although the custom shop was a legitimate business, the origins of some of the parts used to build the machines were often somewhat dubious.) Occasionally the club members stole cycles themselves. Often they were approached by professional thieves who knew the bikers would be able to find a ready market for whatever they picked up.

One time, Boone was asked if he could get hold of a Triumph Bonneville so he put out a few feelers. A pristine late sixties model turned up a few days later. The machine had been lovingly restored and, despite being nearly twenty years old, seemed to be in showroom condition. It was clear that the owner had poured an enormous amount of blood, sweat and tears into the project. As a custom cycle builder himself, Boone knew exactly how much work had been involved and how heartbroken the owner would be to see it gone. "I'll give you the money for it," he told the thief, "but you have to take it right back to where you got it. Right now." He knew that neither he nor any of his fellow Pagans would feel right about stripping down such a beautiful specimen.

Anything standard was fair game and, with practiced hands, could be liberated in a matter of seconds. There was a different method for each kind of vehicle: slide hammers for Japanese cycles, mole grips and feeler gauges for Harleys. Any opportunity to steal was seized with both hands.

A favorite hunting ground was outside rallies and motorcycle shows. The Pagans would wait until the festivities had begun, turn up with a couple of trucks and then work their way through the parking lot grabbing any high-value models they could find. In one single busy weekend, the club stole thirty-nine cycles.

Over time, the Pagans' motorcycle-theft network became

ever more sophisticated. Their contact in the Department of Motor Vehicles—the same one who could get addresses for license plates—began selling blank sets of registration papers at one thousand pounds each. Soon after that, one of the Pagans, by all accounts a bit of a math whiz, managed to work out the formula that Harley-Davidson used to produce the vehicle identification numbers stamped on the frames and engines of every motorcycle they made.

With his mastery of the complex alphanumeric code, a combination of a Julian date and a string of letters and numbers based on location, it was now possible for club members to sell stolen Harleys as if they were brand new. Little wonder that there were soon more new Harleys being registered in the UK each year than were being officially imported.

Boone and the others would be particularly delighted when a stolen Harley turned up bearing a sticker reading: "This bike belongs to a Hell's Angel. Fuck with it and find out." Boone would shake the cycle, run his hands over the engine, fiddle with the gearshift and then take a step back with a puzzled look on his face: "Shit, guys, I don't think the sticker is working on this one. I'm fucking with it and nothing seems to be happening." Clubs that hated the Angels—and there were plenty of them around—would happily pay a premium for motorcycles belonging to one of their members.

At the end of the day, however, this was strictly business and not at all personal. The Pagans had always gotten along reasonably well with the Hell's Angels. Boone, in particular, had a number of friends who were members of the Angels, both locally and in other parts of the country, though he tended to socialize with them on a one-to-one basis rather than with the Angel chapters as a whole. The Angels liked the Pagans enough that, after Rabbi died, a few members from the Kent chapter organized a couple of charity runs in order to raise money for his wife and children.

• • •

The other key focus for the Pagans was to build up their numbers by bringing in new recruits. Prospects were always needed. Not only were they an important source of new funds but they were also good for a laugh and an outlet for casual violence.

Every club gave its newcomers a hard time, but some more than others. During the seventies, in a club called Sons of Hell, being a prospect was, in the words of one former member, "nothing short of a series of near-death experiences." Being beaten, stabbed, hung from trees, or ritually humiliated and mentally abused was all par for the course. The club also routinely set its prospects on fire then left them to put the flames out on their own.

The California-based Mongols MC had such a reputation for assaulting its prospects that by the mideighties its membership was in free fall. No one wanted to sign up for a club in which you were likely to receive a savage beating every night for your first year. The club was eventually forced to adopt a new national policy: no assaulting prospects.

The Pagans had long prohibited serious physical and mental abuse, but many prospects still found themselves pushed to their absolute limit. During a Pagan weekend run soon after coming out of prison, Link and Dozer realized that they had lost the stopper valve from their inflatable tent, which meant the air kept escaping. Every time they pumped their tent up, it would slowly deflate. The solution they adopted was a novel one: they ordered their prospect to use the foot pump to continually add more air so the pair were able to get a good night's sleep. The prospect did as he was told without question and kept pumping until he fainted from exhaustion at around four a.m.

The fewer prospects a club has, the greater the workload each must shoulder. When Boone was prospecting for the

Pagans he was one of only two others trying out for the club at the time, and he found himself being run ragged at parties and events. During the rebuilding of the club there were at least seven prospects attached to the Pagans, so even though some of them were fairly useless and clearly never going to make the cut, they were able to share tasks among them in a way that made it seem they were quite efficient.

Other clubs like the Cycle Tramps and the Pariah from Leicester would visit the new clubhouse, see how well things were being handled and quietly berate their own prospects as they headed home: "Why the fuck can't you organize stuff the way these guys do? They make you look like shit!"

Like all MCs there were dozens of rules about conduct and obligations and any time one of them was breached—late to a meeting, missing a run—the guilty member would suffer the humiliating loss of their top rocker or center patch or both. "I'll bust you back to prospect" was one Caz's favorite sayings. Most of the time these temporary prospects would be restored to full-patch members once they had learned their lessons, but there was always the odd member who couldn't seem to cut it and would keep losing his patches until he found himself out of the club altogether.

Despite all the blood, sweat and tears, not to mention the sheer amount of time that went into obtaining them, the Pagans used to joke that their patches might just as well be attached with Velcro.

While a prospect is constantly ordered around or looking to anticipate what he might be asked to do next, full members are able to make their own plans, so long as they stick to the obligations of their particular club. One of these will be to attend all the mandatory runs for the particular club, usually around six per year. Another is to attend church where all the business of the chapter is discussed and voted on.

For the majority of clubs, church meetings last anywhere between one and three hours depending on how much club business needs to be discussed and how long it takes everyone to settle down. Drinking during meetings is allowed, though it is frowned upon to be drunk or stoned while they are in session. The proceedings are highly formal—motions are introduced and seconded, votes are taken for and against, and the president often has an actual gavel. Heated arguments often erupt and the debates can rage on for hours. The philosophy is a simple one: everyone gets their say but not necessarily their way.

Although the president and other officers are technically in charge, absolutely everything is decided by a vote. In clubs like the Pagans with just one chapter, this would be straightforward. For clubs with lots of chapters spread across a wider area, individual chapters have their votes weighted according to the number of members they have. This use of proportional representation ensures that the decision of the large chapters doesn't sweep the smaller ones along.

It was during a church meeting that the Pagans first decided to make full use of the lessons that had been learned from the Scorpio. Although a few members dealt drugs on a casual basis, this was mostly to ensure that there was plenty to go around at parties and to help them get their own stuff for free. The Angels had started selling meth in the seventies to fund their defense of the Monterey rape case; other American clubs had followed suit and several British clubs were also involved. Now a decision was made to formalize the trade within the Pagans and to get everyone involved.

As the members sat around a meeting table, one of the new prospects placed a small bag containing five grams of amphetamine in front of each of them. The terms were simple: the club had obtained the drugs at a bulk discount price. The drugs had a certain street value. Each member had to take the drugs and return a week later with that sum of money.

"If you want to throw it away, you can throw it away," explained the treasurer, "if you want to snort the lot yourself or share it with your mates, that's fine too. If you want to go out on the streets and sell it one gram at a time, no one is going to stop you. The only thing we want is the money."

Several club members opened their wallets then and there and handed over the required sum. Some—in particular those who always eschewed criminal activity—gave the drugs back as soon as they had paid for them, others made it clear that they planned to make personal use of their stash. The rest casually explained that they already had buyers in mind and knew they would have no trouble meeting the cash target.

No one said too much about the development after the meeting had ended but for Boone it marked the beginning of a subtle shift in the way the club operated. Entering the drug trade was a serious step. Boone had no problem with it—he'd been a major consumer for some years and had plenty of experience of selling at a low level. The difference here was that, for the first time, the club as a whole had the potential to start making serious money. How that money would be used and how it would affect them all remained to be seen.

While the club was still about brotherhood, and still about biking, it had now also become a business.

8

FORLORN ANGELS

As the last of the Pagans left prison, bikers from the nearby Wolverhampton chapter of the Hell's Angels began taking a lot more interest in the club, inviting them to rallies and parties on a regular basis. The Angels would also turn up at the new Pagan clubhouse in Nuneaton, often bringing members of other Angel chapters with them. The Angels also invited the Pagans back to their own clubhouse, a huge detached building that club members referred to as The Fort, set well back from the road in a quiet area of Wolverhampton. It seemed as though, having seen them prove themselves through their battles with the Ratae and having watched them develop financial security through growing levels of criminal activity, the Angels had a new level of respect for the Pagans. They were now clearly grooming them, checking them out to see if they had what it took to join forces with the bigger club.

Once the Pagans became aware of what was being offered, the future of the club became a hot topic of discussion. Boone could understand the appeal of becoming part of a big international brand, perhaps the most recognized MC on the planet, but there were downsides as well. For one thing, the Pagans would no longer be in control of their own destiny. Virtually all decisions about runs and regulations and even which clubs they were at war with would be made by national or international officers with whom the individual members would have little or no contact.

Becoming Angels might also affect their existing relationships with local clubs like the Wolf Outlaws, who had already fallen foul of the HA. Long-standing friendships with bikers across the country would come under threat depending on that particular club's relationship with the Angels. Boone didn't like the idea of not being able to have anything to do with people he had known for years and years, simply because the patch on his back had changed.

There was also the fact that, while the Pagans were a serious and long-established MC in their own right, the level of commitment demanded by the Hell's Angels was significantly higher and there was a good chance that some of the existing members would not make the cut.

Boone was further put off the idea after learning that a friend of his, Jake, had been pushed out of the Angels after failing to toe the party line. Jake had been an Angel for many years but fell out of favor with the club soon after a new prospect joined the chapter. The newcomer had very little money and could not afford to purchase the mandatory Harley-Davidson needed to join, but the club was eager to have him in its ranks at any cost. Jake had a nicely customized model that he wanted to sell and the prospect made him a bargain-basement offer. Jake refused, partly because the offer was low but also because he didn't really get along with the guy.

Jake then started getting pressure from senior officers in the chapter to come to some sort of arrangement and finally agreed to sell the cycle on generous credit terms that extended the payments over several months. But once the newcomer had handed over his deposit and got his hands on the cycle, he refused to make any more payments. By this time the newcomer had become highly popular with the rest of the club members and Jake was told to simply let it go. Instead Jake took back his motorcycle.

Jake argued that he was a businessman, that the motorcycle was worth far more than he was receiving for it and there was no reason why he should not be paid its full worth, but his appeals fell on deaf ears. Over the weeks that followed, Jake was increasingly pushed aside and eventually forced to leave the club under a cloud. The prospect eventually obtained a cheap cycle from another source and went on to become a full member.

A concern among all the Pagans was that none of them wanted to succumb to the peculiar brand of arrogance they had encountered among some Angels, an attitude that seemed to go hand in hand with membership of such a powerful brand. For some Angels, the power, worldwide recognition and level of influence simply went to their head.

What was very clear to the Pagans—now more than thirty strong thanks to a combination of new recruits and existing members finally finishing their sentences—was that the bigger a club became, the more difficult it was to control. Rather like a class of schoolchildren, there were always going to be those at the back of the room who didn't pay attention and messed it up for everyone else.

At the weekly church meetings, after the conclusion of regular business, it would be a member's turn to decide where the Pagans should go riding the following weekend, unless there was a mandatory run somewhere. It wasn't a compulsory thing—if a member didn't have any ideas or didn't want to make a suggestion, he was allowed to pass. The system was just a way of ensuring that everyone in the club got a say in the social activities.

In May it was the turn of a new member named Sweeny. He mentioned that he had heard of a party taking place in a biker-friendly bar a couple of hours north and felt that this would make a good destination for a run. The route was quickly agreed and the meeting moved on to other business.

What Sweeny had failed to mention was that he had been to this same bar a couple of weeks earlier and had gotten into a major beef with a member of the National Chopper Club, an organization for enthusiasts of heavily customized or "chopped" motorcycles that shares many MC values without actually being an MC itself. Following delicate negotiations with the major MCs, NCC members are allowed to wear a single back patch, without rockers.

As the last of the long line of Pagan motorcycles entered the parking lot of the bar where the party was taking place, the exit was immediately blocked off by a couple of vans, which had been waiting inconspicuously on the side. Dozens of cars appeared on the scene and dozens of bikers poured out, all of them wearing NCC patches on their backs and virtually every one of them brandishing a shotgun or other weapon. There were at least one hundred of them and no more than thirty Pagans. They were totally outnumbered and completely outgunned.

One of the Chopper Club members stepped forward, tightly grasping a sawed-off, one hand by the trigger, the other around the barrel. "Now you're going to get it," he hissed. "You've come here for trouble and now you're going to get it."

Caz immediately stepped forward to meet the aggressor, his hands held up in a gesture of surrender. "Whoa, hold up. Wait a minute, guys. I honestly don't know what you're talking about. If we'd come here for trouble, don't you think we'd have brought some weapons with us?" Caz turned gently to the left and right, his jacket falling open slightly to show that he was unarmed.

By now the remaining Pagans also had their hands up and one by one they all did the same. "You see," Caz continued. "Nothing. I really don't know what you're on about."

"He does," said the NCC biker, pointing toward the middle of the Pagan pack. All eyes turned to the tall, gangly Sweeny, who immediately began babbling. Yes, he'd fallen out with someone from the NCC and no, he hadn't bothered to mention it, but he hadn't started it and it was all the other guy's fault and he was the one who had been threatened and he thought going there with the rest of the club might teach the guy a lesson, and so on.

Caz marched over to Sweeny and began ripping his Pagan patches off his back. When Sweeny tried to resist, Switch, the sergeant at arms, and a couple of others went over to help. "Right, fuck off," said Caz. "Get out of here. You're not in the club anymore."

Sweeny made himself scarce, knowing he was lucky to get away without a beating.

Caz turned back to the NCC leader. "Do you mind putting the fucking guns down now?" he asked.

There were some murmurings among the gunmen but the NCC leader was far from happy. He looked across at some of the others, still shaking his head slowly. "Nah, this is some kind of setup." One of the officers shrugged: "Then why have they just kicked out their own man?"

Gradually, men on both sides began talking to one another. The guns were put away and everyone moved into the pub. Beers started flowing and the situation started to resolve itself. Best of all, neither side had been forced to back down—it was all a genuine misunderstanding. A few of the Pagans wanted to kick up a bit of a stink and hit back at the NCC but Caz overruled them. It wasn't going to happen. The tensions eventually ebbed away and the two clubs partied until the wee hours.

While the Pagans were making nice with the NCC, the Cycle Tramps MC was heading down to Hastings, a resort town on the south coast of England famous for its connection to the Norman Conquests, for a run of their own.

Whenever a club rides in formation they do so in strict order of seniority. As the Cycle Tramps made their way down south, Bruno "Brewer" Tessaro was at the head of the pack. At forty-two he was a good few years older than most of the club members in the whole of the Midlands area and was seen as a father figure by many. Although the clubs had all clashed and fought at one time or another, Brewer was always the one who would spot trouble before it broke out, take the agitator to one side and try to make peace. Deeply respected, he was one of the key reasons why the Cycle Tramps had become such a major presence in the area.

The club was originally located just outside Birmingham, but soon began recruiting most of its members from within the city and so based itself there. Originally, club meetings were held in the back rooms of a number of pubs, places that soon developed a reputation as being the best places to score drugs in the city, making them hugely popular with members of the local hippie scene.

It was Brewer, along with his fellow founder Anthony "Jake" Tracey, who had negotiated a difficult peace treaty with the Hell's Angels a few years earlier. The bigger club had objected to the fact that the Cycle Tramps' original colors were red on white, which the Angels had long claimed as their own. After many lengthy and occasionally heated discussions, the Tramps agreed to change to red on yellow, thus eliminating the threat of war.

That same year, a club known as the Desperados MC, who were based a few miles south of Birmingham, became the second chapter of the Cycle Tramps, making them by far the biggest club in the Midlands area. By then the gang had become wealthy enough to purchase its first clubhouse and within two years they had moved to an even larger property.

The club arrived in Hastings and headed to the biker-friendly Carlisle pub. Soon after they had settled in, they were surprised to see another group of bikers, members of the Road Rats, turn up at the same venue. The two clubs had never had much to do with each other and were, if anything, united by their desire to remain independent from the Hell's

Angels. The only issue to be settled was which club could drink more and the members rose to the challenge with glee.

As late afternoon turned to evening and everyone was starting to feel a little worse for wear, one of the youngest members of the Rats, twenty-one-year-old Patrick "Baby Rat" Boyle, began to act up. Brewer could see where it was all going to lead and decided to intervene to prevent any trouble. He walked over to Boyle, put his arm around his shoulder, asked if he could have a word and took him off to a quieter corner of the bar.

"You do realize what's going to happen if you carry on the way you've been carrying on, don't you son? It's going to cause friction. It's going to start here and people are going to get hurt. But the thing is, that's not necessary. There's absolutely no need for it. So why don't you calm down and relax so that everyone here can just have a good time."

Brewer was almost twice Boyle's age. His plea had come across more like a friendly word from a respected elder than any kind of macho confrontation. For a while at least, it seemed to have the desired effect. Boyle mumbled an apology and went out of the bar, ostensibly to get some fresh air. He returned a few moments later, walked up to Brewer from behind, placed the barrel of a Luger pistol against the back of his head and pulled the trigger.

Brewer died instantly. It took a few moments for the other bikers in the pub to realize exactly what had happened but once they did, the whole place erupted into a mass fight. The owners called the police, who arrived en masse within minutes and placed everyone under arrest.

As always, the bikers themselves said nothing to law enforcement, determined to take their own revenge. It was only because staff and bystanders had seen what had happened that the police were able to charge Boyle at all. When the youngster appeared in court all the members of the Cycle

Tramps walked past him as he stood in the dock and drew their fingers across their throats in the ultimate threatening gesture. Boyle would be convicted of murder later that year. Constantly aware of the threat of retribution he faced, along with the fact that he was clearly not even safe behind bars, Boyle eventually took his own life.

Brewer's motorcyle was placed in a truck and carried back to Birmingham. It was taken inside the clubhouse and placed in a glass case in a corner of the main room where it remains to this day, a shrine to the man without whom the club would never have existed.

The loss hit the other clubs hard as well. Boone had not been hugely close to Brewer but had enormous respect for him and admired his attempts at making peace between rival clubs. In the same way that the Cycle Tramps had been a pillar of support to the Pagans in the days that followed the death of Rabbi, so the Pagans returned the favor, helping the Cycle Tramps deal with issues of security and fears of further attacks, allowing them to focus on dealing with the funeral arrangements.

The loss of their cofounder was hard enough to deal with but with so much of the club's success being down to Brewer himself, other MCs were starting to question whether they would be able to survive without him. For the first time in a long time, the Cycle Tramps were perceived as being weak and vulnerable.

The following spring, the image of the Hell's Angels as being all but invincible suffered a major setback. Club members were chaperoning the visiting president of a German Angel chapter when they got into a fight with a notorious gang of football hoodlums known as the MIGs—Men in Gear—in a bar a few miles north of London.

Other drinkers ran for cover as both sides made vicious use

of chairs and broken glasses, but it was the MIGs who quickly gained the upper hand, fracturing the skull of the German and forcing the Angels into a hasty retreat.

Retribution seemed inevitable and the local police prepared themselves. Undercover officers were assigned to monitor the movements of the key figures from both groups and for the next few weekends riot teams and firearms units were on twenty-four-hour standby. The Angels put on an impressive show of strength, wearing their colors and riding their motorcycles in ominous formation up and down the streets where the MIGs lived, but the expected bloodbath never came.

"We were certain the Angels would try and get back at the MIGs," said the local police chief later, "but the whole thing just seemed to fizzle out. It wasn't what we expected at all."

It soon emerged that, in order to lift the threat of reprisal, the MIGs had clubbed together and paid the Angels two thousand pounds in compensation. Whereas the Angels of old would have settled for nothing less than an old-fashioned beating, business had been allowed to take the place of "pleasure."

Once the rumors started flying around that the Angels had taken cash to restore their honor, the gang knew they had to make sure people knew they were still the number one MC in the country. Around this time the Wolverhampton chapter of the Angels took on a new group of prospects, many of them a little on the young side who brought with them a lot of attitude and were happy to throw their weight around to reinforce the image of the club.

When it came to the Rock and Blues Custom Show (a festival in Derby organized by the Road Tramps MC), one of these new Angels, Scooter, got into an increasingly heated argument with a Pagans' prospect named Lee and began racially insulting him. Lee was eager to get busy with the Angel but under MC rules the minute the pair started to fight, all the other club members would have to join in. As a prospect, Lee knew he risked being kicked out if he forced the club into a battle, so he held back.

Scooter, who viewed himself as an expert bare-knuckled fighter, demanded satisfaction. He loudly announced that this was a personal dispute, that he and the Pagan would fight one-on-one and that no one else from either club should join in.

Lee happily agreed and the Angels and Pagans formed a circle around the two men as they began to fight one another. Scooter threw a hard right that Lee easily ducked. His return blow put the Angel flat on his back and he then knelt over his opponent, pinning his arms to the ground, landing punch after furious punch on his unprotected head, turning his face into a bloody, bruised pulp.

Dragging their fallen member away, the Angels decided the fight had been far from fair, regrouped and returned to make a show of force. This soon turned into a small fight with Lee and a few other members of the Pagans, but once again the Hell's Angels again fared worse. The losers left the festival, furious with the Pagans for having embarrassed them and equally furious with the Road Tramps, who, they felt, had let them down by not having had sufficient security on hand to keep the two sides apart before anything could flare up.

The burgeoning friendship between the two gangs had already started to cool off once it became clear that the Pagans had no intention of patching over to become Hell's Angels. Nothing was ever said explicitly—that would have been deemed too disrespectful—but Caz had put the matter to the vote and the opposition had been unanimous. After that, the Pagans started making excuses in order to avoid going to parties at The Fort and soon after that the Angels stopped visiting.

Now relations between the two sides had taken a violent turn for the worse. What had started out as a personal dispute had escalated to the point where it had become a matter of club pride. And neither side was willing to back down.

Secure in their belief that their status as the biggest, best-known and most powerful MC in the world was still intact, the Angels gave little consideration to just how much their actions were affecting all the small clubs around them. They were blind to the fact that the many minor resentments that had been building up for years were rapidly reaching the point of no return.

Oblivious, the Angels planned to make a major show of strength a few weeks later at a small biker festival just across the Irish Sea, not knowing that Boone and the rest of the Pagans were also planning to attend. Things didn't go quite as the Angels had hoped and ultimately it all backfired on them in a way more spectacular than anyone could ever have imagined.

9

EMERALD ISLE

With its extensive network of well-maintained roads that wind cheerfully through stunning countryside and meander gently along breathtaking coastlines, Ireland has long been a favorite destination for touring bikers from across Europe and beyond.

Although casual riding clubs have been common there since the fifties, the actual MC scene arrived relatively late—at least a decade or so after the first such clubs began to surface in the United Kingdom. Despite this, Irish bikers have always maintained a certain pride in their refusal to be influenced by outside forces. Rather than copy an existing club or apply for a charter from an established brand, they decided to go their own way.

The Freewheelers MC, for example, started life in 1979. Of the twelve founding fathers, five are still active in the club to this day. The members were initially drawn together by their love of Harley-Davidsons—at the time an expensive rarity in the Republic—and much of their time was spent building highly intricate, customized machines. A desire to share their creations with others led the club to set up the South East Custom and Classic Show in 1987 in the town of Kilmeaden.

The Pagans had missed the first couple of Freewheelers shows, but the event was receiving great reviews and seemed to be getting better every year so, in 1990, the club decided to check it out for themselves. None of the members had ever been to Ireland before and they knew little about the biker scene there. But with the show's organizers making it clear that one-percenter clubs were allowed by invitation only, the Pagans sent a scout ahead to ensure they would receive a warm welcome.

Link volunteered for the job and agreed to travel alone so as not to represent any kind of threat. He was still putting his head into the lion's mouth but the fact that the rest of the club would be arriving a few days later meant that anyone who attacked him would know retribution was on its way. Besides, in the honor-driven world of the one percenters, an attack on a lone club member under such circumstances would reflect badly on the aggressors.

After catching a ferry to Ireland, Link rode his way to the outskirts of Dublin in order to meet up with members of a club called the Devil's Disciples, known to be a gregarious group. Several of the club's members were involved in the pub trade, providing a focal point and regular employment for a significant proportion of the membership. And they were planning to attend the Kilmeaden event hoping to pick up a few tips for their own soon-to-be-launched show.

Like the Freewheelers, the Disciples had formed in the late seventies. At first their members rode British-made Triumphs (most MCs have a rule that bans Japanese motorcycles, derogatively known as "rice burners"), but slowly they switched to Harleys as they became more affordable and a lack of parts for classic British cycles rendered them too unreliable. In 1986, eager to form strong bonds with other Irish clubs, they changed their colors from red on white to black on white, lest anyone mistake them for associates of the Hell's Angels, who were yet to appear in the province.

Link arrived at the Disciples' pub and formally introduced himself as an ambassador of the Pagans—a gesture that was very much appreciated by the members. After a few drinks, and then a few more, he headed down south toward Waterford to meet the Freewheelers. The Irish guys couldn't have been friendlier—in fact, Link was initially highly suspicious, convinced they were trying to get him drunk so they could steal his cycle. But he soon realized the warmth was genuine, and once he was introduced to the club's officers, he got along with them like a house on fire. "The Pagans are more than welcome to come to the show," the president told him. "Especially if they're all like you."

After enjoying the camaraderie with the Freewheelers for a couple more days, Link headed off to the ferry port to meet the rest of the Pagans. He arrived just in time to see them disembark and could immediately tell that something was terribly wrong. "Get us out of here, get us the fuck out of here right now," gasped Caz.

Once all the bikers had reached a safe distance from the docks, Caz filled Link in on what had happened. The Pagans had not been the only MC on the ferry that day. Another club, the south Wales-based Valley Infidels, was there too, also planning to head to the Kilmeaden show. Halfway through the journey one of the Welsh mob started picking on a Pagan called Rocky, trying to get a rise out of him. Rocky totally ignored the insults, a response that only made the other biker angrier. He continued to taunt Rocky, accusing him of being a coward. After all, what other reason could there be for Rocky to walk away every time he was challenged? But the rest of the Pagans knew better. Rocky was one of the club's best fighters with an infamous and utterly devastating right hand. Like Lee, the prospect who had kicked the crap out of a Hell's Angel at the Rock and Blues Show, Rocky could fight but preferred to choose his battles carefully. He would rather fight five men than just one and had, on many occasions. He wasn't scared of the Welshman at all; he just didn't want to hurt the guy.

Members of the Pagans were also under strict orders never to fight on ferries. With regular runs to mainland Europe they were only too well aware that a travel ban as a result of antisocial behavior would seriously cramp their future travel plans. Bikers from both clubs desperately tried to calm the situation but the Valley Infidel just wouldn't hear of it. Eventually he forced the situation and took a swing at Rocky. The Pagan absorbed the blow with ease and then returned a single one of his own. The rival biker fell to the floor and didn't get up again. When he had failed to regain consciousness after two minutes the ferry captain called for an emergency helicopter, which flew in and airlifted the man to the hospital.

As always, the bikers closed ranks and refused to tell any of the ferry staff what had occurred, leading them to conclude that it had simply been some kind of accident. Once they arrived in Dublin, Caz and the others made the decision to make themselves scarce as quickly as possible in order to avoid any more awkward questions.

If adrenaline levels among the Pagans were high when they left the ferry, they went through the roof when they arrived at the show. Unknown to them, Maz Harris, the official Hell's Angels spokesman and the same biker who had almost been caught up in the battle at the George Street clubhouse, had visited Ireland the previous year on the pretext of writing a piece about it for *Back Street Heroes* magazine. In fact, he had been scoping it out as a possible location for an international run (a mandatory annual get-together attended by at least two representatives from every Angel chapter on the planet in order to discuss business and pleasure). Since Harris had visited, in order to bolster their position in the country, the Angels had opened up two chapters in Ireland, one in Armagh to the north and a second just outside Dublin.

As the Pagans pulled into the compound to set up their tent, they quickly saw that they were nearly surrounded by Hell's Angels from all four corners of the globe. Tensions were already high following the incident with Lee the previous year and Tank didn't help matters when he stormed up to Harris the minute he spotted him.

"You owe me an apology," he said.

"You what? I don't think so. Why would you say that?" came the reply.

"You arrogant fucker, you nearly got me killed," continued Tank. "You said not to worry about the Ratae, that it was all a tempest in a teacup. It's a good thing I didn't listen to you or I would have been killed."

Harris looked at the ground and shuffled his feet for a few moments.

"Yeah, I suppose I do owe you an apology then."

"That's right!"

The exchange didn't go down well with the rest of the Angels and the situation rapidly went from bad to worse when the Valley Infidels suddenly arrived on the scene. The antagonism that had erupted on the ferry a couple of hours earlier had not abated. While no longer itching for a fight—Rocky's fighting prowess had seen to that—the remaining members were still furious about what had taken place and took every possible opportunity to make their feelings known, bad-mouthing the club to anyone who would listen.

It didn't take long before the Pagans were completely and utterly fed up with the disparaging sideways glances, whispered insults and pointing fingers. It was all a bit irritating considering the Valley Infidels had started the trouble in the first place. Their attitude was terrible and they were failing to live up to the standards expected of a typical MC member. If they had been members of the Pagans, they would have all been kicked out a long time ago.

Eventually Caz approached the president of the Free-wheelers to explain the situation. "Sorry about this, but they are pissing us off big-time. We're going to have to deal with it. I know you'd rather we didn't do this at your show, but it's happening. We'll do our best to be as discreet as possible."

The Pagans massed and herded the Valley Infidels into a quiet corner of the field. The few who attempted to resist received a sound beating for their trouble and within the space of twenty minutes it was all over. Every member of the Valley Infidels had lost his patch and they left the show as former members of a club that had suddenly become extinct.

Yet more trouble was on its way, this time involving the Hell's Angels. Since the Angels had opened up their first club-house in the Republic, they had been behaving as if they owned the place. Local bikers found themselves being increasingly harassed by the newcomers, who in effect seemed to be questioning whether any of the long-standing indigenous clubs had a right to exist at all. So far as the Angels were concerned, Ireland was now their territory and all its members wore an "Ireland" bottom rocker, a provocative move that proclaimed the Angels as the dominant one-percenter MC in the country, something that simply wasn't true.

What was particularly irritating to the natives was that many of the newcomers were not even Irish but had been picked from clubs around the UK in order to form the two new chapters.

While the Angels clashed with some gangs they courted others—including the Freewheelers, who happily invited them along to their events never dreaming they had anything other than the most noble of intentions. In fact, the Pagans suspected that the true reason the Angels were being so friendly was that they had their eyes on taking over the Kilmeaden show, which in a few short years had already generated enough profits for the Freewheelers to buy themselves a smart new clubhouse.

Some of the smaller clubs and groups of independent bikers who found themselves on the receiving end of the Angels' wrath didn't take it lying down. A series of ugly confrontations soon spread. "Who the fuck do you think you are, coming to our country and giving us all this harassment?"

While the international Angels contingent who had turned up for the show were well behaved, the British and Irish chapters brought with them a bad attitude that was soon noticed by a good many of the clubs at the event. At one point, Tank was walking through the site when he passed by an Angel who was abusing a local man and his wife. "Cut it out," said Tank, "there's no need for that sort of behavior." The Angel— a grizzly bear of a man—took great exception to Tank's words, pulled out a large hunting knife and began to advance on the Pagan.

Tank was shorter and skinnier than most of the Pagans but still as tough as nails. Utterly fearless in any situation, he didn't bat an eyelid when the Angel came toward him. He reached inside his jacket and pulled out the two plastic lemons he carried on him at all times, both of them filled with ammonia. He squeezed both and two jets of the caustic liquid splattered into the face of his opponent, sending him crashing to the ground, tearing at his face in agony as Tank followed up with kicks and punches.

As the other British and Irish Angels realized what was going on, they rallied round to assist their fallen brother, pulling their man away. The Pagans did the same with Tank and soon the two sides were lined up opposite one another divided by a small area of open ground. What had started out as a one-on-one dispute was about to become club-on-club.

The last time the Pagans had fought the Angels the numbers had been even and they had come out on top, but this time they were hugely outnumbered. Still, the idea of backing down never once occurred to them. "You can fuck off," Caz told them. "You're not treating us like this. We've had it in England, and we're fed up with it there. We're not going to take it over here too." Bravado was one thing but it seemed clear that this time around that the Pagans were in for a severe beating.

But the Angels' antics during the show and throughout the rest of the country had earned them few friends. As word of the impending confrontation spread around the show site, members of the Devil's Disciples rushed over and took up positions alongside the Pagans. So did the members of another Irish club, the Limerick-based Road Tramps (unrelated to the UK club of the same name). Dozens of ordinary bikers from outside the one-percenter scene who were pissed off about being mistreated by the Angels also lined up against them.

Now the odds were almost even. Many of the Angels had knives, the others armed themselves as best they could with whatever they could find. Then, like a scene out of *Braveheart*, the air filled with screams and battle cries as the two massive armies suddenly rushed toward one another and smashed together in a mass of blood and guts and broken bones.

Savage kicks and punches flew in all directions. Bikers fell on both sides, some unconscious, others in terrible agony. Some donned crash helmets, lowered their heads and rushed at their opponents like deranged bulls. Faces were ripped and torn apart and opponents came together in terrible fury. The center of the fight was pure chaos. Everyone was hitting everyone else, whoever was nearest. It was hard to tell friend from foe. Many of those with knives found they were unable to use them in such close quarters or ended up having them turned back on themselves.

The noise of bone against bone, wood against bone and the screams of agony were almost unbearable. Link was whacked across the back with a lump of wood, Boone was virtually knocked out from a blow to the head. Dozens fell. Fountains of blood were spilled.

The whole thing had lasted only a few seconds but in that time there had been dozens of appalling injuries. One of the Devil's Disciples suffered a major stab wound as did at least two of the Angels. Dozens of bikers had major head wounds. There was a short pause—an eerie silence filled only by the groans of the wounded—as bodies were dragged from the battlefield and both sides regrouped. The hosts of the event, the Freewheelers, could only sit and watch the chaos taking place in front of them. A couple of smaller scuffles followed before it was clear that the situation had reached a stalemate and it was time to talk.

But it was already too late. Although the biker gangs liked to think they owned the place, the real power in Ireland then was still in the hands of the paramilitary groups like the IRA. Summoned by friends and relatives who had witnessed the goings-on at the festival, these groups soon turned up at Kilmeaden in force, armed to the teeth, and demanded an explanation from the Freewheelers about what was happening.

After that first meeting was concluded, the paramilitaries did their own research, walking around the site, keeping a low profile while speaking to locals and some of the other biker clubs, building up a complete picture of what had taken place during the preceding hours. When they were satisfied, they arranged to have a second meeting with the Freewheelers. This had been going on only for a few minutes when a member of the Irish club emerged and asked the Pagans to attend the meeting as well.

"All of what's happened here, this entire problem, it's all up to you guys," said the spokesman for the paramilitaries, pointing an accusing finger at the Pagans. "We know you didn't cause it, but ultimately it's up to you because you've brought something here that started out in England.

"Now we don't have a problem with you. We know you were trying to stand up for some of the locals and we're grateful for that, but this thing needs to be sorted out right now." After a few more discussions, the paramilitaries arranged for a meeting with the Hell's Angels. "Basically you've got two choices," the leader of the paramilitaries told them in his thick brogue. "There's a ferry leaving at eight a.m. tomorrow. Either you and all your little friends get on it and you leave, or you stay here forever—six feet underground.

"As of this moment, the Hell's Angels no longer have a presence in Ireland. You're finished as far as this place is concerned. Any of you who are still in the country tomorrow morning will be considered a legitimate target and I can guarantee you that you will never, ever leave. This is your one and only warning."

The Angels may have been a well-organized gang with strong international connections but, when it came to sheer efficiency, the paramilitaries had them beat, hands down. At the same time that the meeting at Kilmeaden was taking place, two teams of heavily armed men wearing helmets simultaneously attacked the Angels clubhouses in Armagh and Dublin, ejecting all the occupants and setting both buildings on fire.

It was bad enough that the British Angels were being expelled, the fact that it happened during the World Run just made it all the more humiliating. The UK contingent were forced to go around to all of their esteemed guests from across the globe and tell them that the weekend had come to a premature end and that they would all be reconvening in England as a matter of urgency.

Both Irish chapters were closed down immediately, their members either leaving the club or moving to England. It was the first time in the history of the Hell's Angels that they had ever been forced to abandon one of their territories.

The fight that had led to the expulsion quickly achieved legendary status among the bikers throughout the Republic and the event was soon commemorated by one of the Freewheelers who had always had powerful literary aspirations. Within the space of a month he had composed an epic poem, "The Battle of Kilmeaden," that read like a cross between Tennyson's "The Charge of the Light Brigade" and "Beowulf." A framed version of the poem can still be found inside the Freewheelers' clubhouse.

The Battle Royale started a powerful chain reaction no one could have foreseen. The Angels had always been feared and revered, achieving a near mythic status, but the fight had proved that if the indigenous clubs combined forces, they were more than strong enough to take on Big Red.

In the months that followed, the bond among the Freewheelers, the Devil's Disciples, the Road Tramps and another Irish MC, the Vikings, grew closer and closer until the clubs eventually formed the "Alliance Ireland"—a group of MCs that had combined forces to "keep Ireland free of international biker politics." In other words, to prevent the Hell's Angels from ever setting foot in the Republic again.

The Pagans remained at the Kilmeaden festival for the rest of the weekend, caring for their wounded and enjoying the festivities as best they could, trying hard not to think about the storm clouds that were now gathering on the horizon. As Boone, Link and the others rode back to the UK on the ferry, they all knew that they had finally sealed their fate.

The previous altercation with the Angels had driven something of a wedge between the two clubs but now that had expanded into a gaping chasm. In the space of a year the Pagans had gone from potential Angel prospects to firm Angel enemies. Once the dust had settled, all that would remain would be a state of war.

The Hell's Angels were also thinking to the future. As soon as they got back they called a series of urgent national church meetings with representatives from every chapter called in to discuss the crisis. The Irish incident was just the latest in a long line of humiliations that the club had suffered. There was now a significant danger, as there had been following the incident on Chelsea Bridge in 1970, that the club's charter might be withdrawn. If the UK Angels were going to retain the right to wear the winged death's head, they were going to have to prove themselves worthy. And the easiest way for them to do that was to spill the blood of a rival MC.

10

REINCARNATION

Just before nine p.m. on a Tuesday evening in March 1992, two full-patch members of the Cycle Tramps, accompanied by their old ladies, emerged from the heavily fortified door of the gang's Birmingham clubhouse. As they climbed into a nearby Ford Fiesta, a silver BMW screeched to a halt alongside the car. Guns appeared at the windows and at least twelve shots were fired before the attackers sped off.

Twenty-four-year-old Francesca Fischer was hit in the arm and back and needed emergency surgery to save her life. Bullets also slammed into one of the bikers and the other woman but the fourth member of the group miraculously escaped unscathed.

Suspicions briefly fell on the gang's old enemy, the Road Rats, before focusing instead on the nearby Wolverhampton chapter of the Hell's Angels. Over the years the Cycle Tramps had worked hard to try to maintain good relations with the bigger gang, even changing the colors of their patches in order to avoid any antagonism. But ever since Brewer had been shot dead, the Angels seemed to have sensed a certain vulnerability and were slowly but surely trying to drive the gang out of existence.

The approach the Angels took was a tried and tested one, which meant that every member of the Tramps and every member of all the nearby MCs could see exactly what was going on. If the Angels could pick off a few of the enemy and make them feel constantly vulnerable, members would start to drift away. Once the numbers were low enough, the Angels could launch an all-out assault and seize the patches of all remaining Cycle Tramps members, a move that, by the rules of the back-patch world, would force the club to close down. Though it would be easy to simply go out and get another set of patches made for everyone, there is no honor in doing so and any MC that did would be an absolute laughingstock. Losing a patch or two in a battle is considered shameful. Losing all your patches is simply unforgivable. Without them, a club simply cannot exist.

If the Angels managed to reach that point, they would take over the clubhouse and invite any former Cycle Tramps members who they deemed to have the right stuff to prospect for the Angels, but the Tramps themselves would be no more.

The Cycle Tramps were not the only ones feeling the heat. Since 1985 the Derbyshire-based Road Tramps had run the Rock and Blues Custom Show, which had rapidly grown to become the largest motorcycle and music festival in the north of England. Just as they had muscled their way into the small gathering run by the Wolf Outlaws at Long Marston and turned it into the generous cash cow that was the Bulldog Bash, so the Angels were now eyeballing the Rock and Blues with the idea of making it their own, with or without the Road Tramps' blessing.

The Staffordshire Eagles had also clashed with the men from The Fort from time to time and, while the Leicester-based Pariah did not consider the members of the Wolverhampton club to be their enemies, they certainly didn't see them as friends and tended to give them a very wide berth. In the meantime the once healthy and respectful relationship between the Warwickshire Pagans and the Angels had fallen apart as a result of the Battle of Kilmeaden, so it seemed a fair assumption that their names had also been added to the Wolvo's hit list.

Every patch holder in every club could see that, to all intents and purposes, the Angels were hell-bent on butting heads with every motorcycle gang in the Midlands area. The smart money agreed that it was only a matter of time before all opposition to the Angels was completely wiped out.

The attack on Albert Road may have brought the dispute to the attention of a far wider public but for those involved in the biker scene, the shooting was merely the most serious of a series of smaller spats involving the Angels and the Cycle Tramps that had been going on for more than a year and had involved beatings, shootings and stabbings, though none of this had led to any fatalities. Any individuals or small groups who ran into the Angels would come under attack and often have their patches taken. Being a biker in the Midlands was becoming more and more like living in a war zone.

The initial solution the Cycle Tramps and other clubs had settled on had been to seek strength in numbers: events that had once been exclusive were increasingly being opened up to MCs from neighboring counties, enabling the clubs to travel en masse and watch out for one another. As the weeks and

months went by, strong friendships were forged among the
members of the different factions and a sense of true camaraderie began to emerge.

For Boone and the other Pagans in particular, the lesson
they had come away with in the aftermath of Kilmeaden
was that if the clubs banded together, they could easily stand
up to the Angels. But while they all remained separate clubs
there was always a chance that any individual group could
get taken out.

The idea for what happened next was not suggested from
the top down—the egos of the officers of the MCs were far too
fragile for them to want to propose anything so controversial.
But the more the rank-and-file members of the various clubs
rode together, partied together and hung out with one another, the more obvious the way forward became: it soon
came to seem like the most natural thing in the world.

They all hated the Hell's Angels and they were all being
targeted for destruction. Individually they were weak and
vulnerable. Strength and security lay in unity. If the biker
clubs of the Midlands were going to survive, they were going
to have to join forces on a permanent basis. They were
going to have to become one club.

The name was the last thing to be chosen. It had taken
months of backroom machinations, innuendo and semisecret negotiations for the Pagans, Cycle Tramps, Road Tramps,
Staff Eagles, Pariah and Wolf Outlaws to finally agree to
unify. But reaching a consensus on what they were going to
call themselves and what their new patch would look like
turned out to be almost as big a challenge as bringing them all
together in the first place.

The key stumbling block was that each club had its own
proud history and every individual member had worked long
and hard to earn their patches. No club was willing to throw

away that kind of legacy without a fight, even in the face of imminent destruction. During the early days of discussion, the Cycle Tramps suggested that everyone simply join their club, as they were the oldest and largest. The Road Tramps and the Pagans made similar suggestions but it soon became clear that the only workable solution was to start anew.

Even this was not without its difficulties. Boone attended dozens of heated discussions in which the smaller clubs expressed particular concern about being railroaded down whatever route the larger clubs decided to go; an agreement was finally reached. They would accept any patch design just so long as it met two stringent conditions: it should not look anything like a Pagans' patch and it should not look anything like a Cycle Tramps' patch.

Coming up with an acceptable design represented a significant challenge. The new colors had to be striking enough to show that the club meant business and intimidating enough to be worthy of the MC tag. Although no one in the new alliance would ever have admitted it in public, none of their individual patches had looked anywhere near as good as the Hell's Angels' infamous winged death's head. Truth be told, some of them were pretty awful.

The patch of the Staffordshire Eagles featured a large golden bird of prey sitting astride a skull, but it wasn't particularly scary and behind their backs other MCs referred to the gang as "the budgies." The Road Tramps had a hooded grim reaper as the centerpiece of their colors, but it looked as though it had been produced by a small child using a blunt crayon; the Pariah favored the head of a Viking, complete with horned helmet, which looked as though it had escaped from the pages of a kids' comic book. The Wolf Outlaws' logo featured two joined heads—one a skull, one a salivating wolf—looking in opposite directions. It was a combination that drew a single response from all those that saw it: What the fuck is that supposed to be?

The back patches of the Cycle Tramps and the Pagans were undoubtedly the best of a poor bunch (hence the collective objection), but still not anything to write home about. The Pagans featured a side view of a skull with no bottom jaw and a full head of flowing hair kept in place by a leather aviator helmet, while the Cycle Tramps had a crudely drawn forward-facing skull wearing an oversize, Native American-style headdress.

Members with rudimentary design skills were sent away with a brief to come up with something that not only had a significant visual impact but also summed up some essential aspect of each original gang, as a way of keeping their legacy alive.

What they eventually came back with was a grinning side-view skull with prominent fangs, a single, flowing lock of hair gathered into a ponytail and a tribal headdress composed of multicolored feathers. It was, in essence, the bastard child of the Cycle Tramps' and the Pagans' patches. For the smaller clubs the design would have been their worst nightmare made real, but for one single redeeming feature—it looked absolutely brilliant.

The real clincher was the headdress itself; each feather was a different color combination, based on the ones that had been used by the original gangs: blue and white for the Pagans, red and yellow for the Cycle Tramps, red and blue for the Road Tramps and so on. The overall colors for the new club would be black on yellow.

The text for the bottom rocker of the patches had been agreed upon without too much fuss. It would read "Midlands"— a territory that not only perfectly described the exact area occupied by the new club but had the added advantage of not encroaching on any existing MC. The nearest chapter of the Hell's Angels had "Wolverhampton" as their bottom rocker, a city that fell within the county known as the West Midlands. Although a strong chapter, it certainly wasn't yet strong enough to lay claim to the whole region, let alone the west of it. The Angels wouldn't like it that the new club had gotten there first, but they were just going to have to accept it.

Choosing a name to appear on the top rocker took significantly longer. Dozens of suggestions were made and dozens were shot down, often accompanied by loud laughter. Everything from the Warpigs, the Cobras and the Leathernecks to the Iron Horses, the Misfits and the Skull Crew came up but none of them quite seemed to fit. At the end of yet another futile meeting one patch holder shrugged his shoulders in frustration. "We should call ourselves the Outlaws, because at the end of the day that's what we all are—outlaws."

A rumble passed through the room and heads bobbed in agreement like a miniature crowd wave in a stadium. A vote was taken and quickly passed with a massive majority. The Midland Outlaws had been born and were ready to stake their claim on the MC world.

The only flies in the ointment were the Coventry Slaves. While the rest of the gangs in the Midlands area got along with one another, the Slaves had never been particularly popular and had not been privy to the initial discussions. The Pagans in particular had never fully forgiven them for cooperating with the Ratae during the raid on the George Street clubhouse. The Slaves were considered something of a throwback, but because they were another MC it was agreed that they had to be treated to a modicum of respect.

It was only when the formation of the new club was a foregone conclusion that they were informed about what had been going on behind their backs and offered the gentlest of ultimatums: either join forces with the new MC that was about to surround them on all sides or risk being destroyed by the Hell's Angels. The Coventry Slaves quickly chose to join the newcomers and a seventh feather—black with a white tip—was added to the headdress of the Midland Outlaws' back patch.

A few weeks before the opening of that year's annual Rock and Blues, the local police received a tipoff that the Hell's Angels were planning to mount an attack at some point during the proceedings. The police promptly told the Road Tramps MC that they would allow the event to go ahead only if the Hell's Angels were not allowed to attend.

This was the first time such a ban had been imposed at the festival, and in passing it, the authorities unwittingly cleared the way for one of the most significant events in the British biker world to take place totally unhindered.

A few hours after the show opened on July 17, 1992, all 122 members of the Pagans, Cycle Tramps, Road Tramps, Coventry Slaves, Pariah, Wolf Outlaws and Stafford Eagles moved into a secluded marquee, removed their old tattered patches, and replaced them with pristine sets featuring the new name and logo.

The new club had no single leader. Instead, each of the original clubs retained its structure and elected officials but as a chapter of the Midland Outlaws. Nothing like this had ever happened before. Clubs had been patched over one at a time and occasionally multiple chapters of a single gang had all switched allegiances en masse, but for a brand new gang to emerge out of so many others in this way was completely without precedent.

Having bonded over a common enemy, the members of the new club were determined to be a class apart from the gang that had caused them so much grief. As they admired their new club colors, one of the senior officers put those thoughts into words. "There's one thing I would like to say that I hope we can all agree on," he said, marching up and down the line like a leather-clad William Wallace, "let no man here ever act like a Hell's Angel and bring this club into disrepute."

They had all seen other biker gangs, and members of the Hell's Angels in particular, being overly aggressive and picking on members of the public for no good reason. They had all learned the hard way that if you treated people with respect and didn't abuse them, they tended to treat you with far more respect as a result. The Midland Outlaws were keen to continue that philosophy.

There would be no bullying, no elitism, no riding rough-shod over the rights of ordinary bikers. If a civilian was deemed to be out of order, rather than beating him half to death the way certain other clubs might, the Midland Outlaws would have a harsh word and embarrass the person in front of his friends. If it became necessary to get physical, they would bitch-slap the person down rather than kicking his head in. If someone was found to be in breach of their rules and regulations by, for example, taking photographs of club members at a show where signs specifically asked them not to, rather than smashing their camera to pieces and putting them in the hospital, the Midland Outlaws would take the camera off the person, remove the film and then give them some money so they could buy a replacement.

Having established the ground rules for behavior, it was time to go public. With onlookers wondering just what on earth was going on, Boone and the other members of the new club emerged from the tent proudly flying their new colors, and lined up for a series of official photographs.

Details of the launch had supposedly been kept from the partners of the patch holders, but in reality many of them were fully aware of what was about to happen. Soon after the unveiling, all the old ladies gathered on the pedestrian bridges over the nearby highway, cameras at the ready, to capture the moment as all the members of the new club went out on their inaugural run, down to the city and then back up to the festival.

It was a moment that none of them would ever forget. Not only were they witnessing the birth of a brand new club, they were also proud members of the single largest MC anywhere in England. Not only were they now bigger than the Hell's Angels but the Midland Outlaws were far more united than their rivals could ever dream of. All the members of the new club were within, at most, a couple of hours' ride of one another while the full strength of the Angels was spread across the country. While the Angels knew the members of their own chapter well, virtually every member of the Midland Outlaws knew every member of the entire club.

The Angels may have been one brotherhood, united by a patch, but the Midland Outlaws were well and truly one, single club. And unlike the individual clubs the new gang had replaced, they were a force to be reckoned with.

It took only a few hours for word of the new club to reach the collective ears of the Hell's Angels and for a moment it was as if all the shit in the world had hit every fan ever made. The response from Angel's HQ in California was equally dramatic: What the fuck is going on over there?

Within a couple of days, senior officers from the Angels had gotten in touch with the newcomers and demanded they attend a meeting at The Fort. The response was curt: No. If you want to meet with us, you come to our clubhouse. The Angels said they would agree only if the Midland Outlaws would guarantee their safety with a verbal peace treaty, which in the MC world is considered wholly binding. The new gang pointed out that if the Angels only want to talk, there was nothing for them to worry about.

The meeting took place at the Derby clubhouse—formerly home to the Road Tramps—which had been fully refurbished to reflect the colors of the new club. All the chapters' premises had been done up accordingly, but Derby was the ultimate showpiece. Constructed in sparkling stainless steel and dark veneer, with highly polished wooden surfaces and low-level mood lighting, it looked more like a plush city-center bar than a biker hangout. All those who visited agreed it was a truly stunning place and the Midland Outlaws couldn't wait to show it off.

The Angels, who had been expecting something of an motley group, were in for a shock. As they left the highway at the Derby exit they were greeted by teams of outriders displaying their shiny new patches, who then escorted them through the outskirts of the town and right up to the clubhouse door.

Looking distinctly uncomfortable and more than a little intimidated, the six Angels fought to compose themselves as they sat down in the meeting room on one side of the large oblong table. Boone and the others could sense that what they really wanted to do was shout and scream and kick, but under the circumstances they felt compelled to remain relatively restrained.

The first words they spoke betrayed their true emotions. "You can't do this," said the lead Angel.

Joey Lagrue, a senior officer from Birmingham, acted as chair for the meeting.

"What are you talking about?" he replied. "We've already done it. It's a done deal. Build a bridge and get over it."

For a few moments the Angels were rendered speechless.

"Well you can't call yourselves Outlaws."

"We are Outlaws. And we're certainly not changing it for you."

"But listen guys, this would be much less of a problem if you changed your name."

"It's not going to happen. We're not changing anything. We haven't done it to upset you. This is a new club. Anything that happened in the past is ancient history as far as we're concerned. We just want to be left alone. You do your thing, we'll do ours."

The Angels demanded to know exactly how many full-patch members the Midland Outlaws had. Lagrue refused to say. In the spirit of détente the Angels then revealed exactly how many members they themselves had in the country at that moment in time. Lagrue would only reply cryptically: "That means there are more of us than you. But don't worry, we're not planning on coming after you. We haven't all gotten together to seek retribution."

The idea that anyone other than themselves would raise the issue of revenge attacks really put the Angels on edge. "How dare you say there won't be any retribution," their spokesman said. "We're the ones who will—"

"But there *won't* be any retribution," interrupted Lagrue. "We forgive you everything that you've done to all of us in the past. This is a brand new start. The slate has been wiped clean."

The Angels went off for a private group huddle, animatedly discussing the situation, while the Midland Outlaws sat back and enjoyed the fact that they had made their once-formidable adversaries quite so uncomfortable. A few minutes later the Angels returned to the negotiation table.

"Okay, we've talked about it and the only real problem we have is the name. If you change your name, then we can all get on and party together."

Lagrue snorted dismissively. "But we don't want to party with you!" he said. "We'll get on with you if you want, but if you don't, then we don't care. We really don't care. Either way, changing the name is out of the question."

"But the thing is, we're at war with the Outlaws in America."

The men on the Midlands side of the table paused briefly and exchanged glances. Then they all shrugged their shoulders. The club members had precious little interest in what was going on outside the Midlands, let alone outside of the UK. Up until that moment, it simply hadn't occurred to them that they were about to become namesakes with a big American club. After all, the Wolf Outlaws had existed for many years without anyone claiming they had connections overseas. Similarly, the Pagans' in Pennsylvania had never seemed concerned about the Warwickshire club. So far as they knew, the American Outlaws had no chapters outside of the United States and had no plans to open any. If the choice of name made the Angels uncomfortable, that could only be seen as a good thing, but it certainly hadn't been a deliberate ploy.

"We don't care about who you're at war with," said Lagrue. "We're not the same club as the Outlaws in America. We don't have anything to do with them whatsoever."

"Then why did you call yourselves Outlaws?"

"Because we had to come up with a name and that was the one that fit best. That's what we are. We're outlaws from society and most of the biking world now. It's our name and you're just going to have to live with it."

"Well I'll tell you this much; if you start going over to America and hanging out with the Outlaws there, then we will be at war."

Lagrue looked into the faces of the men sitting on either side of him and then leaned forward toward the Angels, his voice low and slow. "You still don't get it, do you? You can't tell us what to do anymore. You're not in charge of any of us and you don't make decisions for us. We'll do what we want."

The meeting ended soon afterward. As the Angels rode off, their frustration was plain. It had been a pretty futile exercise for them. They had left with little information and went away shaking their heads, not knowing what to say. One thing was clear to all: there were unlikely to be any more cozy chats between the two sides.

On August 8, a few days after the meeting, there was a bungled attempt to nip the new alliance in the bud. A former member of the Cycle Tramps narrowly avoided death after answering a knock on his door. As he walked down the hall to see who was there, someone pushed the barrel of a sawed-off shotgun through the mail slot and fired.

Two weeks later, at the Bulldog Bash, two Angels kidnapped a member of a neutral biker club who was known to be friendly with several members of the Midland Outlaws. He was tortured until he told everything he knew about their reasons for forming and their plans for the future.

For Boone and the others the fact that the Angels were running scared was a good thing. It meant they had lost the initiative, they were on the back burner and with any luck, they would realize that the best thing they could do would be to leave their former enemies alone. The Angels saw it differently. Whichever way they looked at it, the choice of name was anything but coincidental and this new club had firmly allied itself to their biggest global enemy. That in turn meant only one thing: a new front in the vicious and brutal war that had been raging across America since the late sixties had now been opened up in the UK.

11

BLOOD FEUD

The hatred between the Outlaws and the Angels is epic in nature and deeply ingrained in the psyche of both clubs. The Hell's Angels consider themselves to be the premier back-patch motorcycle club in the world. They have more than thirty-six hundred members in at least thirty countries, a proud history that can be traced right back to the end of the Second World War and, thanks to an ill-informed public at large that consider virtually all bikers to be Hell's Angels, a name that has become synonymous with a drinking, fighting, rule-breaking lifestyle.

Their ultimate aim is nothing less than global domination of the entire biking brotherhood. Back in 1969, the controversial underground magazine *Oz* featured an interview with Crazy Charlie, then president of the newly formed London chapter. Speaking about the club's plans for the future, he said: "We're going to get bigger and bigger. There's no limit. One day it's not going to be Hell's Angels London or Chapter California. It's going to be Hell's Angels, Earth."

The power of their legacy combined with the might of their marketing and public relations machine means that outsiders can easily be forgiven for assuming that the Hell's Angels were the original driving force behind the creation of the alternative biker movement.

But the simple truth is that the Outlaws were there first. According to the official history of the Hell's Angels, the club was born on March 17, 1948, in the San Bernadino district of California. The official history of the Outlaws states that their club was founded in 1935 in Matilda's Bar on the old Route 66 in the town of McCook, Illinois, just outside Chicago.

Originally known as the McCook Outlaws, the gang hand painted their colors—a winged motorcycle—onto the back of their leather jackets and spent their time either racing or going on long-distance motorcycle tours, in between drinking and partying. Despite most members being called up for active duty and several being killed or wounded in combat, the club did not disband during World War II and continued to meet, albeit on a limited basis. It proved it was once again a force to be reckoned with an appearance at the first major postwar biker rally in Soldier's Field, Chicago, in May 1946, nearly two years before the Hell's Angels were even founded.

The club grew rapidly and by 1950 had moved to a new base

in Chicago and changed its logo to a small skull with Old English-style lettering above and below. At this time, members also voted to adopt a new name: the Chicago Outlaws. Three years later, *The Wild One* hit screens across the United States. Starring Marlon Brando, the iconic biker film shocked the mainstream, and became a cult favorite with MC members across America. The Chicago Outlaws loved the film, and in particular, they loved the back patch worn by the Black Rebels Motorcycle Gang. Like their own design, it featured a skull but with the addition of two crossed motorcycle pistons underneath, giving the effect of a modern-day Jolly Roger. They quickly incorporated crossed pistons into their own logo, placing them behind a larger skull in an arrangement that would affectionately become known as "Charlie."

By 1964, the original contingent were joined by clubs from Milwaukee and Louisville so the "Chicago" part of the name was dropped and the various chapters united as one Outlaw nation—incorporated as the American Outlaw Association, or AOA, on New Year's Day 1965. (The Hell's Angels did not incorporate their own club until the following year.)

One notable Outlaw member from this time was Danny Lyon, who in 1965 was a twenty-year-old student at the University of Chicago. A self-taught photographer, he joined the club and began snapping pictures of his buddies at every opportunity. His photography book, *The Bikeriders*, was published in 1968 and depicts a time when most MCs across America considered one another to be brothers above all things. One particularly iconic picture shows a smiling Hell's Angel wearing his colors while riding "two up" behind a Pickelhaube-wearing Outlaw, also in full colors. The peace between the two gangs lasted only a few more years.

The seeds of the clubs' lifelong enmity were sown in the summer of 1969 when a young man named Sandy Alexander traveled from his New York home to California to ask Sonny Barger for a Hell's Angel charter. Alexander had been a member of the Aliens Motorcycle Club, which had chapters across New York state, but after learning to kill with his bare hands during a stint in the marines and fighting as a professional boxer, Alexander found that the Aliens were simply not tough enough for him.

He persuaded thirteen other Aliens to break away and form a gang of their own with the hope of eventually becoming Angels. But while Alexander was away, a fellow Alien, Peter "Greased Lightning" Rogers slept with his wife. Alexander returned and searched high and low for Rogers, only to discover that he had fled to Florida.

Alexander had not returned empty-handed: he received his charter, became president of the Manhattan chapter of the Hell's Angels and went on to become one of the most powerful figures in the organization, second only to Sonny Barger himself. He demanded absolute loyalty and introduced a rule that all prospects had to commit a murder before earning their colors. They were instructed to pick a target from extensive files of enemies kept by the club's security officer and provide documentary evidence of the deed once it had been done.

In the meantime, Rogers remained in Florida and joined the Outlaws. In time, he too rose to become an important figure in his club. He returned to New York in 1974 to visit old friends and was soon spotted by two bikers who remembered that this was the man Sandy Alexander had been trying to get his hands on for the past five years.

Forcibly held until Alexander himself arrived, Rogers was offered a fair one-on-one fight. During the event, there was nothing fair about it. Alexander spent the next twenty minutes beating Rogers to a bloody pulp and then left him for dead. Battered, bruised and brutally humiliated, Rogers returned to Florida and told his club mates a face-saving lie: he had been attacked by more than a dozen Angels who jumped him from behind. Now it was the Outlaws who needed to save face, something they could only do by taking revenge on the Angels.

They got their first opportunity a couple of months later when Big Jim Nolan, president of the fearsomely brutal South Florida chapter of the Outlaws, heard that three Angels from Lowell, Massachusetts, were in town. One of these, Albert "Oskie" Simmons, had left the club in "bad standing" before drifting down to Florida. The other two, Edwin "Riverboat" Riley and "Whiskey George" Hartman, both of whom were wanted for murder, had tailed Simmons to the sunshine state to supervise the covering up of his Angel tattoos—required action for all those leaving the club under a cloud.

The Outlaws confronted the trio and Riverboat and Whiskey explained that they were not wearing their colors out of respect for the fact that they knew they were in Outlaw territory. Seemingly impressed by this gesture, the Outlaws invited the Angels back to their clubhouse where they all drank and partied until the early hours. At which point, the atmosphere changed. The smiles and laughter suddenly gave way to frowns and scowls. The Outlaws chatted among themselves and agreed that they shouldn't be drinking with the scum who were responsible for beating one of their beloved brothers half to death.

Their guests were swiftly tied up and loaded into a van by four Outlaws, including Norman "Spider" Risinger, then driven to a flooded quarry pit near Andytown. There they were made to kneel down facing the water, arms tied behind their backs and concrete blocks attached to their legs. Risinger then shot each man in turn through the back of the head with a 12-gauge shotgun and pushed their bodies into the water. The trio of corpses were discovered just a few days later when a passing motorist spotted a foot with a blue sock bobbing in the water.

The Angels launched their own investigation into the murders, fearful that their guys had in fact been killed by the police in order to set one club against the other. It didn't take long to establish that the Outlaws were truly to blame and, at a national meeting in Cleveland attended by representatives from all chapters, the Hell's Angels declared all-out war on their rivals.

The Outlaws were more than ready to fight. When the Florida chapter suspected those on the fringes of the biker world of gathering home addresses of full-patch members for the Angels, they kidnapped the "snitches," tied them up and dunked them into tubs of water into which were dipped live electrical wires. When the terrified victims still refused to talk, they were taken out into the swampland of the Everglades and made to dig their own graves. When they *still* claimed to know nothing, the Outlaws finally realized that the people they had abducted were actually innocent after all.

Chicago-based Harry "Stairway" Henderson, national president of the Outlaws, ordered that all Florida clubhouses were to be surrounded with cinderblock walls equipped with gun ports. Guards were posted twenty-four hours a day and clubhouses had to be stocked with enough weapons and ammunition to fight off enemies. (In the mobile home that served as HQ for the South Florida chapter, the weapons were hidden inside a box of children's toys.) The precautions proved well worthwhile. In 1975, the Hell's Angels launched frantic machine gun attacks on Outlaw clubhouses in Atlanta, Jacksonville, South Florida and Ohio, but no members were injured.

Soon every Outlaw clubhouse featured a sign reading "All Hell's Angels Must Die," and "ADIOS" (Angels Die In Outlaw States) became a popular slogan alongside the favorite, "God Forgives, Outlaws Don't." Schedules were reorganized and one member from each chapter was assigned to collect all the old ladies and girlfriends from their jobs, rather than each member picking up his own. The move ensured there were always enough people in each clubhouse to fend off a potential attack.

Outlaws from northern chapters were transferred south but told not to wear their colors so they could gather intelligence. Stairway Harry also ordered members to get rid of their stolen motorcycles and any other obvious contraband so they minimized their chances of being arrested. Every available man was needed to fight and the Outlaws didn't want to lose anyone for the sake of petty crime. Members were expected to contribute to a war fund to buy guns, explosives and grenades. At a training camp in the Everglades later that year, a former U.S. Navy commando taught attendees how to use explosives and set booby traps, a move considered prudent as both sides seem to be upping the levels of violence.

The Angels were on the attack too. Clarence "Addie" Crouch and two other members from the Cleveland chapter set up a hit at an Outlaw meeting. Crouch was armed with a shotgun while his two partners in crime carried a machine gun and a .45 pistol.

"There was a bunch of people standing outside and it was dark and we pulled up and stopped and the machine gun opened up, and I started shooting. I shot a window out, I shot a bike, I shot up the driveway and I hit somebody. It turned out to be a seventeen-year-old kid."

Crouch redeemed himself in 1976 while in Memphis. "I was in a tattoo shop getting a tattoo on my arm and a lot of Outlaws walked in. One had 'Outlaws, Memphis' on his back with their center logo. I put eighty stitches in his back with a big X through it. I made him an X member. Ha ha."

The state of war did nothing to slow the global expansion of the MC scene. In Canada, a major Hell's Angel stronghold, four chapters of the Satan's Choice MC patched over to become Outlaws in the spring of 1977. Outlaws from across

America clubbed together to provide machine guns and grenades for their new brothers.

With three heavily armed Hell's Angels' chapters nearby, the two Outlaws chapters in North Carolina—one in Charlotte, the other in Lexington—were always on a higher war footing than most. Midway between Miami and New York, maintaining a firm grip on the area was key to being able to run drugs between the two cities. Neither gang wanted to lose out. Both sides reinforced heavily. The Outlaws surrounded one of their clubhouses with a twelve-foot-high fence reinforced with concrete on both sides and called it Fort Lexington. The Angels replaced the windows of their clubhouse in Charlotte with gun slits and called it The Alamo.

In the summer of 1979, sixteen-year-old Bridgette "Midget" Benfield was well on her way to becoming an Outlaw old lady. She had begun seeing William "Waterhead" Allen, a full-patch member of the gang's Charlotte chapter and soon decided to run away from home to be with him. She called her parents every few days but refused to come home, assuring them that she was all right. But then, in a call made at the beginning of July, five-foot-nothing Bridgette sounded as though things had taken a turn for the worse. "Mama, I'm into something," she said.

"We'll help," her mother Sue replied. "Tell us."

"I can't. I got into it. I have to get out."

In the early hours of July 4, chapter president William "Chains" Flamont returned to the Charlotte clubhouse and found a gruesome scene. Allen was slouched on a seat on the porch, a gun nestled in his lap and a bullet hole in his head. Inside the house, Bridgette, two more Outlaws and a club associate were also dead. They had been hit with shots fired from outside the house and then finished off with shots to the head from close range.

At least two suspects wielding a 9 mm and a .223 semi-automatic fired around forty shots. It looked like Allen was talking to one of his killers when he opened fire on him. The others probably woke to the sound of the shots but were unable to react quickly enough to escape. The shooting lasted less than fifteen seconds. It remains the worst mass murder in Charlotte history and the case is unsolved to this day.

Following the killings, the Outlaws moved their Charlotte clubhouse to North Mecklenburg, a mostly black section of town, on the basis that the snowy white faces of any Angels who came snooping around would stand out like sore thumbs.

Both the bitter rivalry and the body count continued to grow across the United States over the years that followed. By the time the Midland Outlaws unveiled themselves, the AOA had not expanded internationally so the war between the two gangs had not yet reached overseas. But all that was about to change.

12

PAYBACK

The specter of sudden, violent death is a constant backdrop to the lives of one percenters all over the world. Intergang feuds and disputes account for some of the casualties, chronic conditions like cirrhosis that develop from a lifetime of hard partying are responsible for others, but in both cases the proportion is small. Without doubt, the most common cause of a fatality within the MC community is a road accident.

It's not that club members are bad riders—far from it: speeding along in neat formation is nowhere near as easy as it looks and, in most clubs, it is impossible to progress from prospect to full member without demonstrating that you have the required skills to barrel down a highway at eighty or ninety miles an hour with fellow bikers just a few feet in front and behind.

Even when riding alone, the hours that club members spend on two wheels—along with a certain propensity for consuming large quantities of drugs and alcohol—sharply increases their chances of being involved in some kind of accident. In May 2000, the legendary Maz Harris, a Hell's Angel with so much experience that he regularly tested new models for Harley-Davidson, died after plowing a 1200cc Buell into a crash barrier while riding along a freeway. He was fifty years old and just a month away from his wedding.

So many members die in this way that the walls of every clubhouse are adorned with pictures of those who are "gone but not forgotten." Some members even wear special patches in remembrance of fallen brothers who they were particularly close to. Long before the formation of the Midland Outlaws, back even before the shooting of Rabbi, a prominent long-standing member of the Pagans had ended up a paraplegic as a result of a serious motorcycle accident—a powerful reminder to the rest of the club that not all such accidents are fatal. Since joining the club Boone had been to at least one funeral a year and sometimes many, many more.

No one in the club spoke excessively about dying, but everyone was aware that it could happen to them at any time. Boone, in common with the other club members, had only one stipulation for when it came to his turn to meet his maker. It was the same wish he'd expressed shortly before the raid on the George Street clubhouse. He wanted to die with his patches on.

Funerals—which count as mandatory runs for all chapter members—are elaborate, highly ritualized affairs involving mile-long processions of riders who remove their helmets as a mark of respect and rev their engines in unison in order to send their brother to the great chapter in the sky. Popular or high-ranking members can have hundreds attending their services. For Maz Harris the number reached well over three thousand, with attendees flying in from all over the world.

With the former Pagans now members of a much larger organization, the number of accidents (some major, some minor) seemed to soar and quickly reached the point where someone, somewhere, was always in the hospital recovering from a crash.

On one particularly horrific occasion, one of the Outlaws was coming back from a night out, with his old lady riding behind in the saddle. He went to overtake a vehicle in front just as a truck carrying a bulldozer was traveling in the opposite direction. The load was a little too wide for the vehicle and stuck out a little on each side. The Outlaw only just managed to squeeze through the gap.

"Ow!" gasped his old lady.

"What's up, babe?"

"I think that JCB might have caught me on the arm."

Stopping off to check whether the glancing blow had done any damage, he found her right arm had been cleanly torn off at the shoulder. It had all happened so fast that she had felt nothing more than a hard pinch.

The inherent dangers of riding as part of a group cannot be underestimated. A brief lapse of concentration or a simple error of judgment can quickly lead to a major accident. The density of the biker pack means that the consequences of any such accident are almost always catastrophic.

During the tenth anniversary ride of the San Diego-based Saddle Tramps MC, an oncoming vehicle lost control and plowed into the heart of their formation. Four Saddle Tramps died and five more were seriously injured. Similarly, when members of the Brother Speed Motorcycle Club were riding en masse along the I-5 freeway in Oregon and traffic suddenly slowed down ahead of them, all hell broke loose. Three cycles crashed immediately and those behind couldn't avoid the collision. In total, twenty-six motorcycles were involved in the accident and there were dozens of serious injuries. Miraculously, only one club member died of his injuries.

One spring, after the usual drinking and fighting of their first run of the year, the Midland Outlaws decided to take the long way home, driving up through north Wales and across Horseshoe Pass. It was raining as they made their way up the pass but this soon turned to sleet and then by the time Boone and the others were on their way down the other side it had started to snow and conditions had become horrendous.

Of the twenty-eight Outlaws on the run, twenty-two came off their cycles on the way down the pass. Boone took a bend too fast for the conditions and skidded sideways into a tree. Link jumped off his cycle and let it roll into a ditch, the only way he could possibly control it. Caz put his cycle into top gear and used the clutch as a brake to descend the slope as slowly as possible. Halfway down, he heard a scream from behind: "Get out of the way, get out of the fucking way!" Dozer had decided to do the whole thing at full speed and to the surprise of everyone made it safely to the bottom—they all found it hilarious.

As the weather started to improve, a spirit of mischievousness descended on the group. While riding in close formation, those who had already fallen off their cycles would attempt to kick those who hadn't in order to make them do the same. In the meantime, those at the back of the line found themselves constantly dodging and weaving around the detritus—wing mirrors, passenger pegs, heat shields—that fell off the damaged cycles. Spirits were high. No one was seriously hurt and none of the motorcycles were seriously damaged. It was just another anecdote they could tell their friends at the next rally.

At the back of their mind though, every biker felt that it was only a matter of time before they got themselves into a serious accident. There was simply no way to predict who was going to be next or how badly hurt they would end up. So when the news came in March 1993 that Switch, Boone's sergeant at arms, had come off his cycle, the rest of the Warwickshire chapter rushed to the hospital, bracing themselves for the worst.

Switch was lying on a bed at the far end of a busy ward, half propped up by a couple of pillows, looking battered and bruised, especially on his chest and legs where his motorcycle seemed to have rolled over him after he crashed. He was clearly in a great deal of pain.

"What on earth happened?" asked Boone.

"I dunno," came the reply, "I just came off. One minute I was going along, the next I was on the ground looking up at the sky."

It made no sense. Switch wasn't just a good rider; he was excellent, one of the most experienced in the club. He was also as tough as old boots, a former soldier who had been through multiple tours of Northern Ireland during the height of the troubles.

"Did you hit something in the road?" asked Caz.

Switch shook his head, grimacing from the pain.

"Was there something wrong with the bike? Did you have a blowout?"

"I don't think so. I would have known. I just came off."

The club members looked at one another, their foreheads crinkled with concentration.

"Were you on a corner, was there oil on the road?"

"Nah, I was in a straight line. The last thing I remember was being overtaken by a sports bike. After that I went down."

Caz paused for a moment, then, moving with a sense of urgency, made his way over to the other side of the bed and picked up the patches that the nurses had removed from their patient and placed over the back of a chair. He held them up to the light. Two small holes were clearly visible through the leather fabric, one in the center, the other higher and to the right.

"Jesus, mate," gasped Caz, "you've been fucking shot. Twice."

A doctor was quickly summoned and, with the aid of two nurses, gently turned Switch over in the bed to inspect his back. Having assumed that he had simply been the victim of a motorcycle accident they had focused on his more obvious injuries, never expecting there to be anything more.

As Switch growled with pain, his back was exposed and the two small bullet wounds, one in the shoulder, one closer to the center of his lower back, were plain for all to see, even amid the large number of lacerations and bruises. "Looks like a .22," said Boone, "a real assassin's weapon. Lucky they didn't have anything bigger otherwise you wouldn't be here to tell the tale."

The doctor, a middle-aged Indian man with small, round spectacles, turned to the group. "I'm afraid I will have to inform the police about this."

At a signal from Caz, Boone pulled the curtains around Switch's bed, isolating him from the rest of the ward. The nurses made themselves scarce while Caz stood face to face with the doctor, towering over him.

"No, you don't."

"I really should. These are gunshot wounds."

"Listen, there's no law in this country that says you have to report this to anyone. It's entirely your own discretion. I'm sure the police would like you to report it, but that doesn't mean you have to. And I'll tell you one thing, if you even look like you're going to report this, I'll pick my mate up and we'll walk out of here right now and whatever happens to him will be on your conscience forever. And if anything bad happens, all of us lot are going to hold you personally responsible. You understand?"

The doctor looked at each of the faces of the bikers surrounding the bed and saw that they were dead serious. He also knew that they were right about the law (reporting of gunshot wounds by doctors was not made compulsory in the UK until 2004), which left him with no options. "Okay," he said at last. "We'll just treat him. Nothing more."

As the bikers left the hospital, the conversation quickly turned to figuring out who might have been responsible for the hit. There was only ever going to be one set of suspects: the Hell's Angels.

"I think I know who might have shot Switch," said Link. "The bike that he described, it sounds like it belongs to this Angel who was doing time when I was. He and his brother are a couple of psychos. This is just the sort of thing they'd get up to."

All the Midland Outlaws were eager to discuss how they were going to respond to the shooting, but that would have to wait for the next church meeting. What was clear was that the club wouldn't take this lying down. They were going to fight fire with fire. As Boone rode home from the hospital, the chorus line from a Sex Pistols' song kept running through his head: "Oh you silly thing, you've really gone and done it now."

The plan was to mount a revenge attack, but as it happened the club barely had time to catch its breath before the next strike came. Link was on his way to the Rock and Blues festival, driving a Range Rover and towing a large trailer full of supplies for the show, when a couple of Hell's Angels jumped out on him from around the blind corner of a country lane.

They had chosen their ambush spot well. The only place for Link to go was straight up the steep hill, but with his non-turbo vehicle and its heavy load, he struggled to build up any speed, even with his foot flat to the floor.

He could only move back and forth, urging the car to go

faster, and watch in horror as one of the rival bikers produced what appeared to be a semi-automatic assault rifle, took aim and sent a stream of hot lead flying toward him. Glass shattered and metal ripped as the neat line of bullet holes appeared along the side of both the car and the trailer. It was a miracle Link avoided being hit. He breached the hill and drove straight into the campsite, eager to tell his fellow club members what had just taken place.

It didn't end there. Members of the Midland Outlaws found themselves being ambushed at gas stations by teams of Angels who would leap out and pound them with pickaxe handles. Others were jumped on their way to or from their clubhouses and a few ended up with serious stab or even ax wounds. By then, Boone and his comrades had started hitting back, giving as good as they got in many cases by arranging similar ambushes and attacks at places they knew that the Hell's Angels would be.

The Angels made no secret of the fact that they were trying to scare the new gang out of existence, but their tactics had the opposite effect, making them stronger and more determined to survive. Still, the Midland Outlaws were very much hampered by a lack of effective weaponry and because of that felt constantly on the defensive. What they really needed were some guns.

The Hell's Angels had firearms by the bucket load, but they had been around far longer and had made far greater inroads into the criminal underworld, partly as a result of their drug dealing networks and extracurricular work as debt collectors and security guards. When it came to getting their hands on hardware, they were long-toothed veterans.

The Midland Outlaws were, by comparison, infants learning to walk. Theirs was a club of working types who were into their motorcycles, but it was becoming increasingly clear that if they were going to survive at all, that would have to change.

Members in the know were asked to get their hands on as many guns as they possibly could. They were begged, borrowed, and stolen from every possible source. Even then, with the full weight of the club behind the task, certain weapons remained in very short supply. Shotguns were relatively plentiful and always had been, but the only handguns the club could get hold of were old World War I and II relics or deactivated display models that had been restored to enable them to fire once more. Though this was far from ideal, the fact that handguns were far easier to conceal and could fire multiple shots without reloading meant they were the most sought after.

All the weapons gathered were designated property of the club and anyone who spent his own money could be reimbursed out of central funds. The problem with the vast majority of the weapons they accumulated, though, was that you had no idea what they might have been used for previously. It was one thing to risk being caught with a gun, quite another to find that same weapon had been used in a murder. No one wanted to take the rap for someone else's crime.

In a bid to address this problem, Boone and a couple of others traveled to France where brand new shotguns can be bought over the counter simply by producing a driver's license. They smuggled back a couple of models along with a hefty quantity of ammunition, hiding the contraband from the customs officials in a load of discount booze. This still left the club with a chronic lack of handguns—just one per chapter—nowhere near enough to mount any kind of offensive action, let alone fight a full-scale war.

By now the ongoing hostilities were starting to have a serious effect on the day-to-day lives of the members. Because of the constant threat of attack, church meetings of the Warwickshire chapter were rapidly becoming a more somber and serious affair than anything that had taken place during the time of the Pagans. Increasingly paranoid about security, the room would be swept for bugs and every member would be ordered to take the batteries out of their cell phones or leave them outside.

The stress was starting to threaten the most fundamental aspects of the club itself. Everyone accepted that Switch was lucky to be alive but no one wanted to be next. The Midland Outlaws soon found itself in the unique position of being a biker club full of guys who felt distinctly unsafe on their motorcycles.

There were strict rules in place, common with most MCs, that members could only have their cycles off the road for a certain amount of time before being fined or busted down to a three-quarter patch or lower. During church, Caz would be forced to listen through ever more elaborate and ridiculous excuses from increasing numbers of members about why particular motorcycles were not available. Parts were stuck in the mail, essential components had buckled or broken, necessary maintenance was still being completed. Some members even claimed their cycles had been stolen, simply to get out of riding them. Only those with reasons considered genuine and legitimate were given any period of grace, the rest were told to get their acts together as quickly as possible. It was a harsh approach, but the only way to stop the club from completely falling apart.

Having joined forces, the Midland Outlaws were far stronger than the seven founding clubs had been individually, but they had come together with the intention of preventing a war, not starting one. Now that war was upon them the club had little idea of how best to fight it. If they were going to survive, they needed more than just strength of numbers, they needed a way of gaining experience fast.

Although the Midlands club had no affiliation to or connection with their American namesakes, the amalgamation had not gone unnoticed by the AOA. In the same way that the Hell's Angels of the 1980s had sought out every club using their name and sought to bring them under some form of central control, so the Outlaws of the nineties had begun to do the same with the idea of expanding their empire overseas.

The initial approach had been made a year or so earlier when the Wolf Outlaws were still a separate entity. A couple of members had become friendly with a man named Rainier, the sergeant at arms for an Ontario-based chapter of the AOA who also served an enforcer for chapters across the entire province.

A formidable figure, Rainier had even come over to visit with the club and had extended an open invitation first for the Wolf Outlaws and then for the Midland Outlaws to visit him in Canada. It could be just the break they were looking for. If there was one thing that Rainier knew, the former Wolf Outlaws explained, it was about fighting a war with the Hell's Angels. After all, he had killed at least half a dozen of them, and lived to tell the tale.

PART THREE

WORLD
TRAVELERS

13

IN THE LINE OF FIRE

The cult of the one-percenter MC was born and bred in the United States, but when it comes to the other end of the life cycle, Canada has always been king.

More bikers have been killed in its provinces than anywhere else in the world. At the time of writing, the body count is well in excess of four hundred and there is every indication that this will continue to rise. The figure includes two particularly grisly incidents of mass murder: five Hell's Angels from Laval in rural Quebec were executed in March 1985, while in June 2006, eight members of the Bandidos from Shedden, Ontario, suffered the same fate. Both groups died at the hands of their fellow club members in a process the gangs like to call "cleaning house."

Long before the American biker gangs arrived, Montreal, the largest city in Quebec, was home to a thriving native MC scene led by the Satan's Choice in the west (with additional chapters throughout the province) and the Popeyes in Laval, a little way to the north. Although relatively small, the Popeyes had a reputation for being extremely violent. When someone made the mistake of stealing a motorcycle from the gang, one of its members, Yves "Apache" Trudeau, tracked the thief down and shot him dead. Trudeau was an unlikely biker and an even more unlikely hit man. He stood just five feet six inches high and weighed barely 135 pounds. His clean-shaven face had soft, kindly features, reminiscent of a young Elvis. Trudeau had two loves in his life: motorcycles and co-

.er he shot the motorcycle thief, he soon added a
passion: murder.

The other MC in the area, Satan's Choice, had been around since the midsixties and could fight with the best of them if they needed to but they were far better known for their wild social events. In 1968, a reporter from the *Globe and Mail* infiltrated a party hosted by the club and watched in horror as they played a game in which a live chicken was set loose for the bikers to tear apart with their bare hands. The winner was the one who came away with the largest piece of flesh.

During the seventies, the Montreal underworld came to be dominated by Sicilian and Irish American crime dynasties and these mafia groups formed alliances with the bikers. The one percenters sold drugs, smuggled guns, collected debts and worked as bodyguards for the mob bosses, who paid them handsomely for their services.

By 1973, the Satan's Choice MC was so large and powerful that the Hell's Angels sent an emissary from California to discuss their patching over. A brief meeting took place at Toronto Airport but the Canadian bikers made it clear that they would far rather remain independent, and the Angel never even left the terminal.

In fact, the Choice had already been courted by the Outlaws and an agreement had been signed for the two clubs to recognize one another's members as equals and to shelter fugitives from the other side of their respective borders. The clubs produced a special mini-brotherhood patch that combined elements of both their logos to symbolize the new arrangement.

When the Satan's Choice founder and national president was caught red-handed with millions of dollars worth of PCP, a powerful hallucinogen that goes by the street name of angel dust, his replacement decided to embrace the Americans still further. In the summer of 1977, four chapters of the Satan's Choice patched over to become Outlaws. Not all the members went along with the move but those who did—which included most of the Montreal chapter—had the date of the change inscribed alongside their existing club tattoos, together with the inscription "RIP Satan's Choice."

The Outlaws' position as the only American-born MC in town lasted only a few months. On December 5 that same year, twenty-five members of the Popeyes in Montreal (the remainder were judged not to have made the grade) dumped their colors and became Hell's Angels. It was a chapter known for going through vast quantities of cocaine and for having a number of huge and powerful members, some tipping the scales at three hundred and four hundred pounds. But the scariest one of all—the don of the winged death's head—was little Yves "Apache" Trudeau. As he had already proved his willingness to kill for his club, the Angels appointed Trudeau as their point man for all hits on Canadian soil. The scene was now set for the bloodiest biker war ever to hit North America to begin.

On February 15, 1978, Robert Cote was drinking with a friend at Montreal's Brasserie Joey at the corner of Saint-Hubert and Castelnau in the city's Villeray neighborhood. Both men had recently joined the Outlaws and were proudly displaying their colors, unaware that the bar they were sitting in was now a Hell's Angels' stronghold. When supporters from the rival gang turned up, an argument began and Cote was kicked out. He made it only a short way down the street before a volley of shots were fired from a passing car. Cote was hit in the head and died in the hospital five days later.

The hit was carried out by Trudeau and as a result he became the first Canadian Angel to be awarded the "Filthy Few" patch, given out to those who have committed murder to rid the club of one of its enemies.

The following month Gilles Cadorette, the twenty-seven-year-old president of the Montreal chapter of the Outlaws, fell victim to a car bomb planted by Trudeau. He had been drinking in a bar on Bordeaux Street with his friend Donald McLean when the two of them climbed into Cadorette's customized Camaro, parked nearby. As he twisted the key in the ignition, a bomb wired to the circuit exploded and killed Cadorette instantly, leaving McLean seriously injured.

Four weeks later the violence between the two gangs intensified over the course of three bloody days. It began when two Angels knocked on the door of the Outlaws clubhouse at 144 rue Saint-Ferdinand. They told the startled bikers that they wanted to sit down and discuss an end to the killings. Initially cautious, the Outlaws eventually let them in. After a few moments, both the Angels pulled out automatic pistols and began firing wildly. Miraculously one pistol jammed and the other gunman failed to hit anyone, despite emptying an entire magazine. The Outlaws were too shocked to chase after the gunmen and both escaped.

The following day Athanase "Tom Thumb" Markopoulos left the Outlaws clubhouse at eleven p.m. to buy cigarettes. The store was closed so he began hammering on the door to summon the owner. She approached just in time to see two men walk up behind the biker and pump six shots into his back.

The shop was just fifty feet from the clubhouse and at the sound of gunshots, the remaining Outlaws fled, fearing they were under attack or being raided by the police. It took several hours before they learned what happened to Markopoulos.

The next night Outlaw Francois Poliseno took his girlfriend out for a drink at a bar on rue Notre-Dame. Soon after the pair sat down, a masked man burst in and sprayed them both with bullets. Both were seriously injured. Police later determined that the gun used to shoot Poliseno was the same one used to shoot up the Outlaws clubhouse.

The Outlaws attempted to strike back on May 12. Four bullets were fired at Hell's Angel Rene Hebert as he stepped out of his clubhouse. Three missed their target while the fourth only lightly grazed him. It was clear that when it came to gunmanship, the Canadian Outlaws were no match for the Angels. If they wanted to survive, they were going to need some help.

On October 12, a group of Angels were drinking in a Rosemont bar, Le Tourbillon, when two casually dressed men walked in and ordered drinks. The bikers had seen the pair before—they seemed to have been following them around for the past few days—and were sure that they were undercover cops, trying to infiltrate the club.

The Angels were even more convinced that the men were not Outlaws. For one thing, they knew the faces of all their enemies, having gotten to know them when the clubs were still Satan's Choice and Popeyes. The other thing was that these men didn't look like bikers. They had clean-shaven faces, short haircuts and no visible tattoos. They were so obviously police officers that they might just as well have turned up in uniform.

The two strangers finished their drinks and then walked over to the booth where the Angels were sitting. One of the bikers, Louis Lapierre, got up to confront them but before he could speak the man pulled out a handgun and shot him in the chest at point-blank range. The other man produced a sawed-off shotgun and fired volley after volley into the booth until he was sure all the bikers were dead. The pair then dropped their weapons and ran.

The men had been Outlaws all along, flown in from the United States especially to carry out the job. Two of their targets died instantly, another died in the hospital a few days later. Lapierre survived, while his friend, the diminutive Walter "Nurgent" Stadnick, walked away completely unscathed, having slipped his five foot four inch frame under the table in the nick of time.

The Angels hit back on November 10, sending Apache

Trudeau after former Outlaws president Brian Powers. Trudeau tracked him down to his home and knocked on the door. As Powers answered, Trudeau shot him in the head nine times, dumped the gun and made good his escape.

Trudeau, now known as "the Mad Bumper," was in his element. He received payment of up to twenty thousand dollars a time for each murder he committed, which meant he had more than enough money to fully indulge his growing cocaine habit. It didn't take long for the excessive quantities of drugs to begin affecting his judgment. On December 8, while walking round the West End of Montreal, Trudeau spotted a man who appeared to be Outlaw Roland "Roxy" Dutemple. Trudeau walked up to him and asked in French: "Are you Roxy?" He didn't wait for a reply before shooting him in the head.

The victim turned out to be William Weichold, an ordinary Joe unlucky enough to bear a strong resemblance to Dutemple. Trudeau laughed at his mistake and he argued that he should have been paid for the hit regardless. The following March he righted his wrong by planting a bomb under Dutemple's car, blowing him to pieces. And five days later, he murdered Robert Labelle, the twenty-five-year-old president of a biker gang called the Huns, who were rumored to be joining the Outlaws. Trudeau knocked on Labelle's door and shot him twice in the face the moment he appeared.

A month later, Trudeau took a second turn at Donald McLean (injured in the car bomb that killed Cadorette), attaching another explosive device to McClean's customized Harley. As he and his girlfriend Carmen Piche climbed aboard, it exploded, killing them both instantly.

Even fellow Hell's Angels were not safe. Trudeau killed Charlie Hachez, a member of the north chapter, because he had a heavy drug problem and owed Canada's top cocaine importer, a man who helped supply the Angels and who they were keen to keep in that position, more than 150,000 dollars. Hachez was lured to a meeting, killed, and his body dumped in the St. Lawrence River. And when the coke importer himself was murdered, Trudeau was hired to exact revenge.

He tracked the killers down to an apartment building in downtown Montreal where they were hiding out before making an attempt to take over the business of the dealer they killed. Trudeau learned that they did not have a television, so he paid them a visit, taking with him a gift of a TV and VCR, along with a copy of a film, *Hell's Angels Forever*. The men were keen to do business with the Angels so Trudeau told them to watch the film so they could learn "how the Hell's Angels operate, what they're all about."

The television had been rigged with eight pounds of plastic explosives that would detonate as soon as it was turned on. The resulting blast killed the two targets along with two of their neighbors and injured eight more, knocking a huge hole in the side of the building. Trudeau would later joke to friends: "I guess they found out exactly how the Hell's Angels work."

The war was not going well for the Outlaws. The Angels in general and Apache Trudeau in particular were picking them off as easily as fish in a barrel. They were going down at the rate of one a week. If they were going to save themselves from extinction, the Outlaws needed to find a Trudeau of their own. That man was Rainier.

Rainier made a name for himself in the mideighties, just around the time the Hell's Angels starting killing old ladies. The girlfriend of one of the Outlaws was killed when a bomb exploded in her face—it had been intended for her boyfriend—and so far as the Outlaws were concerned, this was overstepping the boundaries. With the Angels targeting their enemies at home, as well as on club business, the war was threatening to spiral out of control. Rainier volunteered to raise the issue in a way that the Angels simply couldn't ignore.

He acquired his own bomb and planted it on a vehicle belonging to the old lady of a senior Hell's Angel. The woman died instantly when she turned the ignition. The Angels initially swore revenge but Rainier convinced them to talk.

He wasn't after peace—far from it. So far as he was concerned, the Angels were scum and he wouldn't rest until every last one of them was dead. But if they were going to fight, there needed to be ground rules. From that point on, it was agreed that only bikers wearing back patches would be legitimate targets. There would be no house calls, no more attacks on family members or attacks at times or in places where club members were clearly involved with personal affairs.

On the flip side, this meant that every time club members put on their patches, they might just as well have been pinning a target to their back. But every club member knew the risks they faced and accepted them. It seemed only right that their families should be kept out of it.

Rainier was soon hailed as a hero and made a member of the SS, the Outlaws' equivalent of the Filthy Few (and similarly made up of members who have killed for the club). Like other SS members, Rainier had the letters tattooed on the inside of his upper left arm. And as the fighting continued, he took collections for a "war fund" from club members each month. This money would be used to purchase weapons, handguns, dynamite and hand grenades—whatever was needed.

Rainier swiftly became the point man for any offensive action that needed to be taken against the enemy, notching up at least half a dozen kills in the space of five years. Every bit as cold-blooded and ruthless as Trudeau, he helped put the Outlaws back in the driver's seat and show that they could give as good as they got. His one regret was that he never got to go up against Trudeau face to face. The Angels took care of that themselves.

Despite his continued success as a hit man and the fact that he had been made president of his own chapter, the "Mad Bumper" was finding life increasing difficult to cope with. His personal drug habit and that of the rest of the chapter was getting out of control. During one three-week binge he snorted his way through sixty thousand dollars' worth of cocaine. Other club members were using so much that they were dipping into the goods they were supposed to be selling, messing up the profits for the club as a whole.

Trudeau knew only too well what happened to Angels who let their drugs habits rage out of control. He had killed several of them himself, so he checked himself into a rehab facility in March 1985. He was still there when the five remaining members of his chapter were summoned to a meeting in Lennoxville by senior Angel officers so they could answer questions about the crazy killing spree and missing drug money. By the time the meeting ended, all five members of Trudeau's chapter had been murdered by their Angel brothers. As soon as Trudeau came out of rehab, he became a police informant and was later given a new identity.

Having carved out his reputation for fearlessness, Rainier used the onset of peace that followed the massacre of the Angel chapter to build up his personal power base. He began reaching out to clubs across the globe that had "Outlaw" in their name and inviting them to join forces with the AOA. In the early nineties, one of those invitations made it all the way to England. And just around that same time, the war between the Canadian Outlaws and the Angels began to flare up once again.

The cheapest last-minute deal on a flight to Canada the Midland Outlaws could find was with Air India, the second leg of a packed flight from Mumbai, which stopped in London for refueling before heading on to Toronto. The bikers were among only a handful of new passengers to board at Heathrow and the scene that greeted them was more reminiscent of India's notorious railway networks than anything to do with flying. Every conceivable inch of space had been taken up with suitcases and oddly shaped bundles of clothing. All the overhead storage bins were full and the plane was so packed that Boone and the others half expected to find additional passengers squished in between the bags of duty–free goods.

The one percenters began drinking heavily almost as soon as the plane reached cruising height, knocking back beers with whiskey chasers just as fast as the cabin crew could serve them, but Dozer insisted on taking things further. He began swigging down champagne and then, on the basis that "everyone in India smokes weed" he rolled a big fat joint and began puffing away on it.

All the Midland Outlaws were sitting in the smoking section (Air India did not introduce a ban until 1999) and Dozer was probably not the only one indulging, but his behavior became increasingly erratic and of growing concern to the crew. His fellow club members were also worried and decided to try to ignore him so that they would not all get into trouble over his antics.

Well aware that they could face a hard time getting through immigration, they were traveling incognito with their patches hidden beneath their jackets and plans to pass through customs one at a time, hoping to slip through inconspicuously. The last thing they wanted to do was attract undue attention to themselves.

Dozer was having trouble grasping that concept and by the time they landed in Toronto he had evolved into a full-blown pain in the ass. While Boone and the others did their best to keep their distance, he stood in the line for passport control spinning one of the metal poles used to hold the rope barriers and lighting up another spliff.

It was as if he somehow believed that the law no longer applied to him. He was wrong. Much to the relief of those around him, the security staff came along, shackled his hands and feet and dragged him away. He looked over at Boone and the others, wondering why they were doing nothing to help him. They did their best not to meet his gaze. It was pretty clear that Dozer wasn't going to make it into Canada. Unless they were extremely careful, none of them would.

Boone was first in line at the customs desk. The stern-faced woman in the booth eyed him up and down carefully. "Before you say anything, I want you to be clear that it is an offense to lie to a public official," she said. "Do you understand?"

"Sure," said Booth.

"Do you have a criminal record?"

"Does a parking ticket count?"

The woman shuffled forward and angled her computer even closer toward her to ensure that no one else could read the screen. "The information I have in front of me includes every detail about your life so I ask you once again. Do you have a criminal record?"

Boone cocked his head to one side. "If you've got all that there, then you already know whether I've got a criminal record or not."

The woman scowled then tried a different tack. "Are you a member of a biker club?" Boone racked his brain. He had to find a way to answer the question without lying. It was like a weird version of the Yes! No! game.

"What exactly do you mean by that?"

"Are you a Hell's Angel?"

At last Boone could be completely honest. "No I am not! How dare you. I am most certainly not a Hell's Angel."

"Okay," said the official, stamping his passport. "Through you go."

The rest of the Midland Outlaws made it through and gathered together outside the terminal where they slipped on their patches. The mood was buoyant and even the news that Dozer was being immediately deported did not dampen their spirits. Many were still buzzing from the combined effects of huge alcohol consumption at high altitude. None of them realized that they were stepping into conflict that would make what was going on back in England look like a Boy Scout picnic.

The Canadians turned out to be gracious and clearly wealthy hosts. As soon as they had dropped off their bags they insisted on taking their British brothers out to a lap-dancing bar. By then, having checked in ahead of time, crossed the Atlantic, waited in line for immigration and then driven across three hundred miles of Canadian wilderness, most of the Brits had been up for thirty hours straight and were starting to feel a little worse for wear.

Boone tried to stay focused as the Canadian president pointed out various aspects of the club and highlighted some of the extras, such as private dances, available from some of the women. "Finally," he said, "you see that woman over there?" He pointed to a statuesque redhead with enormous fake breasts dancing on a podium at the far end of the room. The Brits all nodded. It was hard to miss her. "Well that's my wife. So if you do decide to take advantage of any of the extras. . . ." Boone held up a hand—he knew exactly what the biker was about to say. "If you fancy any extras with her," he continued, "I'd appreciate it if you only go as far as a blow job. We're trying for a kid."

Boone lowered his hand. He had been wrong. He hadn't known what was coming after all. In truth, they were all ex-

hausted and a lap-dancing club was the last place any of them
wanted to be. As one of the scantily clad women began gyrat-
ing between the legs of one of the English guys, he pushed her
away. "Leave it out, love," he said, "I'm really not up for this."

Their Canadian hosts were horrified. "Hey man, what's
wrong?"

"Nothing. We're just not interested."

"What? Are you guys gay or something?"

"Huh?"

"Do you guys like women?"

"Oh yeah, we're just a bit washed out. We've been up all
night and we haven't had anything to keep us going. No coke,
no speed, nothing. We just can't do it."

The president breathed a big sigh of relief. "Oh, thank God
for that. Tell you what, we'll get you back to the clubhouse and
let you get your heads down. We can come here tomorrow
night."

Once they had returned to the clubhouse, a few of the Midland Outlaws crashed right away while Boone and a few others, feeling too wired and too worried about what might be
happening to Dozer, stayed up drinking and trying to relax.

As Boone sat in a corner, his mind buzzing with anxiety, he
noticed the club's sergeant at arms staring at him strangely. It
made him feel uncomfortable and he averted his own gaze.
But every time he looked over, the club's enforcer was still
staring directly at him.

Eventually the man came over to him, lifted the front of
his jacket to reveal the gun stuffed into his belt, pulled the
weapon out and slammed it down on the table next to where
Boone was sitting.

"Take it," said the sergeant.

Boone didn't know much about the rules and regulations
that governed the American Outlaws but he imagined that,
rather like his own group's rules, there were certain restrictions about who was allowed to be in possession of weapons

at any time. There were almost certainly also rules about when you are allowed to attack a fellow club member. Boone knew that the instant he picked up the gun, he would technically be armed. That wasn't something he wanted to be, so he remained perfectly still. He didn't want to give the man any justification to shoot him.

"I said pick it up."

"No," said Boone. "I'm all right. I don't need it."

"But I want you to have it."

"I don't want it."

"It's yours. Keep it. I'll get it off you when you leave."

"Really, I don't need it. I feel safe here."

"But you're not safe."

A shiver went down Boone's spine. Maybe the whole thing was a ruse. Perhaps the Midland Outlaws had been lured to Canada not to bond with the AOA but as a way of getting rid of them. Perhaps the Outlaws were about to clean house.

"What do you mean?" asked Boone.

"Come with me."

The sergeant tucked the gun back into his belt and then he and Boone made their way to the front door of the clubhouse. The sergeant first checked the CCTV cameras that monitored the entrance to make sure the coast was clear, then swung open the heavy reinforced door. He pointed directly ahead, at a cluster of buildings around half a mile away.

"You see that big white building there?"

"Yeah."

"That's the clubhouse of the Hell's Angels. That's how close they are. They already know you guys are in Canada and they have already been trying to get to you. We've had a couple of drive-by shootings, people taking pot shots, but so far no one has been hurt. Because you're over here, you're our guests and we're responsible for your safety. If they can kill one of you, it will embarrass us and it obviously won't do you guys any good either.

"Now we haven't been hit yet, but it's only a matter of time. We don't know what they might do so we have to be prepared for everything and anything. I know you already know how to use a gun. I want you to take this. That way, if we do get hit, you might be able to keep some of us alive."

Boone felt his cheeks flush with embarrassment.

"I'm sorry. I think I took it the wrong way."

"I guess you did. Here, take it."

Boone took the gun and tucked it into his belt. He made sure that while he was in the clubhouse, it was always within reach.

Rainier finally arrived on the third day of their stay. The minute he entered the clubhouse it was as though a Hollywood film star had landed. Boone saw people point and whisper in hushed tones. Those members of the AOA who had not met him before gingerly shook his hand and asked if they could have their photographs taken with him. They would stand beside him and smile for the camera and then make themselves scarce as quickly as possible. It was obvious that, although they were grateful for the work that he did, most people were absolutely terrified.

Despite knowing what he was capable of, Boone almost felt sorry for him and made a special effort to get to know him. The first time he got close, he realized that Rainier was even bigger than he appeared from a distance. Heavily muscled and as solid as a tree trunk, he was clearly a man who spent a great deal of time at the gym. He greeted Boone warmly and the pair began to chat but Boone's eyes were immediately drawn to the SS patch on his colors. Boone had heard about such patches, of course, but had never seen one in the flesh. The Pagans had been too small to have any such patch themselves and the Midland Outlaws were still finding their feet.

Wearing such a badge always struck Boone as being a

rather odd thing to do. Surely you were just marking yourself out for additional attention from the authorities—and making sure that, in any battle with a rival club, you'd be the first one to get taken out. Boone longed to asked Rainier about it, but knew enough about club protocol to know that some things are never discussed.

As the pair chatted, Boone found Rainier to be a surprisingly deep thinker, concerned about the future of the club, the quality of its prospects and the continued loss of good friends through killings and accidents.

"We're supposed to be part of the AOA up here," he told Boone, "but they don't give us any support. People are dying—our numbers are down. They want us to hold onto the town but to do that we need more people. We've been asking for months for them to send additional resources up here, but we haven't heard anything from them. I'm hoping that by bringing you guys here, it will set a cat among the pigeons and we'll finally see some action."

It certainly had the desired effect. Fearful that Rainier was attempting to build an empire of his own, some of the AOA top brass made the trip to Montreal to see why the Brits had traveled there first rather than to the mother chapter in the United States. When the AOA bosses arrived at the Montreal clubhouse, they saw a large "N" had been painted above the AOA logo on the wall.

"What the fuck is that?" asked one of the Americans.

"It's what we are. The North American Outlaws Association."

"You can't have that!"

"Are you saying we're part of the AOA then?" asked Rainier. "Because I was starting to feel as if we were all on our own."

The AOA immediately agreed to send up teams of bikers from chapters across America to support the Canadians. Rainier got one of the prospects to paint over the "N" and returned the logo to its original state. He had accomplished his mission and, though Boone suspected that he and the other Midland Outlaws had been somewhat used in the process, he could see that Rainier was a powerful ally and that whatever happened, it was far better to have him as a friend than as an enemy.

The Midland Outlaws had traveled to Canada partly to find out what benefits joining the AOA might provide but more important, they wanted to learn what it was like to live day to day in a war zone and pick up tips for improving their own security.

The first rule seemed to be that no one was allowed to go anywhere alone. Officers in particular had to have a team of bodyguards and lookouts with them wherever they went. Even if someone simply wanted to pop into a bar for a quick drink, he needed to have a full security detail with him. As well as armed guards, a full detail for anyone traveling by motorcycle included four security cars, two at the front and two at the rear, to look out for snipers and frustrate any attempts at blocking roads or isolating club members traveling on two wheels.

Motorcycles were kept in a secure compound next to the clubhouse, which was monitored by surveillance cameras twenty-four hours a day. Whenever cycles had to be left in a public place, they were checked carefully for any devices before being started. Ideally, a prospect would stand guard over the cycles while other members did whatever it was that they had to do. Every member had been told to acquire a mirror on the end of a stick, which they could use to check the underside of any car before they climbed into it. For the Midland Outlaws these messages initially seemed over the top, but once they heard a few of the stories about the casualties of the war the Canadian bikers had been fighting, saw some of the pictures and shared some of the horror, they realized it was all completely necessary.

Every now and then, someone would slip up and get into a car without checking and the result would be a huge shouting match. It was just about the worst thing you could do and the only way to drill that into people seemed to be to remind them if they messed up in the strongest possible terms. The Brits even saw a few bikers get knocked down a patch or two because they messed up their security protocols.

In Ottawa, the Midland Outlaws were driven around in a huge stretch limo that had a leaky gas tank. "We don't need to worry about the Angels in this thing," said Caz, "one big bump in the road and we're fucking dead anyway."

Every clubhouse had an area at the back with railway sleepers fixed with targets that were used for shooting practice. Most of the time the Outlaws made a game out of it, shooting for shots of whiskey or bourbon. Splitting into small groups, the idea was the person whose shot landed farthest from the bull's-eye had to drink. When it came to Boone's turn, he deliberately shot wide. The longer the game went on, the worse for wear he became and the poorer his shooting got.

"You're really terrible at this," commented one Outlaw.

"Yeah, but I want the whiskey. You guys have got it all ass backward."

With a wide variety of guns legally available, every member of the Midland Outlaws had the opportunity to learn to shoot and become comfortable with a range of handguns, rifles, and shotguns. The only possible downside was that the quality of the weapons available in Canada was so high that Boone knew they would be disappointed once they got back to the UK. No doubt, they'd miss the top-quality drugs too. The Midland Outlaws had used cocaine on a recreational level and at parties back home, but in Canada there was a mountain of the stuff and their hosts seemed to insist on taking it at every opportunity—breakfast, lunch, and dinner. At least one of Boone's colleagues had to go into detox back home.

By the time they returned to England the Midland Outlaws were a very different gang. The bikers had grown in confidence. They had gotten a taste of what it might be like to be part of a larger, more powerful international organization, one with the money and resources and the manpower to compete with the likes of the Hell's Angels on more or less equal terms. They had learned how to survive in the middle of a gang war and seen that, although it generated its own unique difficulties, it was still possible to live a mostly normal life. More important, they had once again seen just how much money could be made from getting seriously involved in the drug trade. It was time for the club to do the same.

If the Angels in Canada knew about the arrival of the Midland Outlaws, then it was a fair assumption that the Angels in England had also been made aware of the trip. Having initially denied that the group had any affiliation with the AOA, the Midland Outlaws had now been caught partying with the sworn enemy. They might just as well have gone up to the Angels clubhouse in Wolverhampton, knocked on the door and given the entire chapter the finger. So far as acts of provocation go, they did not come much more blatant than this one. Once they were back in the UK, everyone expected the Angels to try to teach them another lesson. This time, they were more than ready for them.

14

THE FAT MEXICAN

May 1993

Before the Midland Outlaws could put any of their new-found skills to the test, they received another opportunity to broaden their travel horizons. Days after they returned from Canada, Rainier called to tell them about a forthcoming party taking place at the Paul Ricard Circuit, a motor-sport race track in Le Castellet near Marseille in the south of France. The event, organized by the sole European chapter of an MC called the Bandidos, was strictly invitation only but Rainier said he would arrange everything and meet them there.

Boone and the others found it all quite bemusing. As individual clubs of twenty or thirty members, no one outside of the UK would have given them the time of day. Now that they were all together, everyone wanted to be their friend. The reasons were clear. With more than 120 members, the Midland Outlaws were not only bigger than the Angels in the UK, they were bigger than just about any other club in any other European country. Even most clubs in most American states had fewer members than they did. The Midland Outlaws had discovered that they had real clout, and they were happy to make the most of it.

Beyond the obvious attraction of a long May weekend spent drinking and partying on the banks of the Mediterranean—and the secondary benefit of having a chance to shift a load of stolen travelers checks that Boone had managed to acquire—the invitation also represented an opportunity to get to know members of a fast-growing gang that was increasingly being seen as a real contender to unseat the Hell's Angels from their position as the biggest MC in the world.

In the spring of 1966, in the tiny shrimp and oyster fishing community of San Leon, Texas, a thirty-six-year-old longshoreman named Donald Chambers read about the exploits of Sonny Barger and company and felt certain he could go one better.

A former U.S. Marine, Chambers had been hooked on motorcycles from an early age and was national secretary of a small MC called the Reapers. Although he enjoyed the camaraderie, the parties and the women, the Reapers were just a little too tame for him, so Chambers decided to launch a club of his own. A huge admirer of Pancho Villa and other Mexican revolutionaries who had lived as free men outside the rules of society, he named his new club "Bandidos." For a logo he chose a cartoon image of a big-bellied bandit wearing a sombrero and brandishing a pistol and a machete. (A common misconception is that Chambers was inspired by a TV advertisement featuring Frito Bandito, a sombrero-wearing Mexican bandit who stole the popular brand of corn chips, but the commercial first aired *after* the MC was launched.)

Chambers liked to drink, loved to fight, and wasn't afraid to use his knife. When it came to finding recruits for his club, he wanted men just like himself—total badasses. He trawled local bars and found them among the thousands of disillusioned Vietnam veterans who returned from the killing fields of Southeast Asia only to learn that they no longer fit in. They were men who had gotten bored sitting at home trying to be nice after the government had trained and taught them to be anything but.

The club grew rapidly and soon had several chapters in

Texas and a few in neighboring states, helped in no small part by Chambers's attitude to race. While the Hell's Angels operated a strict "whites-only" policy, Chambers not only welcomed Hispanics into the Bandidos but also used Spanish for the titles of its officers: el presidente, el secretario, sargento de armas and so on. While officers in other clubs wore their titles discreetly on the front of their patches, the Bandidos wore them on their backs in place of their bottom rockers.

Chambers printed up special gold-colored calling cards for members to give out to people they encountered. Embossed in red at the top of each card was the club motto: "We are the people our parents warned us about." In the lower left corner were the initials FTW—fuck the world. And in the middle of each card were the words "Bandido by profession, Biker by trade, Lover by choice, You have just had the honor of meeting . . . ," followed by that particular member's signature.

Although mostly composed of working stiffs like Chambers himself, it didn't take long for the Bandidos to make the move from riding and partying to involvement in a range of criminal activities including motorcycle theft, prostitution and drug trafficking.

In 1972, Chambers and two other Bandidos abducted a couple of drug dealers from El Paso, Texas, who had made the mistake of attempting to rip the gang off. They had sold the bikers a quantity of amphetamine, which turned out to be baking soda. The two men, one age twenty-two and the other just seventeen, were tortured for several days before being driven out to the desert north of the city and forced to dig their own graves. The pair were then shot dead and their corpses set on fire. Chambers and his cohorts were convicted of the murders and sentenced to life in prison.

Another ex-Marine, Ronnie Hodge, once known as "Mr. Prospect" because he had earned his full colors in only a month, was elected as the new national president and immediately set about purging the club of any members he felt were not sufficiently hard-core to wear the patch. At least two entire chapters were closed down as a result of his actions but the end result was a club with members every bit as vicious, brutal and dedicated as the Hell's Angels, if not more so. Under his reign, dozens of Bandidos were arrested for dealing drugs, running prostitution rings, extorting money from the owners of bars and strip clubs—even operating illegal pit bull fights.

In 1978, Hodge led a contingent of the new and improved Bandidos to Bike Week in Daytona Beach. It was their first time at the rally and while there they met up with members of the dominant MC, the Outlaws. It was the beginning of a beautiful friendship. The Outlaws had forged links with Colombian and Cuban dealers who provided them with cocaine, while the Bandidos had mastered the art of manufacturing high-quality methamphetamine from numerous household products. Joining forces allowed both clubs to massively expand their drug interests.

Ultimately the two clubs signed a nonaggression pact and began to refer to one another as "sister" organizations. Some members went so far as to tattoo themselves with the colors of the other club as a further mark of respect.

Around this same time, the Bandidos received their own Monterey-style bad publicity boost when they became prime suspects in two of Texas's most notorious shootings. The first involved the attempted murder of San Antonio assistant U.S. attorney James Kerr, who was shot at several times while near his home. A few months later U.S. district judge John Wood Jr., known as "Maximum John" for his merciless sentences for drug offenders, was shot in the back outside his home and killed.

Kerr identified three Bandidos in a police lineup as his possible assailants while in the Wood case more than one hundred Bandidos were subpoenaed to appear before a federal grand jury and the whole organization came under the glare of the media spotlight. *Newsweek* described the Bandidos as "the single greatest organized crime problem" in Texas, and a segment on ABC's *20/20* news magazine show observed that seven of the club's eight national officers had criminal records "involving drugs, guns, or violence."

The Bandidos insisted that they had not shot at the prosecutor or murdered the judge and that the only reason they were being harassed by police was their antiestablishment way of life. As Ronnie Hodge put it to *Newsweek*: "We're the last free Americans." As with the Angels at Monterey, the Bandidos were eventually vindicated. Members of an El Paso crime family, the Chagras, were eventually convicted of hiring hit man Charles Harrelson, father of actor Woody Harrelson, to carry out both attacks. The Bandidos celebrated by throwing huge parties and giving the finger to any cops that they saw. Not only were they innocent but the club was now more infamous than ever.

Consummate politicians, the Bandidos took advantage of their raised profile to continue expanding by offering the Hell's Angels a deal they could not refuse. Concerned about the potential expansion of the Outlaws, the Angels happily agreed to allow the Bandidos to open up chapters in free states in order to act as a buffer between the two clubs.

In 1983, the same year that founder Donald Chambers was released from prison and retired from the club, the Bandidos stumbled across a golden opportunity to expand overseas into Australia. It was a move that, within the space of a year, would lead to one of the most notorious and bloodiest incidents in biker history: the Milperra Bikie Massacre. This gun battle in a Sydney suburb between members of the Bandidos and a local MC, the Comanchero, would leave six bikers, and a fourteen-year-old girl who was hit by a stray shot, dead.

In the spring of 1989, the Bandidos expanded into Europe for the first time when nine members of the Club de Clichy in Marseille flew to South Dakota in order to attend the Sturgis

Motorcycle Rally. Once there, they officially joined forces with the Bandidos during a ceremony presided over by Ronnie Hodge himself. Clichy had spent three years as a prospect club before being judged to have reached the standard required for its members to wear the Fat Mexican on their backs.

Alarmed at this incursion onto a continent they had always seen as their own, the Hell's Angels responded in typically bloodthirsty fashion. In August 1991, the vice president of the Marseille chapter of the Bandidos was killed and two others injured in front of the clubhouse in a drive-by shooting by four men on motorcycles. The murder turned out to be the joint work of two Hell's Angel puppet clubs, one of which had provided the manpower and the other the stolen motorcycles to be used as getaway vehicles. By now the message to the MC world was loud and clear: wherever the Bandidos went, violence seemed certain to follow.

Just a few short years earlier—despite their close friendship with the Outlaws—the Bandidos had been considered neutral enough to host peace talks between the two rivals (these took place during the Sturgis rally and ultimately came to nothing). Now they had just as much reason to despise the Angels as their sister club, and all the more reason to befriend those who felt the same way.

In May 1993, Boone and nine other Midland Outlaws arrived in Marseille Provence Airport and made their way to the Paul Ricard circuit in a small convoy of hired cars, expecting to receive a warm welcome from the Bandidos. Not only had Rainier, one of the leading lights of the AOA, personally arranged their invitation, they also fully shared their hosts' animosity toward the Angels. In the event, both trump cards turned out to be worse than useless.

Boone and the others arrived at the entrance gate and gave

the club name. The prospects who were on guard duty went away to check and asked them to wait. And wait. And wait. Eventually a more senior Bandido appeared at the gate.

"Who the fuck are all you?"

"We're the Midland Outlaws from England," said Boone.

"Never heard of you."

"We're still quite new. We were all different clubs and we came together last year."

"Ah yes, I remember hearing something about that. But what makes you think you can come here?"

"Well Rainier from the Montreal AOA said he had arranged our invitation."

The Bandido shook his head. "No he didn't. So far as I can see, you don't have an invitation."

"Then someone must have messed up. Is Rainier here?"

"No. There's no one from the AOA here. No one at all. Except you guys."

"Oh, we're not part of the AOA."

"You're not affiliated to them, even though your patches say Outlaws?"

"Well we're all outlaw clubs aren't we," replied Boone. "But we're independent. We don't answer to anyone."

What Rainier had failed to explain was that at the time he made the call to the Midland Outlaws, relations between the AOA and the Bandidos were going through a period of extreme strain. Rainier had been invited to the party himself but suspected it might be a massive setup and that he and the other Outlaws would be walking straight into a trap. In order to test the water, he had sent Boone and company in his place.

Luckily for the Brits, the Bandidos quickly read between the lines and realized what was going on. The fact that they were not affiliated to the AOA also worked greatly in their favor. The organizers allowed the Midland Outlaws to attend the gathering and offered them a level of hospitality appropriate to a fellow MC, but remained extremely wary of them throughout.

All around the circuit, more than five thousand bikers from all over the world had gathered in Marseille for a weekend of racing and partying. As well as the Bandidos there were dozens of smaller, fiercely independent clubs like the Bones MC from Germany, the 666 Undertakers from Denmark and the Morbids MC from Sweden, many of whom had long and proud histories of their own.

Perhaps the most glamorous contingent came in the form of the Desperados Harley Davidson Club, led by its lifetime president, Johnny Hallyday (aka the French Elvis Presley). An icon in France, Hallyday has sold more than one hundred million albums throughout his career, performed on the *Ed Sullivan* show (with the Jimi Hendrix Experience as his support act) and collaborated with everyone from Peter Frampton to Bono. He had always dreamed of being a biker but unable to commit enough to join an established MC, he decided to form his own—the Desperados, who also doubled as his personal security entourage.

The Midland Outlaws found Hallyday a real laugh riot and loved hanging out with him. The fact that he was not seen as a threat to the Bandidos also helped ease the tension that Boone and the others were feeling. Their every move was being watched, with several Bandido prospects charged with keeping a close eye on who they were talking to and what they were up to. Boone couldn't help but make a game of it, trying his best to lose the men who were tailing him.

Although Boone did his best to mingle, the language barrier soon became a problem. But then he noticed that when the French, German and Danes were talking to one another, they used a form of broken English. "Hell, I can do that," thought Boone and within a matter of minutes he and the rest of the Midland Outlaws were drinking and partying with clubs from around the world as if they'd known them all their lives.

In particular, the Brits found themselves bonding with the Undertakers and the Morbids, both of whom seemed to share the same spirit of adventure and determination to survive as independent MCs in a world increasingly dominated by the global biker brands. Boone felt particularly drawn to Michael "Joe" Ljunggren, an officer with the Morbids and a true kindred spirit. "Good morals, good principles," he told friends later, "a real diamond geezer. He's just like one of us. Totally sound."

By the end of the first day, the tensions had eased considerably and the Midland Outlaws were invited into the VIP enclosure to meet some of the Bandidos. Members had flown in from all over the world including a significant contingent from the Texas chapter.

The Midland Outlaws generally knew very little about the Bandidos at the time. To Boone, the logo on their backs looked like a cartoon character—he couldn't take it seriously. And when he caught sight of one particularly large man, standing on the edge of the enclosure, staring into space with "El Presidente" plastered across his back in red and gold lettering, it was all he could do to stop himself from laughing out loud.

One of the Bandidos suggested that Boone thank the president for showing them such generous hospitality, so Boone bit his tongue and walked over to him. The closer he got, the more uncomfortable he felt. In general, the Bandidos were a smart but ragged gang who looked like bikers through and through. Their president, on the other hand, looked like someone who had picked up a costume from a fancy dress store.

His boots were so highly polished that they had a near-mirror finish, his colors were totally immaculate, completely unblemished. It wasn't just that they were new—Boone took every possible opportunity to change his colors in order to keep them looking smart—it was that they looked as if they belonged to someone who had simply never done any real biking.

Boone stood next to the man, who continued staring off into space, deliberately ignoring him. It was a game that two could play, but rather than standing there in silence Boone instead decided to forgo the usual respectful formalities and treat the president like any other biker.

"Oi, mate," he said, nudging the man on the arm. "Any idea where I can get rid of these travelers checks?"

The face of el presidente was incredulous; he could scarcely believe what he was hearing. He was accustomed to constant deference and a certain level of respect. If anyone from his own club had addressed him in that way they would have been thrown out on the spot. "What did you say?"

Boone pulled out a wad of checks from his pocket and waved them in the air. "Travelers checks, any idea where I might be able to cash them?"

The man's mouth opened and closed but no sound came out. He was completely lost for words.

"Forget it," said Boone and walked off with a smile on his face.

After partying into the small hours, the Midland Outlaws were getting on so well with the Undertakers that the latter insisted they visit them in Denmark. Boone and the others readily agreed. A few weeks later in early July, they arrived at Copenhagen Airport and made their way through immigration and baggage to the main roadway just outside the arrivals terminal where members of the Undertakers were due to meet them.

Although the group had gotten to know several Undertakers during their weekend in Marseille, no one recognized any of the men who arrived at the airport and claimed to be there to pick them up. To make matters worse, neither of the two men—most likely prospects—were showing their colors or had anything on display to show any kind of club affiliation. Instead they wore large hooded jackets that totally covered up whatever they had on underneath.

"Why are you guys covered up, what the fuck's going on?" asked Boone.

"Don't worry about it. You're safe," came the reply.

Alarm bells started ringing immediately. Without seeing their patches, there was no way of confirming exactly which club these men belonged to. For all the Midland Outlaws knew, they might have been Hell's Angels luring them off to their deaths. Even if they were Undertakers, the fact they were covered up did not bode well. They could have been expecting an ambush and carrying concealed weapons. Another possibility was that something had happened earlier in the day that had made it necessary for them to cover up to avoid becoming targets. Whatever the reason, the fact that the Midland Outlaws were flying their own colors and had no way of hiding them was a major cause for concern.

Boone explained his unease and appealed to the men to properly identify themselves. They replied that they were under strict orders not to tell the Brits what was going on or to show their patches. The only way the Midland Outlaws were going to get to the party would be to get in the car. If they did not want to do that, they might just as well turn around and go home.

The Outlaws had a quick conference among themselves to decide how best to proceed. No one was 100 percent happy about the situation but at the end of the day they outnumbered the men picking them up by four to one. If it looked as though it was all turning to shit, they would have little difficulty overpowering their captors and getting away, just so long as the other side didn't have a chance to call in backup.

They arrived at the Undertakers' clubhouse just as it was getting dark and were quickly ushered into a garden area where more than one hundred other bikers were waiting. A signal was given and one of the Undertakers lit a fuse at the side of a large metal structure that towered some fifty feet into the air. As the fuse burned it set off a series of fireworks and sparklers attached to the frame that, within a few moments, had spelled out the message: "Denmark welcomes a new nation of Bandidos."

At that same moment, every member of the Undertakers unzipped his jacket and revealed himself. After twenty years of total independence, the entire club had joined forces and the Bandidos now had its second European chapter.

Boone knew precious little about the Bandidos but he knew that Denmark had long been considered a Hell's Angels' stronghold. The Big Red Machine might be happy to coexist alongside a small, local club but the presence of a second American gang would be like a red rag to a bull. Add to that the fact that the Angels had already attacked the first Bandido chapter in Europe and the chances of the conflict escalating seemed almost certain.

As if the Midland Outlaws didn't have enough problems of their own, their presence at the launch party would without doubt get back to the Angels. From the outside looking in, it would be assumed that Boone and the others had planned it all in advance and known all along that they were going to a launch party for the new club and had wanted to be a part of it. Their cards were well and truly marked. Now any club that was at war with the Bandidos would be at war with the Midland Outlaws as well.

15

SEX AND VIOLENCE

Boone loved being part of the Midland Outlaws and relished the fact that they had stood up to the Angels and were now the biggest MC club in the country. He also loved the fact that the club was now developing close friendships with allied clubs all around the world. At the same time, he couldn't help but miss his time with the Pagans. Back then the club was a law unto itself and did whatever the majority of members were in favor of. Now the Warwickshire chapter were just one small part of a far larger club and, though it hadn't happened to any great degree yet, there was always a danger their individual voices could get lost among the crowd.

Boone was also concerned about the baggage they were taking on. The incident when a Pagan had fallen out with members of the National Chopper Club and they had all ended up being held at gunpoint played on his mind. All it would take would be for one of the other chapters to get into a dispute and his chapter would be in the firing line as well. The "one in, all in" philosophy had its upside, but it meant you had to take the rough with the smooth.

The upside of the arrangement was that whenever things got rough at home and Alice, the girl he had been seeing for more than a year, started giving him a hard time about the club, he had plenty of hideouts to escape to. Alice had been a biker old lady long before she met Boone and knew the kind of things he got into when he was away from her. The agreement between them was she never wanted to hear about his exploits and he wasn't allowed to flirt while she was around.

The pair ended up having a huge argument after Boone took Alice to a club party. Depending on the event, club members either take their old lady or pick up some action while they are there. Boone had missed the meeting prior to the event and had not realized that this was the latter. Alice was the only old lady there and while every other member of the chapter got laid at least twice by a bevy of biker babes, Boone was told that he would be fined for having brought Alice with him. To make matters worse, Boone made no secret of the fact that he resented missing out on the action and Alice spent the whole night giving him the evil eye.

The following weekend Boone decided he needed some time away and went to spend a couple of nights at the clubhouse in Leicester. The members there had been eager to get him up there for a while, promising they had something special to show him. After a drunken evening he woke the next morning and was told the surprise had already arrived and slowly made his way downstairs.

"What is it?" Boone asked.

"We got a cleaner," came the reply.

The Leicester clubhouse had a reputation for being one of the filthiest around because the chapter never had enough prospects about to keep it clean. Back when the club had been the Pariah, no one much cared about the fact that they were living in filth. Once they became Outlaws they had to adopt higher standards and the state of the clubhouse was repeatedly raised on the agenda of national meetings.

Boone was happy that the Leicester gang had finally figured something out but he couldn't quite see what the fuss was about until the cleaner entered from the next room. She was in her early thirties with short blonde hair and a good, if slightly stocky body, large pendulous breasts and no pubic hair. Boone knew all of this because she was stark naked.

She smiled at Boone and the other bikers and then moved to the corner of the room, got down on all fours and began to dust some shelves. After a few moments, one of the bikers got down behind her, dropped his pants and began to have sex with her. The woman moaned softly and shifted her body to make things easier for him, missing several dusty spots on the shelf as a result. A few moments later, a second biker joined in.

"She'll do us all before she's finished," the local biker told Boone. "Can't get enough. Goes home and tells her husband about it every afternoon, which is a bit fucked if you ask me, but what do I care. Just jump in whenever you're ready."

Boone smiled. He really did love being a biker.

Ask a typical MC member what they like most about being in a club and they'll talk about biking and brotherhood. For many, an equally important part of the equation revolves around the almost endless opportunities for sex. Bikers have long reveled in the fact that they have a reputation for extreme sexual prowess and it seems to be the case that, no matter what they are up to, certain types of women—usually referred to as "patch snatch"—remain hopelessly drawn to them.

Back in 1972, seven years after the Angels were cleared of the Monterey rape, a series of similar scandals emerged in England, leading to several Angels and other bikers being convicted of rape and sexual assaults.

In March that year, an army nurse alleged that she had been raped by up to sixteen Angels in a candlelit garage. The jury heard she had removed her own clothes before lying back on a mattress and boasting of having been in the same situation with twenty-three bikers in Scotland. After the sixteenth Angel had finished, she announced she was worn out and wanted to stop. She claimed the bikers took no notice. When the men were acquitted of rape, the club president appeared before reporters and announced that the club would be celebrating by hosting a new gang bang that very evening.

"Our status has gone up as a result of this case because no other Hell's Angels have been to court for something like this and been cleared. We have never had any trouble finding birds. When birds hear there are Angels in town they come flocking out of interest. But now some parents may lock up their daughters. But we'll still get birds."

This was true for other clubs just as much as it was for the Angels. More times than Boone could remember as both a Pagan and an Outlaw, a group of club members would ride out to a country pub, enter the bar and watch as the barmaid vanished for a few minutes before returning in a low-cut top, miniskirt and freshly applied makeup. The signals were loud and clear. The only thing Boone and the others then had to establish was whether she wanted just one of them, or all of them. The fact that some women preferred the latter option was often a source of frustration.

One time Dozer was chatting with a woman at a bar who agreed to return with the bikers for a party at the clubhouse. Dozer was traveling in the security van along with a few others, got the woman into the back and started kissing her passionately. Encouraged by her moans of excitement, Dozer believed he was working his magic. It was only when he ran his hands down her body to between her legs and discovered two other sets of hands had beaten him to it that he realized just why she was so hepped up. "For fuck's sake guys, can't I just have this one on my own first?" he gasped. It was a rhetorical question.

When it comes to biker gang bangs, members have to stick to the same hierarchical order that they do when they are out on runs, with the most senior members at the head of the line. At least that's the idea. One time Boone and the VP of another Outlaws chapter were lined up at the bottom of the stairs of a clubhouse, waiting their turn for a woman who was servicing the troops in the main bedroom. When the door opened,

Boone pushed his way past the VP, who grabbed his leg and pulled him back down. The two then started wrestling on the ground.

"I'll have you up at a meeting for this," bellowed the VP. "I'll talk to Caz. I'll bust you down to prospect. I'll have your patch, you fucker."

Boone managed to break free and sprinted up the stairs to claim his prize. "Not for this you won't," he called back as he slipped in through the door. Boone's reasoning was simple. He knew the VP was still being treated for a dose of gonorrhea he had contracted following an earlier encounter and wanted to go first to avoid picking up the infection himself. Mentioning it to the woman was never part of the equation.

Not all the women associated with biker gangs are quite so easygoing. Many, such as Alice, demand and, for the most part, get at least the semblance of a committed relationship. For Boone, Alice was his number one old lady. That meant no one else was allowed to mess with her. All the bikers had a number one old lady—even the ones who were married. Most also had a number two old lady, but had to accept that this one would be fair game for other bikers—otherwise they were just being greedy.

Both wives and old ladies have to get used to playing second fiddle to the club, even if it means their partners miss out on birthdays and other celebrations. One group of women got so fed up of constantly being told their men were out on "business" that they decided to form a club of their own.

Better organized, less given to bouts of drunken rowdiness and with great taste in nicely customized motorcycles, the new women-only club quickly thrived. At first the men paid little attention—the fact that the women were no longer giving them such a hard time was all they cared about. But then the women decided to take things a step further and began organizing runs, rallies and parties of their own. In keeping with the rules of the MC world, they reached the point where they needed to seek permission from the main club in the area, so they arranged a formal meeting with their men.

Boone, Caz, Switch and a few other Outlaws soon found themselves sitting at the clubhouse table opposite the president, treasurer and sergeant at arms of the female club. The women requested permission to stage a party. The men said no. The women tried offering a compromise, the men still said no. Part of the problem was that other clubs were started to attend the women's parties, clubs that included the Angels. It was all getting too complicated so the Outlaws had decided to put a stop to it.

Tempers started to flare on both sides with the women convinced the concerns about the Angels were just an excuse and that the real issue was one of gender. Eventually the female sergeant at arms could not control her temper any longer. She stood up and slammed her fist on the table. "For fuck's sake, all we want is to be treated the exact same way you'd treat us if our club was full of men."

Switch leap to his feet, his face red with rage, stormed over to his female counterpart and punched her in the face, knocking her out cold. "Anyone else want to be treated like a man?" he asked. The female club disbanded soon afterward.

In March 1994, Rainier suggested the Midland Outlaws travel to Florida in order to attend Daytona Beach Bike Week, a ten-day-long festival that competes with the Sturgis Motorcycle Rally for the title of biggest in the United States, so that he could introduce them to senior members of the AOA.

Arriving at Miami Airport, with their patches covered up, they again split into small groups in order not to draw too much attention to themselves as they walked through customs. Boone, Link and Dozer lined up and approached the counter one at a time.

"What do you do for a living?" Link was asked, as he approached the booth. He hesitated a moment too long and the official immediately became suspicious. "Come on, come on, tell me what you do for a living. You shouldn't have to think about it."

"I'm a mechanic," said Link, and soon afterward was allowed to pass through.

Boone was next. "What do you do for a living? Don't think about it, just tell me."

"I'm a mechanic too," said Boone. "I work with that guy who just went through."

"Okay. Where are you staying?"

Boone fished into his pocket and pulled out the note with the address the Florida Outlaws had given him. Having come direct from them, Boone assumed it was a "safe" address that would not draw any undue attention. But as he read it out, Boone could see a deep frown appear on the official's forehead.

"Give me that again."

Boone quickly transposed some of the numbers in the address, hopefully choosing a property on the other side of the road and pretended like he'd made a mistake.

"I should hope so. That first address you gave me is the headquarters of the notorious Florida Outlaws. They're one of the worst, organized crime gangs in all of America. They've been responsible for a least eighty unsolved murders in the last couple of years alone. Whatever you do, don't have anything to do with them."

All the Midland Outlaws made it safely through immigration, but started to feel uncomfortable after Boone repeated what he had been told, a feeling that got worse when they received a text message telling them that Rainier wasn't going to be able to make it to the show and that they would be on their own.

They had been to war with rival gangs, they had shot at their rivals and been shot at on countless occasions. They had fought and fucked and partied the way only Outlaws can. But, as they realized just how little they knew about their hosts

and contemplated the fact that, once again, their main contact was not going to be there to make any introductions, they
couldn't help but feel just a little concerned. They exchanged
glances as they made their way to the baggage area.

"It has to be an exaggeration," said Dozer. "I mean, they
can't be that bad." Boone nodded. "They wouldn't be allowed
to exist if they were anything like that. I reckon the guy was
talking out of his ass." As it turned out, the truth would be far
more brutal than any of them could ever have anticipated.

With its near-constant sunshine, glorious beaches, vibrant
party scene and heavy emphasis on a laid-back lifestyle, Florida has long been a biker's paradise. The first race meeting at
Daytona Beach took place in 1937 and, apart from a hiatus
during World War II, the rally has taken place every year
since. Today, every March, some half a million bikers from
around the world attend the ten-day-long event, making it
one of the largest gatherings of its kind on the planet.

As in California, clubs based in the region have the chance
to ride all year around, but while the West Coast will forever
be associated with the Hell's Angels, Florida has long been
seen as exclusively Outlaws territory. This started during
the late fifties, back when the club was still known as the
Chicago Outlaws and several members began spending the
winter in Florida to escape the bitter north. The visitors
from Illinois soon became friendly with a club based in the
small city of Hollywood, midway between Miami and Fort
Lauderdale. Known to local media as the Iron Cross MC—
their patch featured an oversized red cross pattée on a white
background—the club's official moniker was actually Outlaws MC, a name that appeared in red on white lettering on a
small rocker just above the cross.

Led by the formidable James "Big Jim" Nolan, a flame-
haired Goliath of a man with a black belt in taekwondo, the

club first gained a reputation for extreme violence in 1965 when members followed home a farm worker who almost swerved into them on the Florida turnpike and shot dead his wife.

The shared name led to an instant bond between the two gangs and Nolan and his comrades soon agreed that, of all the many, many bikers they had met over the years during Daytona and other events, the Chicago Outlaws were by far their favorites. The feeling was mutual and when the Outlaws dropped "Chicago" from their name and began to expand into other areas, the Florida bikers were among the first gangs they asked to join their brotherhood.

In July 1967, Outlaws national president Harry "Stairway" Henderson and a few other members traveled down to Hollywood to meet up with Big Jim, hand over two dozen sets of new black and white "Charlie" patches and personally sanction the charter. It took only a few weeks for the new chapter to hit the headlines once again with another act of violence, but this time the reverberations were felt all the way around the world.

On Sunday November 12, 1967, two Florida Outlaws pulled up outside St. Mary's hospital in West Palm Beach and dropped off a red-haired, freckle-faced eighteen-year-old girl named Christine Deese. Clearly in terrible pain, she showed the doctors her hands and explained that she had fallen on some boards with two protruding nails, which had then passed right through her palms. Staff at the hospital were immediately suspicious and, after administering treatment, called the county sheriff: the nails had passed through the exact center of each hand and it seemed highly unlikely that this could have occurred by accident. The sheriff shared their suspicions and tracked down the girl's father, an auxiliary police chief.

Christine's father arrived on the scene within the hour and

took her alone to a quiet room. The pair emerged fifteen minutes later with the young girl in a flood of tears but willing to
tell the whole truth: Deese was the old lady of Outlaw Norman "Spider" Risinger, the same man who seven years later
would help spark the global war between the Outlaws and the
Hell's Angels by literally blowing the heads off three of his rivals with a shotgun.

Spider had become furious when Christine failed to hand
over ten dollars she had made working as a prostitute earlier
that day. By way of punishment, Spider and four Outlaw buddies decided to nail Christine to a tree in a remote part of
Juno Beach, ten miles north of West Palm. She stood on tip-
toe and placed her palms on the trunk but didn't scream or
fight as they hammered the four-inch-long, iron nails through
her flesh: "They said they would bash my face in with a hammer if I did," she said later.

Christine spent half an hour hanging from the tree while
Spider and the others drank beer, smoked dope and tossed insults at her. They eventually pulled her down and took her
back to the clubhouse. The Outlaws finally agreed to take her
to the hospital when the wounds looked as though they were
becoming infected, but only after they had dreamed up what
they believed was a plausible story to explain the injuries.

The shocking case made local, national and international
headlines and prompted state governor Claude Kirk to declare
war on the gang. Risinger and another Outlaw were quickly
jailed and a posse was set up to track down the three others
involved who had fled first to Chicago (where they were hidden by members of the mother chapter) and then to Detroit,
where they hid out with a local gang called the Renegades.

The governor was there in person at Palm Beach International Airport when the fugitives were brought back in. "This
bunch of bums has got the word they're not welcome in Florida," he told the massed ranks of reporters who had come to

witness the scene. "I hope young, thrill-seeking girls who go with them know now they can get their fingers burned—or, in this case, their hands nailed."

But Risinger had simply been following protocol. The chief source of Outlaws income at the time came from old ladies working as prostitutes or dancers, and Big Jim Nolan had set up strict rules and regulations about how the business was to be run. The women wore special patches that designated them as the "property of" either individual Outlaws or the club as a whole.

The old ladies were put to work in brothels, strip clubs and topless go-go dancing bars on the understanding that they would give all the money they earned to their Outlaw men and do whatever was asked of them without question. They were also told to refrain from taking drugs unless they had been given permission to do so.

If any of the old ladies withheld earnings or tried to run off or broke the rules in any other way, her Outlaw could administer whatever punishment he felt suitable—most often a lengthy beating. If the behavior was deemed more serious, the woman might be subjected to "training"—which often involved being sent to a prostitution "lockup" at a truck stop. There the woman would be on call for twenty-four hours a day for as long as the "training" lasted, often a period of several weeks.

Despite all this becoming known to a wider public, Governor Kirk's warnings fell on deaf ears. Dozens of young women still flocked to the sprawling mobile home that served as clubhouse for the South Florida chapter of the Outlaws. Even Christine Deese herself continued to hang around with the gang once she had recovered from her ordeal, proudly wearing the nails they had used to crucify her on a chain around her neck.

Under Big Jim Nolan's leadership, the club grew rapidly throughout Florida and soon had the largest concentration of

Outlaws anywhere in the entire United States. Along with founding members like James Starrett, Frederick Hegney, Michael Cave, Clarence Smith and Timothy Duke, Big Jim found himself at the helm of the most ruthless biker gang in the world.

The killing of the three Hell's Angels in the spring of 1974 was just the start. They spent the next decade killing and maiming people with virtual impunity. Anyone who threatened to talk to the police or betray their secrets was ruthlessly executed. In all, the Florida Outlaws would be responsible for more than eighty brutal murders. And much of the violence was directed against the very women whose income they relied on to support the club in the first place.

Joyce Karleen first met the Outlaws in August of 1974 when she was hanging out in Daytona Beach and looking for a job. She met a couple of guys who invited her to a party in Hollywood and said they might be able to help her find some kind of employment. They took her to the Outlaws clubhouse and she soon met Big Jim Nolan.

Karleen had been in the house for only a few hours when Nolan ordered her to fetch him a beer. Unfamiliar with the role of women in the biker world, Karleen replied that if he wanted a beer he should get it himself. Nolan hit her, then pulled out a gun and asked her to accompany him to a back room so he could educate her about how Outlaws expected their old ladies to behave.

Nolan explained that Karleen would be expected to work and give over all her earnings to the club. She would also have to do exactly as she was told. He then ordered her to give him a blow job. Karleen hesitated until Nolan placed the barrel of the gun to the side of her head and repeated the order. This time Karleen complied.

Nolan then raped her and was soon joined by eight other

Outlaws. Leaving, he told Karleen to do exactly what the others wanted or he would beat her again. Once he was out of the room Karleen began to struggle. Nolan returned and punched her in the mouth several times until she was too weak to resist.

The next day Karleen was taken to a local lounge to work as a topless dancer alongside several other Outlaw old ladies. Every penny she earned went directly to members of the club. At the end of that first week the awful nightmare that had become Joyce Karleen's life took a turn for the worse. Several bikers at the club came to believe she was responsible for stealing some clothes from a "patched" old lady and decided that the newcomer needed to be punished.

As she left the lounge after work, Karleen was abducted and taken back to the clubhouse, tied to a chair and stripped half naked. The bikers then took turns punching and kicking her. When she refused to admit to the theft, they heated up a spoon on the stove and used it to burn her arms and breasts. When she passed out, they covered her head with a sheet and fetched the other Outlaw old ladies from around the clubhouse and escorted them into the room. They removed the sheet from over Karleen's head and told the women to take a good look. This, they explained, would be what would happen to them if they misbehaved.

The Outlaws then took Karleen and dumped her in a field where they expected her to die. She didn't and would later be a witness against the gang.

Outlaw old ladies get few privileges but one is that if they ever have problems with "outsiders" they can count on the club to come to their rescue. In early 1980 Mary Lou Rodriguez was a popular girl who wore her "Property of Outlaws" patch with pride. When someone slashed the tires of her car one night after a party, she naturally asked some of the more senior club members, including Timothy Duke, to help her figure it out. When they failed to do so to her satisfaction, Rodriguez was furious.

Back at Duke's house, Rodriguez and Duke got into an argument and she stormed out. Duke then told the rest of the Outlaws in the house that he was worried that Rodriguez was going to "rat him out," and that the only way to stop her was to kill her. Duke grabbed an old telephone cable and ripped it away from the baseboard, telling his companions he planned to use it to strangle Rodriguez.

When Rodriguez returned to the house later that same evening, an Outlaw named Hawkins asked Duke if he wouldn't mind waiting an hour or so before he killed her as Hawkins wanted to have sex with her first. Duke agreed and after Hawkins was through, Duke followed Rodriguez into the bathroom and started to strangle her with the telephone cord. He released his grip once she stopped struggling but as her body slumped to the ground, he heard Rodriguez start to breathe again. Duke ran off to his bedroom and returned carrying a high-powered spear gun that he then used to shoot Rodriguez in the head, killing her instantly. Her body was left in a trailer on his property for a few days before he finally asked Hawkins to get rid of it.

Around the time of the Rodriguez murder, Big Jim Nolan spent time in Florida state prison on drugs charges. Ever thoughtful, one of his fellow Outlaws, Ronald Watchmaker, arranged for him to receive a "gift" when he was released—a young woman named Iris Geoghagen.

Wanting to get some use out of the "gift" himself, Watchmaker ultimately decided to give Nolan 49 percent of Geoghagen while he was in prison and keep the rest. Having met Geoghagen, Nolan decided he wanted the whole package and offered to buy out Watchmaker for two thousand dollars. Unable to decide whether to take the deal, Watchmaker asked Geoghagen whose old lady she would rather be. Believing that being connected to the more powerful Outlaw would entitle her to more privileges, Geoghagen chose Nolan. She then visited Nolan every weekend in prison, usually smuggling in cocaine and marijuana for him to use and sell to other inmates.

In the meantime, Geoghagen stayed at Nolan's house in Fort Lauderdale with another founding member, Michael Cave, who Nolan had told to watch over his new old lady. Geoghagen was having a hard time finding a job as a topless dancer, so Cave told her to get a job as a nude dancer instead. She explained that she wasn't at all happy with the idea of dancing totally nude so Cave proposed a novel solution. He would put a dog collar around Geoghagen's neck and make her parade around the house naked in front of his friends until she got used to not wearing clothes. To emphasize that he was serious, he told her that if she ever tried to run away, he would find her mother, stick a baseball bat up her ass and take pictures. It was clear he wasn't kidding: Geoghagen applied for a nude dancing job that same afternoon.

Nolan was released from prison in September 1980 and he and Geoghagen moved to Tucson, Arizona, where he had been ordered to serve out his parole away from the rest of the club. Nolan had led Geoghagen to believe that she would be treated to a thirty-day "honeymoon period" during which she would not be required to work as a prostitute. Nolan had also told her that he would refrain from bringing any other old ladies home during the honeymoon. Neither turned out to be true.

Nolan became increasingly violent. One time Nolan found Geoghagen in tears and asked her what was wrong. She told him that he had hurt her feelings by not taking her out to dinner as he had promised, a few days earlier. Nolan exploded with rage. He threw his boots at Geoghagen, punched her in the face, then grabbed the money she had made from working as a prostitute that evening and shoved it down her throat, forcing her to swallow every last note.

Another time, Geoghagen could not find a bag of marijuana that she had hidden somewhere and that Nolan wanted to sell. Nolan kicked and punched her on the chest and back so hard that she ended up with broken ribs.

A few weeks later, Geoghagen went out of state to visit her sick mother. Nolan could not go with her because of the terms of his parole so he needed to find another way to ensure she would return. Nolan explained that if she stayed away, he would beat her stepfather to death, leaving her mother without anyone to look after her. Geoghagen asked Nolan if she could buy her freedom, and he said that it would cost her 125,000 dollars to be free, but that she could not pay him with her prostitution earnings—her only income—because that money was already his anyway.

By March 1981, Geoghagen was living on tenterhooks, worried that she was going to be the next one to end up dead. After another argument while out at a bar, she became convinced that Nolan would kill her the moment they arrived at their home. At a stop light, she jumped off the back of Nolan's motorcycle and began to run. Nolan ran after her. When he finally caught her he punched her in the face again and again until she finally agreed to get back on the cycle with him. As they rode back, Nolan held a fistful of her hair to make sure she didn't try to escape again. Once in the driveway Geoghagen, who was terrified that Nolan would kill her right there and then, started to scream, hoping that one of the neighbors would help her. As Nolan screamed at Geoghagen to shut the fuck up, he grabbed her face, lifting her off the ground by her chin. Nolan's crushing grip was too much for Geoghagen's lower jaw, which snapped like a twig, causing her to pass out.

Geoghagen remained in the hospital for a week and had a steel pin implanted into her chin and the rest of her jaw wired shut. During her stay, Nolan brought another old lady to the hospital to visit Geoghagen. As he stood over the battered Geoghagen, Nolan turned to his companion: "You see what I did to her? . . . I'm in love with her. I don't even like you, moth-erfucker. Go ahead and piss me off."

One night, soon after Geoghagen got back from the hospi-tal, she got out of bed and saw Nolan in the living room orally sodomizing his latest old lady, who was just thirteen years old. Dismayed, she gathered up all the pills she could find in the house and tried to commit suicide. Nolan found her un-conscious and could not contain his anger at what she had done. He dragged her from room to room and beat her for more than three hours with the heavy buckle of his belt, leav-ing her covered in a mass of blue and purple bruises and welts.

The next day Geoghagen escaped with the help of a friend and soon made her way back to her parents' house in Florida. Her horrified mother and father called the police, and Geogh-agen, who had finally been pushed too far, eventually agreed to make a statement. Nolan missed Geoghagen right away, but it wasn't her company he longed for, rather the income she had brought him through her prostitution. He quickly made arrangements with another Outlaw friend to purchase another woman to make up his losses, but also began mak-ing arrangements to move the gang into a whole new area of business.

Prostitution income had been on the decline for some time when Nolan decided to expand the Outlaws' criminal activi-ties into the field of narcotics trafficking. As with the sex trade, strict rules of conduct were introduced, partly to maxi-mize income but also to protect the club (as far as possible) in the event of a bust. For the most part, Outlaws only dealt with other Outlaws in order to reduce the risk of detection. On the occasions where Outlaws dealt with outsiders, they would ensure their association with the club was well known in order to intimidate the new customer into remaining silent. Drugs were dealt directly from the clubhouse and also while members of the gang were traveling or on regional, national or local runs.

As had been the case with Geoghagen, old ladies were drafted to assist the trade by weighing and repackaging the drugs prior to resale, and sometimes by smuggling contraband into prison. The move into a new business area was a huge success and the money flew in almost as fast as the bikers could launder it. The Florida Outlaws subsequently used the proceeds from the sale of narcotics to purchase at least one of their clubhouses and its members became increasingly affluent.

Five years before Boone and the other Midland Outlaws arrived in Florida, Nolan and five other members of the Florida Outlaws had been jailed following what turned out to be the longest federal trial in the state's legal history.

Previous murder, rape, and kidnapping trials had fallen apart because witnesses tended to have poor memories or vanished shortly before they were supposed to testify. Eventually, the authorities had utilized RICO legislation, a set of laws first introduced in the 1970s in order to combat the Italian mob, which allowed them to prosecute the likes of Nolan for directing others to commit crimes that he himself did not personally take part in.

It wasn't the first time the legislation had been used against a biker gang. In 1979 the target was the Hell's Angels, pursuing them as a criminal organization rather than a collection of individuals who sometimes got involved in criminality. Sonny Barger was arrested along with dozens of other Angels and charged with a range of activities including drug trafficking, prostitution and the attempted murder of two police officers. But the case was poorly prepared with no independent corroboration of what the witnesses and informers were alleging. Barger and the others were cleared of all charges scoring a massive PR victory in the process.

In the past, the FBI had massively underestimated the

power and sophistication of the biker gangs so when it came to the Florida gang, no one wanted to take any chances. This time around, the case was rock solid and the government got the victory it so greatly desired. By finding the six men guilty, the jury was essentially accepting the government's argument that the Outlaws acted together to run a criminal enterprise that was supported by prostitution and drug trafficking. Although this did not make the group illegal, it meant they were clearly identified as an organized crime gang, not as they claimed a group of motorcycle enthusiasts.

But although the old guard were all gone, the new generation of Outlaws in Florida were smarter and better organized than ever before. And, as the Midland boys were about to find out, they were every bit as deadly.

16

DAYTONA BEACH

By the time the Midland Outlaws had collected their bags and emerged into the arrivals terminal, they were feeling considerably more apprehensive about what was to come. They had already made the mistake of underestimating the situation in Canada and had been determined to be better prepared this time around, but somehow no one had found much time to do their research.

With only the chilling warning of the immigration officer to go by, Boone had to assume (despite it being Daytona Beach Bike Week with tens of thousands of other bikers in the area) that they were once again stepping into the middle of a war zone. The fact that their patches read "Outlaws" meant it would be impossible to escape being associated with the AOA. They would be considered prize scalps by any of the gang's enemies.

If the Midland boys hoped for reassurance from the man who came to collect them from the airport, they were sorely disappointed. Instead, the man in Outlaw colors striding toward them looked like a throwback to the hippie days rather than a biker, and wore baseball boots that were so worn that his toes showed through and the soles flapped up and down as he walked. He spoke in an agonizingly slow drawl, sounding like Forrest Gump played at slow speed, stretching out every letter of every word. Boone was immediately reminded of the films *Deliverance* and *The Hills Have Eyes*.

"My . . . name . . . is . . . fly . . . ball," he told them, before leading the group out into the parking lot where a battered old VW camper van with no side window was waiting to take them away. He was so scruffy and laid back the group assumed he was just a prospect. In fact, he turned out to be president of the Orlando chapter.

Flyball seemed relaxed, singing along to the radio as they drove out of the airport down toward Daytona Beach, but every member of the Midland Outlaws was on edge, scanning the road ahead and behind for any signs of the HA. Finally Boone worked up the courage to ask the question that was on everyone's lips: "Do you get many Hell's Angels around here?"

Flyball moved slowly, as though he were underwater. He turned down the radio. "Hell's Angels?" He then began to sing again, a kind of mock gospel spiritual. "Oh Lord, won't you send me an Angel. Please Lord, send me an Angel. Hell with it. Send me two of the motherfuckers and I'll shoot them both." With that he reached down and turned the radio up once more.

Boone and the others looked at each other, none the wiser.

"Is that a no then?" asked Boone.

Flyball smiled, "There's no Hell's Angels round here man—

none in Florida. If they ever show up, they know they'll get shot, so they stay away. What we have here are Warlocks, but not for much longer. You guys relax. You're on our home turf. You've got nothing to worry about."

Although the Brits were exhausted from their long journey, they had significantly more energy than they had when they arrived in Canada. The minute they got to the clubhouse they all trooped out of the camper van and headed straight for the bar. They were all delighted to see that the prospect serving drinks was someone they had met in Canada the year before.

It was more club than house, with loud music blaring away and people standing around drinking and chatting. Boone tried to say something to the barman but he could not make himself heard. He leaned in to try again but to no avail. In the end Boone tried shouting, raising his voice to its loudest just as the music ended.

"I said are there any fags in this clubhouse?"

Bikers from around the country all stared at him open-mouthed as the next music track began and filled the awkward silence. The prospect leaned forward. "I told you before Boone, we don't call them fags here, we call them cigarettes."

"Oh yeah, right. Sorry."

Later that evening, as the visitors began to relax and get into the swing of things, their Florida hosts explained that it was getting close to the designated time that one of their Lounge Lizards would be calling the clubhouse for a chat. It might, they suggested, be a nice boost to his morale to chat to some overseas one percenters.

The call from "Smitty" came in and the phone was passed around a few of the Florida bikers, for a few rounds of "Hi, how are you?" before being passed to Boone. The pair chatted briefly about the biker scene in the UK and how the Midland Outlaws came to be visiting the United States, before Boone decided it was time to ask some questions of his own.

"So what are you going to be doing for the rest of the evening?"

Having spent time inside, Boone expected Smitty to describe a typical prison routine with a sloppy meal in a large refectory followed by lights-out at a seemingly ungodly hour. The answer surprised him. "Well I've just finished my washing and ironing. I think I'm going to cook myself a pizza tonight, that's what I feel like, then I'll watch a film and after that I guess I'll go to bed."

Boone sat up, his jaw dropping a little in shock. "Fuck me, talk about having an easy life. I thought American prisons were supposed to be tough. I mean, that sounds more like a fucking holiday camp." All around him, members of the AOA were frantically waving their hands and shaking their heads in an effort to get Boone to stop, but he was on a roll. "You wouldn't last five minutes in England, mate. We have proper prisons there. I can't believe they make everything so easy for you."

There was a long, long pause before Smitty eventually replied. "Well, they tend to give you a few more privileges when they put you on death row."

Boone felt himself flush crimson. "Ah. Shit. Sorry about that, man. I didn't realize."

"No problem, brother, I know you didn't mean anything by it."

Flyball later explained that Smitty—one of four Florida Outlaws on death row at the time—had been jailed on four counts of murder and one count of attempted murder, after allegedly breaking into the home of a man who had assaulted his old lady. A woman who survived the massacre by playing dead had identified Smitty as the assailant, but he had an appeal coming up and hoped to eventually be cleared of the crime.

As the evening wore on and the beers flowed, the Midland Outlaws eventually started to tire. Because of the Daytona festival, dozens of bikers had already arranged to stay at the clubhouse itself so the Florida hosts had arranged for the Brits to stay in a nearby hotel. At the front of the clubhouse the visitors watched as dozens of available taxis sped by. "What are you waiting for?" asked Boone, who had by that time drunk so much that he was struggling to stand up straight.

"You'll see," replied Flyball.

Eventually the largest stretch limousine Boone had ever seen pulled up in front of the building. At the rear of the vehicle was an open-top hot tub with four silicone-enhanced, drop-dead gorgeous, scantily clad women sitting inside.

"Everything's paid for," said Flyball. "Including the women. You guys have a good time."

The Midland Outlaws looked at one another. By now they had been up nonstop for twenty-four hours and were drunk up to the eyeballs. Flyball could sense their hesitation.

"You guys do like women, don't you?"

"Of course," said Boone. "It's just that . . ."

"Just that what?"

Boone thought for a moment. At this rate the Midland Outlaws were in danger of developing a reputation on the international scene as the guys who always turned down women. If they didn't step up to the mark soon, the rumors were going to be impossible to shed.

"Nothing," replied Boone. "Come on guys. Let's go."

After a short tour around the town, the limo driver eventually pulled up at the hotel. Three of the four Midland Outlaws got out and headed for bed, Boone remained behind for another tour, determined that all four women should be left in no doubt whatsoever just how debauched and depraved the British bikers could be.

The following day, the Midland Outlaws got their first chance to meet up with Harry "Taco" Bowman, international president of the Outlaws and one of the most notorious and dangerous bikers on the planet.

Based in Detroit, Taco lived and breathed the biker ideal and controlled the Outlaws' empire with an iron fist. At the same time he lived in an affluent suburb, sent his children to private schools and, when not on his motorcycle, drove around in an armor-plated Cadillac.

Taco had been appointed international president in 1984, right in the middle of a major war with the Hell's Angels, and demonstrated his absolute ruthlessness right away. Hearing rumors that a member of the club was thinking of talking to the police about the whereabouts of a fugitive, Taco decided that something needed to be done. To alleviate his concerns, he asked Wayne "Joe Black" Hicks, then the vice president of the nearby Toledo chapter, to track the man down and kill him. Ultimately, Hicks was unable to find his target but Taco was so impressed by his dedication that he appointed him president of the key chapter in Fort Lauderdale, Florida.

By 1990 Hicks had become regional president of Florida, with the responsibility for overseeing the activities of all six chapters in the state, many of which were heavily involved in the drug trade and bringing in massive profits for the club overall. Maintaining absolute control of this territory was absolutely essential.

Taco's biggest fear came not so much from other clubs—though they were a constant concern—but from members of his own club ratting out others to save themselves. With all the Outlaws getting involved in increasingly serious organized crime and the authorities increasingly conducting prosecutions under the RICO laws, striking a plea bargain and testifying against former club members was often the only way to avoid a draconian sentence.

Taco launched an aggressive campaign to prevent this from happening with his club. He issued T-shirts and patches that read "Snitches are a dying breed" and made it clear that anyone who conspired against the club would not live to regret it. One member who decided to testify to a grand jury was lucky to escape with nothing more than a severe beating and the revoking of his membership.

Although the Hell's Angels had no chapters in Florida, they could see the value of the area from a commercial point of view. In the early 1990s, they formed an alliance with a small club called the Warlocks, who began selling drugs on the Angels' behalf. Taco was furious and immediately declared war on the club. He became even more incensed when he learned that a former Outlaw, Raymond "Bear" Chaffin, had defected to become president of one of the Warlock chapters. He ordered Hicks to track Chaffin down and kill him.

A prospect named Alex "Dirt" Ankerich was offered the job and eagerly agreed after learning that, if completed successfully, he would immediately receive his full patches. After gathering intelligence on his target for a night, Ankerich shot Chaffin in the back of the head four times as the Warlock president worked on his bike in the garage adjacent to his home—his body was found by his twelve-year-old daughter when she returned home from school.

The murder was reported to Hicks, who in turn reported it to Taco, who in turn complimented Hicks on the quality of his work. Ankerich was told that he had not only earned his patch but was also entitled to a set of "SS" lightning bolts as he now belonged to the elite group of Outlaws who had committed murder on behalf of the club. Newspaper articles on Chaffin's murder were copied and sent out to other Outlaws chapters around the world.

In March 1992 during Daytona Bike Week, Irwin "Hitler" Nissen, a one-time Outlaws prospect who had failed to make the cut, got into a fight with James "Moose" McLean, president of the gang's Atlanta chapter. Taco heard about the fight and ordered Nissen to be brought before him.

The following morning Houston Murphy, president of the Fort Lauderdale chapter, and another Outlaw, Christopher "Slasher" Maiale, took Nissen up to a hotel room where Taco greeted him with a solid punch to the face. Then, while Murphy held Nissen down, Taco put a knife to his ear and threatened to kill him if he ever raised his hand against another Outlaws officer. Taco then told Murphy and Maiale to give Nissen a sound beating and then throw him off the third-floor balcony of his room. Nissen survived but with severe injuries including a shattered ankle.

Under Taco's rule the Outlaws went from strength to strength. It was he who had personally supervised the opening of the club's first European chapter in France in June 1993 and he was determined that this growth should continue, both overseas and at home.

On December 31, 1993, just three months before the Midland Outlaws arrived, Taco arranged for all the Outlaws in Florida to attend a huge New Year's Eve party in Fort Lauderdale. "It's time to put a stop to these clubs that are enemies," Taco told them. "This is the year that we are going to be more rottener than ever before." Hostilities would be escalated and there would be no tolerance for the Hell's Angels or their sympathizers.

When Taco met with Boone and the rest of the Midland Outlaws he greeted them warmly and posed for photographs. He seemed genuinely interested in their ongoing war with the UK Hell's Angels and eager to give them advice about how they could maximize their income through his personal connections in the drug trade. More than anything he made a solid case for the club to become a prospect chapter for the AOA so they could come directly under his wing.

"You guys have done well against the Angels. We're impressed," he told them. "But now it's time to take it to the next level. You should consider patching over. We could use guys like you in England. That way the Angels would know that if they mess with you there, they are messing with the AOA everywhere in the world."

It was an offer the Midland Outlaws had more or less expected, but one that none of them was willing to act on at that time. They were still getting used to the idea of being one club and suddenly having enough power to be players on the world MC stage. Although they found the AOA to be kindred spirits in many ways, they had also enjoyed partying with the Bandidos.

Another possibility for the future, and one that had been the subject of much discussion among club members at all levels, was that they should retain their own brand and expand internationally themselves. It had started out as a bit of a joke during some of their travels, telling smaller clubs that they would be welcome to apply for a charter from the Midland Outlaws, but as time went on, Boone and many of the others began to realize it was a genuine option for them all. It would be tough surviving internationally without the support of an existing club, but it was far from impossible. In the meantime they would try to maintain good relations with as many clubs as possible, no matter how trying it could be at times.

The Midland Outlaws, like most MCs, had strict rules when it came to members and their patches. They had to be worn or kept with the member at all times and could never be left unattended except inside a locked safe. In Florida, Boone quickly learned that the AOA was far more relaxed. It was, for example, permitted to leave patches in the clubhouse and head out without them.

With the AOA's rules over patches far softer than those in the UK, Boone felt able for the first time ever to leave his patches in the Florida clubhouse while he went out shopping for some Harley-Davidson accessories, taking advantage of the exchange rate. He had noticed some trade stalls down one of the back streets a few blocks from the clubhouse and headed there. He soon realized he was being flanked by two men, one of them an Outlaw who had been at the clubhouse the previous day, though he hadn't actually spoken to him.

It was clear they were lining up for an attack, so Boone decided to take the initiative. He was sure it was all some simple misunderstanding but if he made any sudden moves or spooked them they might take him out of the game before he'd had a chance to explain. He turned and headed toward them, arms spread out at shoulder height with palms wide open. Then, in his best English accent, greeted them warmly.

"Hello, chaps. How are you? Do you remember me from yesterday?"

The two men looked at one another.

"No," said the taller of the two.

"I'm from Outlaws, England. We met at the party."

"Outlaws? Then what the fuck is that?"

The man pointed to the tattoo on Boone's arm that read "Pagans."

Boone had forgotten that America had its own MC called the Pagan's. He had no idea what the relationship between them and the Outlaws was like, but he was getting the distinct feeling that at that point in time, it wasn't great. Formed in 1959, the Pagan's were the fourth largest MC in the United States with around four hundred active members, though the club had shown no sign of wanting to expand overseas. Boone remembered that, a few years earlier, when letters were being exchanged between the Warwickshire club and their U.S. namesakes, it emerged that the latter were heavily involved in the drug trade and had ties to the New Jersey mafia among other organized crime gangs.

While most MCs wore a bottom rocker to display their territory, the Pagan's chose not to in order to make it more difficult for the police to identify members of individual chapters.

He could understand why the potential presence of even a single member of the club would make the Outlaws nervous.

"I was with the English Pagans, then we became Outlaws."

"English Pagans? Never heard of them."

"We were pretty small. Just the one chapter."

"Where are your patches?"

"Well, I took them off and left them in the room because it's so fucking hot. Is there some kind of problem?"

The only problem was that Boone was completely unaware that Taco had ordered any members of certain rival gangs, the Pagan's among them, turning up during Daytona week to be killed on sight.

"When we clocked your Pagan ink, we were going to take you around the corner and shoot you."

"Seriously?"

"Yeah. We hate Pagans. It's a good thing you said something. You'd be dead by now."

"You'd have just shot me right there?"

"Yeah. We've got a 'gator farm we use to dispose of the bodies. You wouldn't believe how many have been dumped there. Guess you won't be joining them after all."

"Guess not."

Following that narrow escape, Boone took his patches with him wherever he went, no matter how hot it was.

The Brits spent their days traveling around Daytona, meeting up with other groups of bikers, enjoying the sunshine and drinking as much as humanly possible. A few days into their trip they met up with a group of guys from Australia and hit it off like a house on fire. The Oz gang were also called the Outlaws and just like the Midland boys, they were a separate group from the AOA.

Based in Hobart in Tasmania and Melbourne in Victoria, the Australian Outlaws wore a patch that depicted a horned skull with a rope noose hanging down beside it. As the beers flowed and the anecdotes went back and forth, the Australians told how some of them had actually been present during the notorious Milperra Massacre of 1984 where the Bandidos had fought the Comanchero, though luckily no one on their side had been hurt during the fighting.

"They knew exactly who they wanted to kill that day," said one. "And they went after them one by one. It was truly horrible to see."

The Australians explained that they were officially prospecting to join the AOA but that they had been prospects for the last fifteen years. At this point, the Midland Outlaws had firmly placed any notion of joining the AOA on the back burner but the idea of having to wait fifteen years for the dubious honor turned their stomachs. The more they thought about it, the more unfair the situation seemed to be. And the more beer they drank, the more their newfound Australian friends agreed with them.

Talking until the early hours, a new plan was hatched. The Australians would join forces with the British club, all under the British patch. With one fell swoop, both gangs would suddenly go international and have representatives on both sides of the world.

Rainier was moving through the bar at Daytona, trying to mingle with as many people as possible. When he came across the Brits and the Australians and they told him their news, he went as white as a sheet. The following morning, following a consultation with Taco himself, the Australians were presented with their AOA patches, which had been produced overnight in a special rush order.

The celebrations went on until the early hours of the morning. The Australians realized that, had it not been for the Brits, they would have had to wait around for many more years before being brought into the fold. Although the Midland Outlaws felt a slight tinge of sadness at the thought of not being able to take their own club oversees, they soon got over it in the old-fashioned way—by drinking themselves into oblivion.

On one of these nights, Taco's right-hand man, Wayne Hicks (who had been busy organizing various events during the first few days of the festival) came along to meet Boone and the others. He was a solid man with a short black beard and tiny intense eyes that he normally hid behind dark glasses. Despite his enormous gut you could tell he remained physically powerful and certainly not a man to mess with.

He too pushed the idea that the Midland Outlaws would be welcome to prospect for the AOA. And once again the visitors had to explain, as tactfully as they possibly could, that they had not yet made up their mind about what to do in the future.

Boone and the others remained in Florida after Daytona finished, visiting other Outlaws chapters up and down the coast and getting to know other key figures from the region. Although they were not members of the AOA and therefore were not able to sit in on any of the church meetings, it soon became clear that the level of criminality going on around them was far more intense than anything they had previously experienced.

Not only did the local Outlaws trade drugs but they also extorted money from various local businesses and held the whole place up for ransom. They were considered by many to be public enemy number one and they were proud of it. Once upon a time this might have terrified the Midland club members but they accompanied members of the local clubs as they went about their work and soon got into the swing of things. Within the space of a week, they found themselves fully embracing this kind of behavior and working out whether they could emulate it once they returned home.

The only way to party all night and drink all day was to consume increasing amounts of drugs. It was a philosophy that had worked well for Boone in the UK and one that he intended to stick to during his time in Florida. Although drugs were usually plentiful, every now and then the supply ran dry. When Boone discovered himself short on one occasion, he decided the best man to ask would be the guy in charge.

The next time he saw Taco in the clubhouse, he approached him. "Get us some coke will you?"

Taco smiled, "What do you think I am, a fucking drug dealer or something?"

"Of course not. But get us some coke."

As soon as Boone opened up the small package, he knew it wasn't going to do it for him. Instead of the fine powder he was used to there was a kind of damp sludge. Boone went straight back to Taco.

"I need to have a word with you," said Boone.

"What is it? I'm kind of busy, man."

"I need a word in private."

"No, man, whatever you have to say to me you can say in front of my brothers."

Boone pulled out the drugs packet.

"I don't want this. I want my money back."

Taco held his smile but strain started to show at the corners of his mouth.

"What, man?"

"I don't know what this stuff is, but I wanted coke. This isn't any good to me. I want my money back."

"Are you trying to say I'm ripping you off? That's coke. That's what we have down here. Are you trying to embarrass me in front of my brothers?"

"No, I just want my money back."

Taco stared at Boone for a long while and then burst into a chuckle, "Sure Dog, whatever, you can have your money back."

It would be some time before Boone realized just what a lucky escape he'd had, and that Taco had had men killed for far less. Had Boone been a member of the AOA his attitude toward Taco would have gotten him killed on the spot, but because he was from England and part of a different club, not yet full members of the organization, Taco decided he was happy to give him significantly more leeway than anyone else would have been entitled to. It didn't last long.

One evening, a group of the Midland Outlaws were sitting in the clubhouse chatting, laughing and drinking away with the AOA boys when Taco came in looking even more stressed than usual. He sat down with a beer and began talking to Daytona chapter president Stephen "DK" Lemunyon, not really paying much attention to anyone else.

All of a sudden Taco leapt to his feet and began moving toward Boone. He threw a table to one side, fished his gun out of his trouser belt, pulled back on the slide to chamber a round, and then pointed the weapon directly at Boone's face, his finger tight on the trigger.

"That's it, man," he screamed. "You're dead. You're fucking dead. I don't let anyone talk to me like that. You think you can come in here and disrespect me? You think you can come in here and verbally abuse me? This is my house! I don't have a drugs problem. I haven't fucked up my face, you piece of shit. I'm gonna fucking kill you right now, you limey sonofabitch!"

Most of the time Flyball moved as if he was in a bit of a daze, but this time he moved like greased lightning, racing over in a flash and putting himself right in the line of fire, directly between Taco and Boone.

"Hey, man, put the gun down."

"Out of the way, soldier," barked Taco.

"I can't do that. I can't let you shoot him. He's a guest."

"You're my fucking soldier and I'm telling you to get out of the way."

"I'm not moving. You'll have to shoot me first. I'm not moving until you put that thing down."

"Out of the way right now or I'll shoot you too."

"No, man. You ain't shooting anyone today."

The gun Boone had been issued when he arrived at the clubhouse was tucked into the waistband of his jeans at the small of his back. It had all happened so fast that he hadn't had time to reach for it, hadn't expected to have to reach for it. And now here he was, sitting in a chair with the international president of the AOA pointing a gun at his heart. Even with Flyball in the way, there was every chance the bullet would pass right through and still kill him. And the worst part was that Boone had no idea what he had done, no idea at all what was going on.

Caz hadn't moved quite as fast as Flyball but now he too came over to see if he could resolve the situation without bloodshed. The whole clubhouse had fallen silent.

"Dog, what did you say about him?"

"I didn't say anything."

"You must have said something."

"No, nothing."

"Think. Come on, Dog, think."

Boone screwed his eyes tight shut and racked his brain. "Dozer asked me what time we were going out to eat."

"And what did you say?"

"I didn't know."

"Is that what you said?"

"Yeah. That was it. He asked me what time we were going out."

"And you said . . ."

"Fuck knows."

Taco took a half step forward, pushing Flyball to the side with a heavy sweep of his arm. "He said it again!" he bellowed. "He's disrespecting me. I told you. I'm gonna kill the fucker.

I'm gonna put one in him. He's saying I've got a fucked nose. He's saying I've got a coke problem. . . ."

It took nearly ten minutes to calm Taco down to the point where he was finally willing to put down the gun and another ten minutes to explain that "fuck knows" was a common English colloquial expression, not a sly insult.

"If someone doesn't know something, they say 'Who the fuck knows?'—it's just slang. It doesn't mean anything," said Caz as slowly and calmly as possible.

"Yeah? Well I haven't got a fucked nose."

"No one is saying that you have."

Taco thought about it all for a few moments then stuffed the gun back into his trouser belt. "I've had enough of this—I'm going," and with that he stormed off.

It turned out that Taco had been getting a lot of grief off of some of his senior officers who were concerned about his increasingly heavy drug habit. Taco insisted he was fully in control, but if anyone needed proof that his drug consumption was making him paranoid, the scene that had just been played out at the Orlando clubhouse was all the confirmation they needed.

Unknown to the Midland Outlaws, Taco was also feeling the stress of planning multiple campaigns against various enemies of the club—fulfilling his pledge to make the year the "rottenest" on record.

In April 1994 he arranged for an Outlaw named Donald Fogg, whom he suspected of snitching, to be murdered in such a way that it would look as though an enemy of the club did it. A few weeks later, Fogg's body was found lying face down in the snow close to an Outlaws clubhouse in Gary, Indiana. He had been shot in the head. He received a full Outlaws funeral at which a story circulated that he had been shot by a police officer who had been interested in his girlfriend.

Soon after, Taco decided it was time to take out the War-locks. Flyball and DK began experimenting with different types of explosives they could use to attack the enemy club-house. They finally picked a five-gallon jerry can, which they filled with diesel and a large firework with a long fuse, which they stuffed into the mouth of the can.

One night in May the pair drove Flyball's camper van past the nearest Warlock clubhouse, lit the fuse and tossed the makeshift device inside. The building—which purely by chance had been unoccupied at the time—exploded in a mas-sive ball of flame and was totally destroyed. Several other Outlaws, including Hicks, watched the bombing from a safe vantage point and cheered as the building collapsed.

In September 1994, around forty Outlaws had a showdown with twenty-five Hell's Angels at a public racetrack in Lan-caster, New York. Earlier that year, someone had thrown a grenade into the home of Buffalo Wally, a midlevel Outlaws leader. Bowman called on Outlaws from around the area to congregate at the racetrack as a show of force and to avenge the bombing.

"Good morning, brother," Hell's Angels leader Mike Quale said to Buffalo Wally, as the two groups closed together.

"You're no brother of mine," Buffalo Wally replied.

With that, the fight was on. At first, fists flew and then out came the knives and the guns. When it was over, both Buffalo Wally and Mike Quale were dead.

Buffalo Wally's funeral was attended by a neutral MC known as the Fifth Chapter, a small club made up of recover-ing drug and alcohol addicts who sought to maintain good re-lations with all the major one-percenter clubs. As a mark of respect, the Fifth Chapter members turned their colors in-side out during the service.

A few days later, the Fifth Chapter members attended the funeral of Mike Quale. This time they flew their colors proudly and one of the club members was pictured, in a local newspaper report of the event, embracing and consoling a Hell's Angel. When Taco saw the photograph he hit the roof and immediately asked Hicks to shut the club down in Florida where the Fifth Chapter's national president lived.

In December, DK Lemunyon invited members of the Fifth Chapter to the Outlaws clubhouse in Orlando, ostensibly for a party. Once inside, the members were seated at two picnic tables and surrounded by armed Outlaws. DK then announced that there was a problem and pulled out the article with the photograph of the Fifth Chapter man hugging the Angel. After a brief chat about loyalty, he pulled out a heavy flashlight and began beating the president of the Fifth Chapter with it.

The others were given a good thumping too—several had their legs or ankles broken—and leathers, patches and anything bearing the logo of their club were confiscated. Too injured to walk away, the bikers were hosed down, placed on top of their motorcycles and pushed off down the road. Unable to change gear or brake because of their broken ankles and legs, several had no choice but to keep going until they eventually crashed.

The level of violence being employed by the Outlaws was out of all proportion and one newly patched member, a former dope dealer named Mike Lynn, realized he had bitten off more than he could chew. The last straw was when Outlaw Jimmy "The Pimp" Kinsey, who had bought a house next door to the Orlando clubhouse, refused to give his property over to the club so that the complex could be expanded. Instead of accepting his decision, Hicks arranged to have Kinsey killed.

If the Outlaws were prepared to kill their own, Lynn figured that all the talk of brotherhood and friendship no longer meant anything. Realizing that he knew too much to be allowed to leave of his own accord, and with no desire to spend the rest of his life behind bars, he decided to turn snitch. He trusted that the authorities would be able to protect him from the wrath of the club.

During the course of the next six months (just after the Midland Outlaws had left Daytona), Lynn secretly recorded much of what Flyball, DK and Hicks were saying during church meetings. "We're getting ready. Next week the place is getting torched, you know," said Flyball a few days before the firebomb attack on the Warlocks' clubhouse. "I'm fucking going in there next week come hell or high water. We got it pretty much figured out how we're going to do it."

A few days later, DK was recorded talking about his plans for a local business owner who was refusing to pay extortion. "He's going to feel like he just fucking saw God. I'm gonna fucking cut his fucking face off and all that shit, shut him down, blow his house up, kill all his employees and all that shit."

Slowly but surely, Lynn was helping to build a case against the club that would ultimately strike a crippling blow.

Back in England, the Midland Outlaws kept in touch with their newfound Florida friends and listened with interest to some of the stories of bombings and shootings and murders that were emerging from the region. But ultimately Boone and the others didn't have much time to focus on what was happening on the other side of the Atlantic. The reason was simple: there was a far bigger and far deadlier war going on much closer to home.

17

TWO TRIBES

1994–1997

When the Midland Outlaws unwittingly found themselves at the patch-over party that saw two chapters of Denmark's Undertakers MC don the colors of the Fat Mexican, they had no doubt that the Hell's Angels would have something to say about it.

A couple of years earlier, the Angels had responded to the opening of the first European chapter of the Bandidos by arranging a drive-by shooting that killed the club's vice president. In the aftermath, both sides began recruiting heavily and now the opening of the first Scandinavian Bandidos chapter looked as though it could be the catalyst to escalate the conflict into a full-scale war.

Crucially though, the biker scene in Scandinavia was very different from the scene Boone had grown up with in the UK. For some time, club pride and brotherhood had taken second place to the pursuit of profit for all the MCs. The only real concern the Angels had was to ensure that the hard-won territory that netted them millions in drug sales each year would not be compromised by the new Bandidos. In the end, high-ranking American representatives from the mother chapters of the two clubs met up in Paris and, after lengthy talks and delicate negotiations, agreed on terms.

The Angels wanted Scandinavia to themselves and planned to be the dominant MC throughout the whole region. Just so long as the Bandidos agreed not to open up any more chapters in the area, they would be left alone.

A motley collection of small, independent biker gangs with curiously unconventional names had been a mainstay of Nordic subculture since the late sixties, but it wasn't until 1979 that the Galloping Goose MC moved into the big time and became an official prospect chapter for the Hell's Angels. The Angels' Amsterdam chapter, formed in 1977, was already taking advantage of lax local drug laws to reap massive profits. The Denmark chapter was expected to do the same by seizing control of Copenhagen's lucrative hash and pot trade.

Much of this business took place in Christiania, a former army base in the southeast of the city that was taken over by hippies in the 1970s and turned into a self-contained commune with its own government and education system. Drugs were legal there and more than one hundred thousand dollars of dope changed hands on a daily basis, but the biker gang that supplied the drugs, Bullshit MC, refused to let anyone else have a piece of the action.

The Copenhagen chapter of the Angels received its full charter on New Year's Eve 1980 and soon afterward its leader, a fearsome thug by the name of "Blondie" Nielsen, declared war on the Bullshit. After receiving a tip that four of the gang were in a city bar, Nielsen walked in alone, drew his knife, cut the throats of two of his rivals and stabbed a third before the fourth had even had time to react.

The Angels then went after Bullshit president Henning Norbert "Makrel" Knudsen, emptying the magazine of a submachine gun into his body as he stood outside his home. He died instantly. Over the course of the next five years, at least ten more bikers died, so utterly decimating the ranks of the

Bullshit that it no longer existed as a club. The Angels had achieved their goal and assumed total control of Denmark.

In 1990, the Angels expanded into Sweden using their tried and trusted technique of choosing the most suitable candidates. They would visit the country, party with a few clubs, then sit back and watch them fight with one another over the chance to wear the death's head patch. The last club standing would win. In Sweden, that club was the Dirty Draggles (Swedish for "scum") based in the port city of Malmo, directly across the Øresund Strait from Copenhagen. Following a violent struggle with two other local clubs, the Draggles received their charter in late 1993, much to the chagrin of the rival Morbids MC.

Based in Helsingborg, just thirty miles north of Malmo, and led by Michael "Joe" Ljunggren (the man Boone had met and befriended in Marseille), the Morbids were furious that the Angels had chosen the Draggles and not given them a chance to prospect at all.

Despite having signed the Paris agreement, the Danish Bandido leader, "Big" Jim Tinndahn—a man every bit as formidable as Blondie Nielsen—had no intention of sticking to it. In early 1994, he approached the Morbids and offered them the chance to join him and give the Angels a real run for their money. Joe called Boone to let him know what was happening.

"You're asking for a lot of trouble if you go down that road," Boone told him.

"I know, but we'll have trouble anyway. You know what the Angels are like. They want to take over the whole country. Since they came to Sweden, we've done nothing but put them down. Sooner or later they will try to destroy us. At least if we become Bandidos, we might be able to survive."

The development was discussed at the next national church meeting of the Midland Outlaws, and soon afterward Boone called Joe back with the club's view of the situation.

"We say, fuck 'em," Boone told his friend. "Don't pay attention to anything the Angels are telling you. Put up the Bandidos patch. Don't let them push you around. Go for it."

True to form, the Angels sent a couple of associates to visit the Helsingborg clubhouse and shoot it up. No one was injured in the attack, but soon afterward the Angels opened up a prospect chapter of their own in Helsingborg. Now the scene was set for the war everyone had feared to begin in earnest. And Joe Ljunggren was right on the front line.

By the time Boone and the other Midland Outlaws returned from Florida, there had been another gun attack on the Morbids' clubhouse in which one of the Bandidos had the end of his finger shot off. Then there had been an exchange of gunshots at a Bandidos party that had left one HA hangaround dead and three others wounded. Shootings were now taking place in Helsingborg on an almost daily basis.

While the Midland Outlaws still struggled to find weapons and had to travel abroad in order to receive proper firearms training, the Nordic bikers had no such difficulties. At the time, all the Scandinavian countries had mandatory military training for virtually all males over the age of seventeen, which meant that most of the members on both sides of the conflict had already completed their service. They not only knew how to fire a range of pistols, rifles and submachine guns but they had also been trained in the use of anti-tank weapons, land mines and hand grenades. Furthermore, they knew exactly where they could find these.

In order to support their civilian militias in the unlikely event of war, both Sweden and Denmark had established a network of small arms depots throughout the countryside. The buildings were unguarded and relatively insecure, but this had never been a problem. Knowing their importance to national defense, no one had ever breached one.

Then the bikers came along. In a series of thefts by both the Bandidos and the Angels, around 300 handguns, 272 rifles, 10 machine guns, 16 antitank rockets, hundreds of hand grenades and some 17 kilos of plastic explosives were taken before the authorities wised up and began securing the depots. One of these antitank rockets was fired at the HA clubhouse in Helsingborg soon after the first theft, though no one was injured.

The shootings challenged the public perception of the Nordic biker gangs, who up until then had benefited from incredibly positive PR. In the ten years prior to the first attack, the Angels clubhouse in Copenhagen had received a substantial amount in government grants (subsidized by the liberal Danish state as a place where people could enjoy their "hobby"). High street shops dedicated to selling T-shirts and other biker novelties in support of the clubs could be found all over Scandinavia. Some children even dressed up as bikers at Halloween. The battles were almost tolerated because the bikers were killing only each other. So long as the public were not involved, they seemed content to let the MCs get on with their war.

By June, though, the fighting had spread to Finland and led to the death of the president of the Klan MC, a prospect club for the Bandidos. Increasingly alarmed by what was going on overseas, Sonny Barger summoned the leader of the Swedish HA to California and arranged for talks with the central command of the Bandidos, with the idea of reminding them about the Paris pact. But the pact did not cover Sweden and the Morbids were eager to avenge the attacks the HA had carried out on them. Further talks took place when a group of American Bandidos visited the Hell's Angels in Denmark and Sweden, but they too failed to come to an agreement.

Back in the UK, rumors began to circulate that the Midland Outlaws were about to become an official prospect club for the Bandidos. Boone and the others had no idea where this story came from, but they did everything they could to encourage it. From a PR point of view, they wanted to make the British Hell's Angels as uncomfortable as possible and there was hardly a better way of doing this than to show their support for all those taking a stand against the HA.

As further provocation, Boone led a small group of Midland Outlaws to Sweden to attend a party cohosted by Joe (now president of the Helsingborg chapter) to celebrate the opening of yet another Bandidos chapter.

The day after the party, the Bandidos proudly showed the Outlaws around the clubhouse, which was built inside a large industrial complex. By then the constant state of war and use of high-grade military weapons had dramatically altered the design and layout of all new clubhouses. The security room had a large onyx table, above which hung a bank of dozens of security monitors. Cameras pointed in all directions making it impossible for anyone to approach the site without being seen—the room was occupied at all times.

To the right of the control console was a large red button. This, Boone was told, was the emergency lockdown control. In the event of an emergency, all the doors in the building were automatically closed and secured shut with blasts of compressed air from a central reservoir. Bullet- and blast-proof, no one would be able to get into the building, though at the same time no one would be able to get out until the alert was over. With plenty of food and water as well as a generator, the club would be able to sustain itself in a locked-down state for several days. "If there is ever a nuclear war," one of the Bandidos announced to Boone, "this would be one of the best places to be."

The following day Boone found out just how effective those security measures were. As he and his fellow Outlaws sat in the bar at the center of the clubhouse unit, an alarm sounded and all the doors began to slam shut with incredible force and huge hisses of compressed air. One prospect only barely made it into the bar area after executing an Indiana Jones-style headfirst dive into the room.

"We have a big problem," the prospect announced after catching his breath, "there are maybe two hundred policemen with Heckler and Koch machine guns surrounding the clubhouse."

"Okay," said Boone, fighting to remain calm. "So what do we do?"

"If they come in, you put your hands up."

"I know about putting my hands up. I mean what do we do until we get to that part?"

"Oh, we just wait."

Boone couldn't help but feel a little on edge at the situation but the fact that the local bikers were treating it like something that happened on a regular basis made him feel a little more comfortable. An hour or so later the doors opened up and the alert status was downgraded. It turned out that the police had been unaware that the club had been patched over. Having received reports about a large number of Bandidos in the area, they feared the clubhouse had been attacked and expected to find a total bloodbath inside.

The Midland Outlaws returned to the UK and the war in Scandinavia raged on with a series of tit-for-tat exchanges taking place across the region. In February 1995, the fighting spread to Norway with a mass shootout between members of the Bandidos and the HA that, miraculously, ended with no injuries. The next major incident, however, would hit the Brits and Boone in particular far harder.

In July 1995, Joe Ljunggren, by then promoted to national president of the Bandidos, was riding his Harley on the major E4 highway in Sweden, on his way back from a party in Finland, when he was shot by a sniper who had secreted himself along the roadside. Although Ljunggren was traveling at more than seventy miles an hour, the gunman's single bullet hit him at the base of his neck in an area not covered by the bulletproof jacket he had taken to wearing at all times. He died instantly.

Boone and several other members of the Midland Outlaws who had gotten to know Joe traveled to Sweden for the funeral. It was an impressive occasion, with massive limousines booked to carry the mourners to a large cathedral just outside Helsingborg. The priest performed the service first in Swedish and then in English, for the benefit of the small British contingent. And at the end, they played Joe's favorite song, "Wind of Change" by the Scorpions. Boone had been to plenty of biker funerals before but this one affected him deeply. It was more than just the loss of someone he had felt a real connection with; it was to do with the way he had been killed. The attack had taken place at such a distance and had been so cowardly, so completely without honor. A part of him wanted the Angels to attack the funeral party, just so that he and the others would have a chance to take their revenge.

Boone returned to England with two Danish Bandidos, including JJ, a close friend of Joe's who had been riding with him just half an hour before the assassination. The plan was to attend the Rock and Blues Show, but Joe's absence put a real damper on the whole thing. The trio spent hours talking over their memories of the man and mourning their loss. A few days before the event opened to the public, with the Midland Outlaws camped on the site in order to get it ready, half a dozen police officers turned up at the main gate.

"We're considering canceling the event," the lead officer announced.

"Why?" asked Caz.

"Because you've got Bandidos here and there's just been another attack with an antitank rocket in Scandinavia. We don't want to take the chance that it's going to kick off here. We think the Hell's Angels might try to hit back at you."

Boone knew he had to inform his Bandido guests of what had happened. He made his way over to the portable cabin where the two men were sleeping and gently woke them up.

"I've got some bad news, I'm afraid," he said softly. "Something terrible has happened."

The two Bandidos were already miserable after Joe's funeral and by now they were used to a constant stream of bad news in connection with the ongoing war. They prepared themselves for the worst.

"What is it now?" asked JJ.

"There's been a rocket attack on the clubhouse in Copenhagen."

"Oh God. How bad is it?"

"At least eleven wounded. Could be one, maybe two people dead."

"This is terrible."

"There is one bit of good news though," said Boone.

JJ's brow furrowed—how could anything good come of this? "What do you mean?"

"It was the Hell's Angels clubhouse that was hit, and your lot that did it."

JJ was wearing only his boxer shorts and his patches but he didn't care. He leapt up and began running around the field outside his cabin, cheering, waving his arms in the air and turning cartwheels. By now the police had agreed to allow the festival to continue but the lead officer wanted to inspect the site. He saw JJ running around and asked Boone what on earth was going on.

"I just told him what happened in Copenhagen."

"And this is how he reacts? This is just wrong. You guys are animals. People could be dead."

"I know," said Boone, "you've just made his day."

As the police later found out, the Midland Outlaws had arranged their own security to counter any possible threat of an attack by the Hell's Angels. As two officers patrolled the site, a man in full camouflage gear, wielding a British Army-issued SA80 assault rifle, suddenly confronted them. The stunned officers could only stand speechless as the man waved them on. "You guys better move on," he explained, "I'm trying to do security here."

Once they had recovered from the shock, the officers reported the incident to the head of their unit, who in turn demanded to know who the man was, and where his weapon had come from. But the armed guard had mysteriously vanished without a trace.

"It's nothing to do with us," explained Caz. "We have some friends of the club who have offered to take care of security. We don't have any control over them. I think the best thing you can do is to forget all about it."

Despite Joe's death, the Bandidos continued to expand across Europe, and in March 1996 members from a few different chapters traveled to Finland to celebrate the opening of their newest chapter in the capital, Helsinki. The party was the usual raucous, high-spirited affair and the Bandidos looked as though they had been to hell and back by the time they headed to Vantaa Airport for the journey home.

All the antics of the previous days were swiftly forgotten when a group of Bandidos headed to Copenhagen, arrived at their departure gate and realized that by complete coincidence, a large contingent of Danish Hell's Angels were going to be on the exact same flight.

Fearing an outbreak of violence, Finnish police escorted both groups from the terminal to the plane, only to discover that, rather than being spread throughout economy, both sets of bikers had booked themselves into the business class section of flight SK715 (the drug trade had made all the clubs wealthy and they liked to flaunt their money whenever they could). Somehow, in the panic and confusion, no one from the authorities thought to warn their colleagues in Denmark about the volatile cargo that was heading their way.

Although separated by nothing more than a narrow aisle, the two sides managed to keep themselves under control for the duration of the flight. There's an unspoken agreement among biker gangs that forbids them from fighting on an aircraft because of the risks involved—it can lead to lifetime travel bans for all those involved, in addition to stiff prison sentences. That afternoon, all the nonbikers in business class were, for once, wishing they had flown economy. They spent the whole journey in stunned silence, expecting an outbreak of brutal carnage at any moment, having found themselves unwittingly in the center of a potential war-zone.

The plane landed at Kastrup Airport without incident but as the Bandidos were lining up at customs, their colleagues outside who had come to pick them up in two Opel Kadetts came under sudden and vicious attack. Two vehicles drove toward them at high speed, their occupants firing out of the windows. Screeching to a halt, two men—both brandishing 9 mm automatics—approached Bandido Uffe Larsen in his car and began firing through the windshield and door. Larsen was hit in the head, heart and legs, and died on the scene.

The Bandidos in the other car fared only a little better. Their vehicle had been strafed with bullets, shredding the tires and smashing the windows. The driver escaped by heading the wrong way down a one-way street, narrowly avoiding an oncoming bus. The car jerked to a halt a little farther on and the passengers stumbled out and staggered into the departure area where they collapsed, three of them bleeding from gunshot wounds to the chest and neck.

Nearly three hundred miles away at Oslo Airport, Fornebue, an almost identical attack was taking place. A Norwegian Bandido—also returning from the Helsinki party—had been shot in the chest as he came out of the arrivals terminal.

The Midland Outlaws returned to Denmark for another

Bandido funeral, only to find themselves directly in the firing line. As Boone and the others emerged from the terminal and filed into their pickup car, another vehicle drove past and let off a volley from a submachine gun. Boone was standing beside two Bandidos and threw both men to the ground as soon as he heard the first shot, unsure of whether he was doing so to save them or to give himself a soft landing. Bullets crashed into the car and one ricochet struck him in the back. The bikers left the area before the police had time to question them.

Boone's injury turned out to be minor (and was treated in the clubhouse by a Bandido who had trained as an army medic) but the message from the Hell's Angels was clear: any club that supported the Bandidos was considered a legitimate target.

The Bandidos took their revenge for the airport attack in October 1996 as three hundred revelers celebrated the sixteenth anniversary of the Angels' Viking chapter at the clubhouse in the Norrebro district of Copenhagen. Fliers advertising the event were posted all around the city and, eager to improve their public image, the bikers invited neighbors and members of the public to attend. A large marquee was erected in the garden and a lavish buffet was put out. Around forty police officers put up a security cordon to prevent attacks from rivals. It proved utterly useless.

At around one in the morning, an antitank missile slammed through the clubhouse wall and exploded inside the bar. The shot had come from the flat roof of a one-story building some seventy meters away and another live missile was found at the same spot. It had passed directly over the heads of the police cordon. An Angel prospect died instantly along with twenty-nine-year-old single mother Janne Krohn. Nineteen others were injured. In the wake of the attack, TV pictures were beamed around the world showing banners hanging from the apartment buildings that surrounded the clubhouse. Written on them were the names of the children who would have been killed if the attackers had missed their target.

Shockwaves from the attack were felt throughout Europe and beyond, and as a result a bill was rushed through Danish parliament giving police sweeping new powers. The "Biker Law" was used to prohibit gang members from gathering in residential areas, and allowed police to close down many of the bikers' clubhouses. At the same time, they introduced round-the-clock surveillance of the remaining biker strongholds, and kept a close watch on the key players in the conflict.

Despite the clampdown, more violence followed. In January 1997, a Hell's Angel was shot dead in his car in Aalborg, Denmark, and six months later a car bomb exploded outside the Bandidos clubhouse in Drammen, Norway. A female passerby became the first civilian casualty in the conflict, when she was killed as she drove past. The blast flattened the heavily fortified building, set nearby factories ablaze and shattered windows three-quarters of a mile away. That attack was followed three days later by an even more shocking assault, in which one Bandido was killed and three wounded by a Hell's Angels associate who opened fire outside a restaurant crowded with holidaymakers in the resort town of Liseleje, Denmark.

By this time, both gangs were increasingly aware that the feuding could not be allowed to continue. The massive amount of self-imposed security, as well as the high cost of arms and explosives, had put a major financial strain on both groups. Soon, feelers were being put out in an effort to restore peace.

Officially, the last violent confrontation occurred on June 7, 1997, when a Bandidos trainee was shot dead by a Hell's Angel member in Northern Zealand. The final death toll stood at eleven dead and around ninety-six seriously injured.

Police were investigating seventy-four cases of attempted murder.

Shortly afterward, live television coverage captured the emotive image of high-ranking Hell's Angel Blondie Nielsen shaking hands with Bandidos leader Jim Tinndahn. The pair announced that, following a summer of negotiations, a truce was now in place. "We have agreed to cooperate to stop what has been happening," said Tinndahn.

The truth was that the two former enemies had drawn up an agreement in which every town and every city in Scandinavia had been systemically split up, right down to specific pubs, discotheques and striptease clubs, in an effort to end the disruption to their lucrative criminal activities. Neither side had gained or lost any ground and neither side had won any kind of strategic advantage as a result of the war. Neither the Angels nor the Bandidos nor the Outlaws could claim a victory. As Boone read reports of the truce, he couldn't help thinking that the whole thing—including the murder of his friend—had simply been a colossal waste of time and that Joe and all the others had died for nothing.

18

DOWN UNDER

March 1997

Ever since the Midland Outlaws returned from their first trip to Florida, the newly appointed Australian chapter of the AOA had bombarded them with invitations to head down under and pay them a visit.

The Ozzie Outlaws were eager to play host: as far as they were concerned, it was entirely due to the efforts of the Brits that they had been awarded their charter in the first place. Had Boone and the others not intervened during Daytona Bike Week, they would undoubtedly still be prospecting. Their gratitude knew no bounds and all the chapters across the various states and territories were eager to thank their benefactors in person as soon as possible.

As he boarded the plane, Boone couldn't help but reflect on the fact that he had now been a member of an MC for more than a decade. In those early days, a ride out to Wales and a fistfight with the locals or a ride down to Cornwall to hang out with the Scorpio had been the highlights of the annual calendar. Along with Caz, Dozer and the others, Boone was now a member of the biggest club in the country, with good friends all over the world. When they were Pagans, half the members had never even been abroad. Now they were all collecting air miles. It wasn't all good though. The club also had more enemies than ever, and every time they traveled abroad or got closer to another MC, they were picking up baggage and putting themselves in the firing line. When they were Pagans they could pretty much do whatever they wanted because they were too small for their alliances to have any real consequence. Now every individual member of the Outlaws had to think before he spoke to anyone, just to make sure he didn't inadvertently start a major conflict.

In England, bikers were still far more likely to die in motorcycle accidents than in any other way but in every place they visited—Canada, America, Scandinavia and now Australia—there was a good chance of being shot or blown up. It was great to visit and the sense of camaraderie Boone and the others felt with their biker brothers was incredible, but he didn't know if he could live that way all the time.

After they were collected from Sydney Airport in a series of vehicles and given time to rest, the visit immediately took on a familiar pattern. The Midland Outlaws were taken from bar to bar, clubhouse to clubhouse and all-night party to all-night party. Everywhere they went, they were treated like celebrities and given unlimited access to all the beer, drugs and women they could handle.

Their time in the New South Wales capital included a sightseeing tour. Each member of the club had his picture taken against the backdrop of the Sydney Opera House. In typical one-percenter style, the majority of the photographs were taken with the men facing away, showing their colors, not their faces. They were also taken on a visit to the outskirts of the city to visit a bar called the Viking Tavern, the site of one of the most infamous incidents in biker history: the 1984 Milperra Massacre.

Boone and the other Midland Outlaws remembered hearing a little about the incident at the time. Now, for the first time, they were able to hear the full story from some of those who had actually been there on the day.

In 1966, the same year the Bandidos were founded, Scotsman William "Jock" Ross left his native Glasgow for a new life in Sydney. He was twenty-six but struggling desperately to find the right path in life, having already worked as an apprentice blacksmith and a truck driver and served in the army. He hoped a change of scenery would get him back on track.

A natural leader and true "man's man," Jock soon found everything he was looking for by starting up a motorcycle club that he named the Comancheros after the John Wayne western. Every member had to swear an oath of allegiance until death, and have the MC's colors tattooed onto his arm. Recruits were not allowed to ride "rice burners" and had to contribute to a "war fund"—the proceeds of which went directly to Jock himself. They also had to agree to abide by the club's own version of the Ten Commandments:

1. *The President is the Supreme Commander of the Comanchero.*
2. *Any member found guilty of cowardice will be thrown out of the Club.*
3. *Any member found guilty of stealing from a member of the Club itself will be thrown out of the Club.*
4. *Any member found guilty of screwing another member's real Ol' Lady or taking advantage of a rift between them will be thrown out.*
5. *Any member found guilty of selling, distributing or using hard drugs will be thrown out.*
6. *Any member found guilty of breeding dissension in the Club (i.e., running down the President of the Club or club policies by discredit in any way, shape or form—or bad shit rumors) will be thrown out of the Club.*
7. *Any member found guilty of using their superior ability to con another member or nominated member out of their bikes, money or valuables will be severely dealt with.*
8. *Any member found guilty of not helping another member who is in genuine trouble (not bullshit trouble) will be severely dealt with.*
9. *Any member found guilty of divulging Club business or Club policies to anyone that is not a member, unless directed by the President, will be severely dealt with.*
10. *Any member found guilty of wearing his colors on or in anything other than a British or American motorcycle of 500 cc or more will be severely dealt with.*

Obsessed with the military (he lied and told friends he had served with the elite special forces), Jock insisted that club members take part in weekly combat training sessions and spent time marching in formation around a makeshift parade ground outside their clubhouse in a Sydney suburb. The Comancheros soon became his own private army.

Vicious fights with other biker clubs were commonplace and regularly made headlines in the local press, cuttings of which Jock lovingly kept in a special folder. In one notorious incident, the club butted heads with the Loners, a small city-based MC. After one of the Loners threatened several Co-mancheros with a shotgun Jock launched a counterattack in which several Loners were beaten, and then suggested the two sides meet at a hotel to establish a truce.

The Loners were eager to comply and turned up at the ap-pointed place unarmed, as promised. They were met by two carloads of Comancheros wielding baseball bats and, after re-ceiving a sound beating, were forced to hand over their col-ors, putting the club out of existence. Police arrived on the scene but none of the Loners would press charges. Although their club had been destroyed, they remained loyal to the MC code of silence, knowing that any breach would only add to their humiliation.

In the late seventies Anthony "Snoddy" Spencer joined the club. A former naval officer, he was an orphan who had wit-nessed his own mother's suicide and spent his formative years in and out of care institutions. He was nineteen when he discovered the Comancheros and finally found the family and sense of acceptance he had been searching for. Jock, twelve years older at the time, became like a father to him.

Snoddy's arrival coincided with growing dissent in the ranks: "If I'd wanted to march around all fucking day I'd have joined the army," was an increasingly common complaint. But things got far worse when Jock himself was found to have broken one of the club's cardinal rules.

Comanchero sergeant at arms Colin "Caesar" Campbell and a friend were visiting a club member when they saw Jock's vehicle parked at the front of the house. They looked in through an open window and saw Jock having sex with the member's wife. The two men knocked on the door and when Jock answered, they stared at him and walked off without a word. The supreme commander had breached one of his own commandments. For Snoddy, it was the ultimate act of be-trayal. The man he had looked up to and seen as his mentor had turned his back on everything Snoddy had been taught to believe in.

Campbell tried to force his president to attend a church meeting to answer the charges against him but instead, in early 1982, Jock split the Comanchero into two separate chapters, one based in the western suburbs of Sydney and led by Jock himself, the other in the city-center, led by an increasingly disillusioned Snoddy.

A couple of years earlier, Snoddy and another Comanchero had traveled to America to buy Harley-Davidson parts. While there they had met and partied with members of the Bandidos, who by then had established chapters in more than a dozen states. For Snoddy it was a revelation: here was a club that didn't bother with drills or parades, they were into bikes, partying and making money through crime. They were, thought Snoddy, everything the Comancheros were not, but everything he wanted them to be.

Three months after the split, Snoddy and several other Comancheros resigned from the club, burning their colors in a ceremonial bonfire. The defectors included Caesar Campbell and his five brothers—Bull, Chop, Wack, Shadow and Snake Eyes—a veritable biker clan in their own right. Having obtained permission direct from president Ronnie Hodge, Snoddy then proceeded to set up the first Australian chapter of the Bandidos.

For Jock, this alliance with a foreign club was the ultimate act of betrayal by the man he saw as his "adopted son." He branded all of them traitors and deserters, and would only refer to them as "Bandaids." As the weeks went by, the rivalry between the two groups became increasingly intense and spawned a number of clashes, including roadside beatings, bar fights and several exchanges of gunfire. Both sides tried to negotiate peace but after one particularly heated telephone call, Jock declared all-out war on the newcomers.

At a July 1984 meeting at the Bandidos clubhouse, a furious Snoddy made it clear the dispute would not end without blood being spilled. "Something has got to be done about Jock and the Comancheros and anybody in the club who has got any guts and wants to get rid of the problem, not just by bashing them, meet me in the bar after the meeting. We want to get rid of Jock permanently."

Rules of conflict were quickly drawn up, including a prohibition of members being "hit" at their homes or places of work. Any other location was considered fair game.

Both clubhouses were turned into fortresses with windows boarded up, gun parapets erected and barbed wire stretched across all the entrances.

The Bandidos also called in backup. Ronnie Hodge and three other club members made their way to the Australian Embassy in Los Angeles to obtain visas to travel to Sydney. Their applications were refused.

On the morning of Father's Day, September 2, 1984, the Bandidos threw down the gauntlet by turning up at the home of a Comanchero member (a breach of the rules of conflict) and letting him know that they would be attending the British Motorcycle Club swap meet that afternoon. A family event attended by dozens of bikers and patch clubs from across the country, the meet would take place at the Viking Tavern, a popular watering hole in the western Sydney suburb of Milperra.

The news got back to Jock, who immediately began to organize an attack, arranging to get to the site long before the Bandidos arrived and setting out his forces in a "Bull's Horns" formation similar to that used by the Zulus against British forces, a conflict he had studied in depth as part of his obsession with all things military. Each Comanchero team was issued with a walkie-talkie so they could coordinate their movements.

The original plan was for Jock to lull the Bandidos into a false sense of security by letting them think he was at the

meet alone. Once they approached him, the rest of the Comancheros would launch an attack from their strategic positions. The only glitch in the plan was that, when the Bandidos
failed to show up, their rivals relaxed and began drinking,
discarding their walkie-talkies at the bar.

The Bandidos—included Snoddy and five of the six Campbell brothers—seemed to arrive out of nowhere. For a few moments there was an awkward standoff between the two gangs
as they lined up on either side of the crowded parking lot.
Both sides were equipped with shotguns and rifles as well
as baseball bats, knives, chains and iron bars (although the
Bandidos—having scouted the area earlier and seen no sign of
the Comancheros—had left much of their arsenal in the van).

Neutral bikers, many of who had attended the event with
their families and minutes earlier had been enjoying a jovial,
carnival atmosphere, could scarcely believe their eyes at the
sight of the weaponry being brandished. But Jock was ready.
He raised a machete with the words "Bandaid hair parter"
crudely painted on it above his head and waved it in a small
circle, the signal his club had been waiting for. "Kill 'em all!"
he screamed, and the slaughter began. Two sets of bikers who
only a few months earlier had all belonged to the same club
and considered one another brothers went after each other's
blood.

Jock had issued strict orders to his men about who to target first and Snoddy and the members of the Campbell clan
were on the top of the hit list. In the middle of the parking
lot Geoff "Snake Eyes" Campbell suddenly found himself
staring down the barrel of a shotgun. He had just gotten off
his motorcycle and was armed only with a chain that served
as a belt in his jeans and a four-inch folding knife. He raised
his clenched fists: "Fight with these?" The Comanchero
shook his head then pulled the trigger. The blast hit Campbell
straight in the gut, shredding his flesh. For a brief moment he
felt nothing and stood stationary, wondering whether to

make a dash for the gun, and then the pain hit and dropped him to the ground, blood pouring from his wound.

A second Comanchero, one who had been a close friend of the Campbell brothers, appeared and loomed over Snake Eyes, a shotgun pointed inches from his face.

"Do it then," gasped Snake Eyes.

The Comanchero winked and moved the gun away. "Not today, Snake," he said. "Not today."

Caesar Campbell saw his brother fall and ran to his aid. He managed only a few steps before he was hit with two shotgun blasts in the back and a third that ripped through his shoulder. He spun around and collapsed on his back where he received a fourth shot to the chest.

Mario "Chop" Ciantar, who had been adopted into the Campbell family at the age of twelve, pulled out his .357 revolver and began firing wildly as he ran toward his fallen brothers. At least one of his bullets found a Comanchero target, striking the man dead, but another flew wide and tore into the face of fourteen-year-old innocent bystander Leanne Walters, killing her instantly.

Chop never made it to his brother. As he ducked past the crowds of screaming women and children, desperate to get out of the line of fire, he was struck by a hail of bullets and hit the ground hard. Elsewhere in the parking lot, the youngest brother, John "Wack" Campbell was shot the instant he climbed onto a motorcycle belonging to Philip "Bull" Campbell. The blast catapulted him into the back of a nearby car and left his right arm literally hanging by a fleshy thread.

By now the Bandidos had regrouped and were starting to fight back, forcing the Comanchero to retreat to the back of the bar. The individual Bandidos had also been assigned specific targets with others, appointed "rovers," to back up anyone who was in danger of being overwhelmed. Three more Comancheros were killed in quick succession. One, Ivan "Sparrow" Romcek, was hit at such close range that wadding from the spent shotgun cartridge was embedded in his neck. Another, Tony "Dog" McCoy, was hit in the face and chest and died before he even hit the ground.

Refusing to seek cover so that he could observe and direct the battle, the Comanchero supreme commander Jock was hit in the chest before a second bullet smashed into the left side of his head, shattering several of his teeth and coming to a rest inside his skull.

Friends carried Snake Eyes to safety, but as soon as they put him down he found himself staring at the agonized face of Gregory "Shadow" Campbell, who had been blasted through the throat moments earlier, after challenging another shotgun-wielding Comanchero to put down his gun and "fight like a man" with his fists. "I can't breathe," gasped Shadow, and Snake Eyes knew then and there that his brother was going to die. As he looked on helplessly, Shadow drowned in his own blood.

Over two hundred police officers were called to the scene and one, Detective Superintendent John Garvey, almost got caught up in the tail end of the violence when he came face to face with Comanchero Ray "Sunshine" Kucler, who, despite having suffered a major head wound, pointed his loaded shotgun directly at him. It took several minutes of tense, careful negotiation and reassurances that the police only wanted to disarm the bikers, so that the paramedics could enter and care for the injured, before Kucler agreed to put his weapon down. By then, six bikers were dead and twenty-eight were seriously injured. Incredibly, despite the mayhem, the bar had continued to serve drinks throughout.

The deaths continued even after the shooting stopped. In prison, racked with guilt and feeling personally responsible for the deaths of the two Campbell brothers, Snoddy recorded his feelings, frustrations and depressions in a series of diary entries. "My mind is starting to crack," he wrote. "I just don't understand what is happening to us. I don't know how much longer I can hang on to my sanity. I wish we could get bail soon. It is sending me round the twist."

On Saturday April 28, 1985, at six a.m., Snoddy was found hanging from the shower rail in cell 3233, Wing 3 of Parklea Prison. After his body had been taken down, the other Bandido inmates were allowed to gather around his body and pay their last respects to their deceased president.

Bull, who had spent almost an hour lying on the pavement hugging the body of his dying brother Shadow at the shootout, also died before the court case began—a result, his family insisted, of injuries he received on the day of the rumble.

Thirty-nine bikers were subsequently put on trial. Not one of the accused from either side was willing to testify. Jock—who survived his wounds, much to the utter amazement of his medical team—was singled out by the judge as being primarily responsible for the violence, and sentenced to life imprisonment. Seven other Comancheros also received life sentences. Sixteen of the new Bandidos received fourteen years each for manslaughter. The trial itself was the largest, longest and most expensive in Australian legal history.

The shootout, which ultimately came to be known as the Milperra Massacre, put an end to the undisputed reign of the Comancheros and to their dominance in the Sydney drug trade, and accelerated the rise of the Bandidos in Australia, not to mention further enhancing the club's reputation for violence elsewhere in the world. The incident also acted as a wakeup call in Australia and beyond about just how ruthless and deadly the supposedly lovable rogues in the biker gangs could be.

During the course of their Australia trip, Boone also visited the chapter in Tasmania where they partied with many of the Outlaws they had met in Daytona. They also hung out with Sid Collins, president and founder of the Melbourne Outlaws and famous as the man who was once shot in the stomach by a 9 mm pistol wielded by legendary underworld toe-cutter and hitman-turned-author Mark "Chopper" Read.

The trip was a huge success, but the Brits still struggled to come to terms with the differences between the MC scene in Australia and the rest of the world. Chief among these difficulties was the fact that down under, bikers are known as "bikies." Although the name carries the exact same connotations and strikes fear in the hearts of civilians everywhere, no matter how many times the Midland boys heard or said it, it just sounded ... well ... incredibly lame.

Then there was the problem of the new world order. While the three big international gangs, the Hell's Angels, the Bandidos and the Outlaws, all had a presence on the continent, none of them had anything like the level of gravitas they enjoyed elsewhere. Clubs like the Rebels, the Finks, the Gypsy Jokers, the Coffin Cheaters and the Comanchero were unknown outside Australia, but virtually all of them had a larger and more powerful presence throughout the country than the Outlaws and other international gangs did. Because of this, working out exactly who was friend and who was foe involved a steep learning curve.

Still, despite their lower position in the pecking order, spirits were sky high among the Australian Outlaws. It may have been a relatively small club, but firm power bases in Europe and America gave it a significant boost. In fact, soon after receiving their charter, the Outlaws were one of the major MCs invited to attend a meeting in Sydney where a plan was established to reduce the number of motorcycle gangs operating in Australia.

The best way forward, it was decided, would be for the larger clubs to take over the smaller ones, with or without their agreement. By the year 2000, there would be a maximum of six gangs left on the continent—the Hell's Angels, the Outlaws, the Bandidos, the Rebels, the Black Uhlans and the

Nomads. The thinking behind the consolidation was to limit and control the amount of competition for the shrinking dollar in the illicit trading arena such as the drugs market, and to strengthen the financial position of the remaining players. The plan was dubbed the "Australia 2000 Pact."

This biker blueprint for carving up territory among the strongest clubs to maximize income was later confirmed in a confidential assessment prepared by the New Zealand police on the activities of the Bandidos and the Highway 61 club and an agreement between Australian motorcycle gangs. "This [movement] began in America where most motorcycle initiatives appear to begin, and through the reaches of the empire of the strong gangs, such as the Hell's Angels and Outlaws, spread to Europe through their associated chapters and affiliated groups, and then to other countries of the world," the report said. "Where minor gang entities exist, they were either to be chartered (taken over) or absorbed by takeover, or eliminated completely, often through extreme violence, [including] homicide through shootings and bombings."

Although they were not allowed to attend church meetings or take an active part in club business, the Midland Outlaws were trusted enough to be privy to much of the illicit activity that was going on. It was crystal clear that the manufacture and supply of amphetamine and cannabis were major money earners for their Australian brothers, and that illegal weapons were widely available. In Melbourne they learned that their hosts had a contact at VicRoads, the state government agency in charge of vehicle registration and related matters, who could provide them with fake driving licenses. For a cost of two thousand dollars each, the senior employee would produce licenses that contained their photographs combined with fake name and address details.

The gang would use these licenses to avoid traffic fines and obtain fraudulent mortgages. They carried them whenever they were engaged in illegal activity. During drunken nights at the clubhouse, the Australians regaled their visitors with tales of shootouts, bombing raids and violent takeovers of smaller gangs, all linked to competition for territory that in turn related to opportunities for profit. The great strength of the club to date was that few of their activities had ever attracted much publicity, so they were able to operate without too much harassment from the police.

The final stop of the Midland Outlaws' tour involved a visit to the newly established chapter in the Queensland town of Mackay, some five hundred miles up the coast from Brisbane. Although a relatively small community with a population of just seventy-five thousand, the town had significant strategic importance when it came to controlling the Queensland drug trade. Here the visitors learned of simmering tensions with a long-established local gang, Odin's Warriors, though other than a few standoffs and hand gestures, nothing much took place.

The Midland Outlaws left Australia with an open invitation to return whenever they wanted and firm promises from members of all the chapters they had met there that they would be returning the favor and coming to the UK in the near future. It wasn't until the end of August (long after the Brits had returned home) that those tensions that had been simmering away in Mackay finally boiled over into an event that came close to replicating the horror of the Milperra Massacre all those years earlier.

It started on a Friday night when twenty Outlaws attacked five Warriors with baseball bats at a Mackay nightclub. In a planned revenge attack, a procession of Warriors on motorcycles converged on the Outlaws' clubhouse at three p.m. the following Sunday. However, the Outlaws had been tipped off and were waiting in ambush, armed with an arsenal that included pump-action shotguns and semi-automatic rifles.

At one stage during the standoff the two sides called a truce to allow an ambulance convoy to collect wounded men lying on the road. Later, pizzas were delivered separately to police and bikie gangs. The battle raged on for more than three hours. As darkness fell, many of the Outlaws fled into surrounding mangroves. Police, reinforced by contingents from Brisbane and Cairns, took the entire following day to round them all up.

Two men shot in the head underwent emergency operations on that Sunday night. One would lose the sight in one of his eyes. Another three men were hospitalized with lesser injuries. In all, fifty-three bikers—including two Bandidos who were visiting the Outlaws at the time—appeared in court on charges connected to the shootout. All refused to cooperate or make any kind of statement, making it impossible for police to proceed with anything other than the most rudimentary charges of a fight.

Although police seized dozens of weapons, none of them contained any fingerprints and while more than one hundred spent shells and cartridges were recovered, none of them matched any of the seized weapons. When the case finally came to court, no one was found guilty.

PART FOUR

BROTHERS
IN ARMS

19

PATCH OVER

While some members of the Outlaws craved political power within the organization, Boone had always been happy to remain on the sidelines. Caz wasn't going anywhere—virtually all the individual chapters of the Midland Outlaws were being headed by the same people who had previously served as president of the individual clubs—but the other roles would change hands from time to time to spread out the workload.

During his time with the club, Boone had served two separate terms as treasurer, one as secretary, one as sergeant at arms (while Switch was recovering from his wounds) and one as vice president under Caz. The latter had been by far the most fun. People assumed all the power was in the hands of the president but with Caz attending an increasing number of national meetings as the club grew ever larger, the reality was that on many occasions, Boone would find himself running the chapter. He soon realized that if he wanted to change something within the club, all he needed to do was plant the seed of the idea with Caz and wait for him to suggest it. If the idea worked, Boone could claim part of the credit. If it turned out to be a failure, Caz would have to shoulder most of the blame.

Initially, national meetings required the attendance of each chapter president, but as more clubs joined and the numbers grew, it was clear the existing structure was going to have to change and that a proper national president and executive board would be needed to run things. Soon after returning from Australia, Boone began serving a second term as sergeant at arms for his chapter and it was suggested on numerous occasions that he would be the ideal candidate to run for the national position. Boone wasn't interested: running security for the chapter was tough enough, taking on responsibility for all the Outlaws in the country would simply be too much.

Everything was getting far too serious for Boone's liking. In the Pagans, if a couple of members had been behind with their bar tabs it was all seen as a bit of a joke, unless it got really out of hand. Now, treasurers for each chapter had their financial reports scrutinized at the national meetings and being in the red simply wasn't an option.

Similarly, running national security would have been a complete nightmare. Planning a run for the chapter involved a huge amount of preparation to ensure the route would be safe and not cross into enemy territory, to ensure sufficient weapons were on hand in case of an attack and to ensure that the people who were being issued the weapons knew how to use them properly.

Thanks to the training he had received in Canada, Boone was one of the most confident when it came to handling firearms. Others in the chapter didn't have a clue and needed hours of training to bring them up to speed. They would travel to quiet areas of remote farmland for target practice but would also learn to fieldstrip, load and clean the weapons. The chapter had access to a handful of shotguns and four handguns—two revolvers and two automatics. It wasn't much but in a country where the number of firearms has always been low, where the police remain unarmed and all private ownership of handguns was completely outlawed in 1997, it was quite an achievement.

All too aware of the consequences of indiscriminate use, both for individuals and the club as a whole, Boone would teach his fellow club members to treat their guns with huge respect. They should use guns to win fights, not to commit mass murder. Ideally the guns should be used only as the last, not the first, resort. "I have no respect for anyone who pulls out a weapon and starts waving it about at the first sign of trouble," he told them. "But I have a lot of respect for people who are carrying guns but are being very discreet about it. For me, those are the people you should fear. Sometimes, just the bulge is enough to make the other guy walk away."

Such intensive training was deemed absolutely necessary. Although the Outlaws were now firmly established and growing rapidly—four new clubs had already joined the fold including the Rare Breed, the Strays and the Henchmen, with more expected to follow—the threat from the Hell's Angels had not receded and had, if anything, become greater.

Part of the issue was that the Outlaws had changed their bottom rocker from "Midlands" to "England"—a territory previously claimed solely by the Angels. Another problem was that, inspired by the example of the Outlaws, several other clubs had begun building empires of their own, potentially threatening both clubs.

Of particular concern were the Outcasts, a group that had started life in London in 1969 and strived to remain independent ever since. Unusually media friendly for an MC, they had achieved a certain level of notoriety in 1985 after allowing themselves to be followed by a camera crew from the BBC documentary series *40 Minutes*.

Highlights of the film included numerous scenes of drug taking by the thirty-odd members, as well as footage of the club president, Tramp, talking about his attitude toward the practice: "As long as the lads are fit they can take as much speed as they want, as much coke as they want. Provided it doesn't go into their veins. I will not allow any injecting. I've lost a lot of good lads to the needle."

With several members serving prison sentences for crimes of violence and firearms offenses, they were not a club to be taken lightly, even if some people saw them as something of a joke. Years after the documentary, a group of advertising executives contacted the Outcasts with the idea of using them in a campaign. After visiting in person, the club was rejected as the clients claimed they simply "didn't look like real bikers."

By the midnineties the club had grown considerably and had around two hundred members spread throughout nine chapters in London, Essex and Great Yarmouth in Norfolk. (Members of this latter chapter were among the bikers who joined forces with the Ratae for the attack on the Pagan clubhouse in Leamington Spa in 1986.)

The Outcasts could see other gangs expanding around them and decided to do the same, approaching a small Hertfordshire MC known as the Lost Tribe with the idea of making them a prospect chapter before ultimately joining forces. Once news of the plan leaked out, the Hell's Angels were eager to prevent it. In the summer of 1997, they went to see the Lost Tribe and offered the "most suitable" members the chance to join the Angels instead. At the same time, several Outcasts were invited to join the larger club.

"It was more like a threat than an invitation," one Outcast said later. "The Angels had received orders direct from the United States that said that unless they maintained their position as the premier biker gang in the country, they would lose their charter. They made it very clear that if we didn't join them, they would destroy us."

Soon afterward, a total of twenty-two members of the Outcasts and the Lost Tribe defected to the enemy. According to the Outcasts, the Angels sweetened the deal with promises of an easy time as prospects, and interest-free loans allowed members to purchase the now-mandatory Harley-Davidson motorcycles. Accused of bribery, the Angels claimed that the new recruits simply recognized the superior MC and made the sensible choice.

The remaining Outcasts headed east with the idea of entering into peaceful, sit-down discussions with the Angels. Instead, they found themselves confronted by the entire Essex chapter, heavily armed, and were given a by-now familiar ultimatum: join the Angels or be wiped out.

During the tense proceedings one of the Outcasts, Keith "Flipper" Armstrong, tried to make an objection and was punched to the ground. It wasn't much of a victory—some years earlier, Flipper had lost a leg while serving with the Royal Irish Regiment and wore a prosthesis. Outnumbered and outgunned, the rest of the Outcasts were unable to fight back. Instead they left to contemplate the catch-22 offer that had been made to them.

Ultimately, the Outcasts decided to stand up to the might of the Angels by whatever means necessary. In November 1997, two members of the club were arrested in East London in possession of loaded shotguns, seemingly on their way to confront the Angels. There followed a series of minor clashes between the two gangs and it was clear that it was only a matter of time before things came to a head.

January saw the Outcasts attend the annual Rockers Reunion festival in Battersea, south London, an event that had been trouble free for more than fifteen years. The seventeen hundred-strong crowd of rockers, Teddy boys, slick-haired greasers, and bikers were in high spirits, drinking and dancing the night away, when security guards spotted a tall man in Hell's Angels colors moving across the dance floor.

The guards turned and saw a group of Outcasts hurrying down the corridor toward a side door. Turning back, they saw there were now about a dozen Angels gathering inside the venue, the tall man striding out ahead of them. It was, they said later, like something out of a Wild West movie, with people parting to let them through. In the meantime, outside the Arts Centre on Theatre Street, Outcast Keith "Flipper" Armstrong, the same man who had been attacked at the earlier meeting, was just arriving on his motorcycle.

The Angels attacked "like sharks," going in small groups, kicking and stabbing before retreating and another group taking over. Groups of four or five Angels, armed with knives, axes and heavy clubs, swooped in on their victims in wave after wave of attacks. Unarmed bikers equipped with headset microphones helped pick out the targets.

Flipper was at the top of the list. Five or six Hell's Angels went at him with iron bars, baseball bats and at least one knife. All too well aware of the level of hostility between his own club and others, the Outcast was also armed, but so heavily outnumbered that he didn't stand a chance. He was dragged from his cycle and stabbed repeatedly. He suffered at least four deep wounds to his abdomen and left leg. His lungs were pierced and he was bleeding inside.

Malcolm St. Clair—aka "Mal" or "The Terminator"—an Outcast and a giant of a man, went to help his friend but soon became the next victim. He was hit repeatedly with a blunt instrument, most likely a hammer or the side of an ax. St. Clair hit back with a knife, but was cornered and stabbed. Grievously wounded, he stumbled to Theatre Street where he was attacked again by two more Angels.

Italian photographer Ramak Fazel, who was on his way to take pictures at a rock concert, watched in horror as a bearded biker lay into St. Clair with an ax. "He was bringing his ax up over his head. The victim was lying with his head between his knees." Fazel then saw another man pull out a ten-inch knife and continue the attack. "The knife was thrust in on both sides. Then they calmly walked away. It was cold-blooded."

Jason Wilkinson, whose house overlooked the scene of the attack on St. Clair, said: "The total silence was the surprising thing. I had the feeling it was like a professional job or a punishment beating. The attackers didn't seem to be screaming or shouting like one would expect and there didn't seem to be any noise from the victim. He didn't utter one sound during the whole period of the attack. That was in itself quite shocking."

Immediately afterward, one of the Hell's Angels who attacked St. Clair was heard to say: "I got the bastard. I got him, I did him."

David "Diddy" Treherne, an Outcast, was also wounded in the fight. Treharne refused to make a statement to the police despite being severely injured. The Angels, it seemed, had very specific targets in mind on this night. The whole thing, said one witness, lasted "a couple of sets of traffic lights."

Fazel had seen two of the attackers climb into a Volvo and made a note of the registration number on a napkin. The car was traced to Ronald Wait, vice president of the Essex Angels—known as the Hatchet Crew. Wait, who had undergone triple-bypass heart surgery and suffered from both angina and diabetes, claimed he was too ill to have taken part in any attack but was charged with murder after Fazel picked him out in a lineup.

Police appealed for witnesses, photographs and videotape of the party. A few Outcasts and many members of the public gave statements but the Hell's Angels kept mum. "The rules state that you are not allowed to make a statement to police, or speak to them if it involves another club member," Wait said later. "You have to seek permission to speak to the police."

Wait then came up with a new alibi, claiming he was drinking at a biker's clubhouse in Reading, Berkshire, at the time of the killings. The alibi was supported by several members of the Angels who agreed to go to court and testify that this was the case. Prosecutors couldn't help but be more than a little skeptical and remanded him in custody to await trial.

One Outcast told the police that he and his wife would give evidence only if they were guaranteed anonymity because they were so terrified of reprisals. Their request was initially accepted and the pair were placed on the witness protection scheme, but then the police accidentally revealed their names and addresses to the lawyers for the defense and the pair pulled out. Charges against two other Hell's Angels, Hollingsworth and Raymond Woodward, were dropped because of lack of evidence. Both were former members of the Outcasts gang who had defected to the Hell's Angels.

Retaliation seemed inevitable. In July 1998, the National Criminal Intelligence Service (NCIS), at the time the UK equivalent of the FBI, sent a warning to thirty-seven police forces in England and Wales advising them of the "possibility of armed conflict and the use of automatic weapons and explosives" by biker gangs over the summer.

The warning was issued after a crude bomb, made from fertilizer, gas and a commercial detonator, was found at the clubhouse of the Hell's Angels chapter in March, just two months after the murders at the Rocker's Reunion. A few weeks later, a motorcycle shop in Kent, owned by various members of the Hell's Angels, was the scene of an attempted arson attack involving gas and a pipe inserted through the store's mail slot.

A month later, police received a tip about a potential arms cache being moved around the West Country. They stopped Outcasts member Richard "Stitch" Anderton while driving his Jaguar car with his common-law wife. A loaded Smith and Wesson .45 revolver was found tucked into the waistband of his trousers and additional rounds were found in his pockets. Amphetamines, cannabis and Ecstasy were found in his car, along with scales and self-sealing bags. A search of his apartment uncovered more drugs, hundreds of shotgun cartridges and thousands of rounds of 9 mm ammunition. Detectives were disturbed to discover large numbers of hollow-point rounds, which are designed to expand on impact and cause maximum damage. Such bullets are outlawed under the Geneva Convention because their effect is so devastating.

Decommissioned weapons including an Uzi submachine gun, an AK-47 rifle and a rocket launcher were also recovered. It emerged that Anderton was the Outcasts' main sergeant at arms and was responsible for its armory. Detectives suspected the guns had been purchased with the proceeds of drug dealing. Although large quantities of 9 mm ammunition were found, no 9 mm weapons were being kept at the property, leading to speculation that additional weapons were still in circulation among the club's two hundred or so members.

After his arrest, Anderton claimed he had been told the Angels had drawn up a "death list" containing the names of several Outcasts who were to be "killed on sight." Fearing for his life, Anderton moved from Essex to Dorset and armed himself with the handgun for his own protection. He claimed the other weapons and the drugs were merely being stored at his property as it was considered to be safe. Anderton had previously been a prospect member of the Angels. He left for reasons unknown and rumor had it that he had been placed on the death list because he was considered a traitor.

As a result of the NCIS warning the Hell's Angels approached the organization to ask for more details. NCIS told them that it had the names of fifteen suspects and had traced an amount of Semtex they were believed to be in possession of, but they would not say where the intelligence had come from.

Subsequently, Warwickshire police asked the Angels to cancel the 1998 Bulldog Bash. They refused and the event went ahead under heavy police guard at a cost to the public purse of some 140,000 pounds.

Boone and the other former Warwickshire Pagans who had gone on to become the Warwickshire chapter of the Midland Outlaws observed the aftermath of the murders at the Rockers Reunion with what could only be called wry amusement. So far as they were concerned, the Outcasts were just as much of an enemy to them as the Hell's Angels were. If the two wanted to kill one another, they were more than happy to let them get on with it.

The rest of the Midland Outlaws felt somewhat differently and arranged to take part in a joint run with the Outcasts as a show of unity. Under tight security the combined clubs rode into East Anglia, an area where the Hell's Angels were also trying to expand and which therefore carried a considerable risk of the two sides running into one another.

Still more fond of the press than most, the Outcasts invited a journalist from the UK men's monthly, *Front*, to join them on the trip. "We need to show a presence because the Angels are trying to move in around here," an Outcast called Den told the magazine. "They're trying to grow by absorbing other small clubs, what we call nonleague outfits. They promise them all sorts of things and claim we're going to be finished by Christmas. They say the same thing every year and every year we call them and say, 'Still here.'"

The run went off without a hitch but despite the bravado, both clubs knew the writing was on the wall. The Outcasts were simply spread too thinly across the UK to have any real strength in numbers when it came to taking on the Angels. At the same time the Midland Outlaws were reaching the point where they had to decide what future direction the club was going to take.

Ever since the new club had formed there had been discussions taking place about where it was all going to lead. Despite the choice of name, it was far from a foregone conclusion. Some members, particularly a few from the Derby chapter, remained keen on joining forces with the Bandidos but although a good many friendships had been established with the Fat Mexican crowd, the club had spent significantly more time with members of the American Outlaws Association.

Daytona Bike Week was now a regular fixture on their calendar and there had also been more visits to Canada and

Denmark as members made the most of the opportunities for cheap travel that their friendship with the AOA provided. However, the more time individual club members spent abroad, the greater the pressure for the whole club to join one of the bigger outfits.

At that first meeting with the Angels, after becoming Midland Outlaws, the club had been warned of the consequences of consorting with the AOA. They were now firmly seen as allies but unless they joined forces officially, they would have to face all the dangers of the association without any of the main benefits. They couldn't carry on like this forever: sooner or later, they were going to have to make a decision.

A key objection among members was that they did not like the AOA patch, the skull and crossed pistons, known as "Charlie." There were even discussions among the Midland Outlaws about getting the AOA to change their patch to a design based on the multifeathered skull one they were using, but the American group was simply too large and powerful to even give consideration to such a move. It was the Midland Outlaws who needed them, they insisted, not the other way around. "There's only one way—AOA" became the mantra.

The other major sticking point was the question of exactly what kind of organization the Midland Outlaws would be getting involved with. Although they talked about biking and brotherhood being the main reasons for the existence of the club, they all knew that the AOA had far more going on than that, and the ongoing threat of conflict with the HA in the UK meant such values were far from the minds of most members.

The Midland Outlaws were not an out-and-out criminal organization any more than the AOA was, in the sense that committing crime was not the sole reason for the existence of the group, unlike, say, the Mafia or a drug cartel. However, high-level organized crime was rife within the AOA and Boone knew only too well that joining forces would undoubtedly lead UK members to go in the same direction. Part of this would be because of opportunities to work on a global scale with trusted colleagues in other countries and the rest would simply be because of increased financial pressure to pay "dues" for AOA membership. More crime would also put members at more risk as it would be inevitable that they would be treading on territory run by other gangs—both bikers and nonbikers—the moment they expanded their operations.

Although the Midland Outlaws could pretend as much as they wanted that the American Outlaws had nothing to do with them, they knew it was inevitable that if they joined forces with the AOA, they would be embracing all the club's activities. They would be permanently making the move from club to gang.

Rainier and the rest of the Canadians were making millions from the drugs trade, as were the various European chapters, but just how much of a gang the AOA was had become clear a few months before the attack on the Outcasts when Taco Bowman himself had been indicted for his involvement in a series of bombings and murders, as well as drug trafficking, extortion and firearms violations.

Taco immediately went on the run and, a year later, achieved the distinction of becoming the first member ever of an outlaw motorcycle gang to be placed on the FBI's Top Ten Most Wanted list. While on the lam he continued in his role as international president and maintained regular contact with various members of the Midland Outlaws, intensifying the pressure for them to join the fold.

While Taco remained at liberty, other AOA members were not so lucky. Boone and the others had briefly met an Outlaw named Mike Lynn on their first visit to Florida but now learned that he had become a government informant and recorded dozens of church meetings during which other members of the Florida chapter had been planning their campaign of violence against the Warlocks.

Boone was mortified when he learned that Glen "Flyball" Clark, the man who had essentially saved him from being shot by a drug-crazed Taco and someone he had called a friend ever since, had crumbled under pressure and decided to cooperate with the authorities rather than face life in prison. This in turn led to two further members of the Daytona Beach chapter, DK and Wayne Hicks, also agreeing to roll over.

Taco was finally arrested in Michigan in 1999 and the role of international president was immediately taken over by James "Frank" Wheeler, at the time a fifty-six-year-old native of Indianapolis, whom several Midland Outlaws had met during their visits to Daytona. Wheeler was equally eager to expand the AOA's operations overseas and ensured there was no letup in the pressure for the UK contingent to sign up, making it clear that if they did not do so, the hospitality they were enjoying at AOA events might well dry up. Part of Wheeler's concern was that the Florida Warlocks, though still a small MC, were growing fast and had even opened up two chapters in England. Wheeler was eager to ensure any further expansion was contained as quickly as possible.

Ultimately the issue was put to a vote and the mantra turned out to have been an insightful prediction. Although a small number of dissenters from the Derby chapter opted to leave and join forces with the Bandidos after all, relocating to mainland Europe in order to do so, the remainder of the club voted to join forces with the AOA.

In February 2000, Valentinos bar in Birmingham played host to a massive celebration. The newcomers were joined by Outlaws from Norway, Belgium, Canada, Florida, Ohio, Indianapolis and Tennessee, to name but a few. Guests of honor included Rainier—in many ways the driving force behind the evolution of the Midland Outlaws—and Frank Wheeler himself. The new international president could not have been more unlike his predecessor. While Taco had been volatile and unpredictable, Wheeler was thoughtful and at times philosophical. He even wrote poetry in his spare time. A thirty-year veteran of the club, the party lifestyle had taken its toll on his looks as, although Wheeler wasn't quite there yet, he looked to be ready to collect his pension. Wheeler was one of those bikers who was so determined to die with his colors on, he had taken the ultimate step of having a full-size version of the club's Charlie logo tattooed across his back.

Beers, spirits and the occasional bottle of champagne flowed like water and few of those who attended the joining-forces party remember much about it—always the sign of a good night out.

The change of name also required a change of organization: elections were held to find new officers and Stuart "Dink" Dawson, previously president of the Henchmen MC and one of the most ardent supporters of the move, was elected as the first national present of the AOA in the UK. Shortly afterward, and much to the consternation of Boone and the rest of the former Pagans, the remaining members of the Outcasts also joined the fold.

For the Hell's Angels it was as if all their worst nightmares had come true. Their domination of the UK biker scene was now well and truly over. With a head count approaching 250, the UK chapters of the AOA had at least 100 more members than they did. Furthermore, while their battles with the Midland Outlaws had only been of passing interest overseas, any future conflicts between the two would have implications for every Angel chapter that had Outlaws nearby or ever crossed into enemy territory.

The Angels responded in a wholly predictable fashion: they began recruiting heavily, targeting more small clubs around the country and cherry-picking the best potential prospects, desperately hoping to get to them before they could be approached by the Outlaws.

Although the Angels could still claim to be the best-known MC in the world, they were no longer the only major international club operating in the UK. For the first time ever, smaller biker clubs that wanted to be part of a major global brand had a choice. Any club that had a problem with the Angels in the past or feared a hostile takeover now had an alternative route they were able to consider, preempting the Angels by joining forces with the Outlaws instead.

Once seemingly invincible, the Angels now looked distinctly vulnerable.

20

EVOLUTION

𝕴n June 2001, the Motorcycle Action Group (MAG), a lobbying organization that campaigns on behalf of bikers throughout the UK, called for the Bulldog Bash to be scrapped on the basis that the Hell's Angels were unfit to host it.

In the months leading up to the announcement the Angels had turned up—usually uninvited—to several MAG events, intimidating and sometimes assaulting the group's members, all part of an aggressive recruitment campaign aimed at boosting Angel numbers. The group was eventually forced to hire professional security professionals in an attempt to keep the Angels out.

Neil Liversidge, chairman of the MAG, and several other senior officers received a series of death threats soon after speaking out but ultimately the request fell on deaf ears after both Stratford District council and, in particular, senior members of the local Warwickshire police force fully backed the event, stating it had never caused them any problems during its fifteen-year history.

Regardless of what the Angels might get into the rest of the time, the Bulldog Bash was famous for being almost completely trouble free. The Angels handled security at the event themselves—patrolling the grounds in battered old sedans with all the windows taken out and death's head logos painted on the doors. Among the sea of bikers, the cars made sure the security teams stood out, a perfect deterrent to even petty crime.

Every regular attendee of the Bash knows the story of the young biker who lost his wallet with two hundred pounds in it on the last day of the weekend, went to the lost and found office expecting nothing, only to have it returned with all his cash still inside, or the story of the stallholder who left his cash box on open view all night only to find the contents untouched the following morning.

The 2001 event was the biggest to date, attended by almost twenty-five thousand bikers, and featuring performances from the likes of Terrorvision, Reef, Feeder and The Fall. Despite heavy rain turning many of the campsites into little more than muddy bogs, the four-day festival still went off without a hitch.

Trouble came in the final hours. On Sunday afternoon, as the Bash was winding down, a small group of French Canadian Hell's Angels who had been enjoying the festivities were heading toward London on the southbound highway of the M40 in a three-cycle convoy when they suddenly came under attack.

A dark-colored sedan that had been following them for a short time suddenly accelerated and moved into the middle lane alongside them. A handgun appeared at the passenger window and a number of shots were fired before the car raced off. One of the bikers was hit in the leg three times but managed to stay in control of his machine long enough to pull over to the side of the road, just between junctions 11 and 12. The thirty-one-year-old was taken to the hospital but refused to speak to the police or provide them with any information and discharged himself the following day.

News of the incident spread through the ranks of the Outlaws like wildfire, though no particular chapter or individual was willing to claim responsibility within the club. The general consensus was that it was likely the work of a former member of the Outcasts, a club that had only just joined the Outlaws fold, and revenge for the murders at the Rockers Reunion a few years earlier. "Whoever it was, they need to get down to the shooting range," Boone told a friend. "That way, next time around, they might do a better job."

With little in the way of leads to go on and an uncooperative victim, the police quickly wound down their investigation. So far as they could tell, it had been an indiscriminate, motiveless attack and had no particular link to either the Angels or the Bulldog Bash. It would be six years before they realized their mistake.

There could be no doubt about it: the Outlaws were changing. The constant pressure to obtain more and higher-quality weapons to defend themselves against possible attack, to pay increased dues as a result of their AOA charter as well as more regular demands for additional payments to cover other expenses was pushing an increasing proportion of members into criminality.

There were still plenty of completely legitimate businessmen and law-abiding bikers in the club but Boone couldn't help feeling that they were becoming a minority. As the Hell's Angels had discovered many years earlier, having trusted brothers in other countries made it much easier to arrange deals across international borders and procure everything from precursor chemicals for the manufacture of amphetamine to guns and military-grade weapons.

Dink, the Outlaws national president, personally coordinated much of the drug traffic for the UK Outlaws, taking a lead from Frank Wheeler, the international president, who was doing much the same across large parts of the United States. Dink would arrange for representatives from chapters across the country to travel to north Wales in order to pick up supplies from him on a regular basis. As a result of the ramping up of criminal activity, dozens of Outlaws were spending time in and out of prison for offenses ranging from drug dealing and assault to firearms offenses and vehicle theft. One even opened up his very own cannabis farm in a remote town in Wales.

Church meetings now included regular updates on what was happening with Outlaws around the world. There was more expansion with chapters opening in Sweden, Germany, Ireland and even interest from a Russian MC. There was also a steady stream of reports of stabbings, shootings, attacks—almost all of them the result of the ongoing conflicts with rival gangs—and court cases as the authorities continued to turn their attention to the gang's illegal endeavors.

Chief among these cases was the conviction of Taco Bowman himself. After his first trial ended with a hung jury, a second found him guilty of a range of charges including murder and racketeering and he was given two life sentences. Messages of support—including several from Boone, Caz and other UK Outlaws—flooded in from around the world.

Boone's long-term girlfriend, Alice, had long struggled with his commitment to the club and the fact that she always took second place in his life. Now, his increasing involvement in criminality and regular brushes with the law proved too much and she finally decided to leave. Boone felt torn. He had considered leaving the Outlaws for Alice, but ultimately he knew he could never do that.

Leaving a one-percenter club is hard but not impossible. For those who leave in "bad standing" it means giving back any item bearing the name or logo of the club and often surrendering many of their personal items. The theory is that, because of your membership in the club, you have benefited financially and therefore many of your personal assets actually belong to the club. Any tattoos bearing the club logo must be removed or totally obscured. Some clubs insist on doing this themselves with the back of a hot spoon. Some unlucky former members have even had the skin cut off their arms with a razor blade or burned off using a blowtorch.

Those who leave in "good standing" have it slightly better. The most favored among them are allowed to officially retire, stitching a special patch to the front of their jackets to signify this. You are allowed to retire once and then come back—but only once. Otherwise, people would retire from the club whenever a war was on and come back once the good times started up again.

When you leave the club in this way, you are allowed to keep your tattoo but you must have the date that you left inscribed into it to show that you are no longer a member. If invited, you are allowed to attend clubhouse parties, mandatory runs and funerals, though many retired members simply leave everything about the club behind and get on with their lives.

Boone knew the Outlaws would never let him go voluntarily. He had been there too long, knew too much and was too useful to them. More to the point, the club had been a part of his life for so long—far longer than he had been with Alice— that he didn't really know if he'd be able to live without it.

He would have happily kept Alice around but she made it easy by walking away herself and giving Boone the chance to knuckle down to the business of making serious money.

He soon carved out a reputation for himself as a cool head in a crisis and would regularly get calls from importers linked to the club who had encountered a last-minute problem and needed someone to step in and sort it out. "We need you to put the wheels back on this, Boone," they would say. "You need to fix this for us." He would have to drop everything and take on a huge amount of stress but would be well rewarded for his trouble to the tune of tens of thousands of pounds each time.

A few months after the departure of Alice, Elif came into Boone's life. A drop-dead gorgeous brunette with a dazzling smile and an appetite for trouble, Elif felt no qualms about getting involved with a senior Outlaw. Having noticed Boone's patches at a classic motorcycle show in the north of England, she had made a beeline for him in the beer tent.

"So tell me about yourself. What do you do for a living?" asked Boone.

"Ah, Snake Dog, you don't want to know."

"Does that mean you're a police officer?"

"No, I'm not a police officer!"

"Tax inspector?"

She giggled, flashing the most perfect set of teeth. "No, I'm not a tax inspector either."

"Then I don't get it. Those are the only things I'd be bothered about."

"You really don't want to know."

"Ah shit, you're not a journalist, are you? That might be a problem."

"No. That's not it," she sighed deeply. "I'm an air hostess."

Boone was confused.

"An air hostess? That doesn't seem like it would be a problem. I bet you look great in your uniform."

"You don't understand. I'm a long-haul air hostess. I'm away for ten days at a time and then I'm only back for four. Most guys don't like it because they miss me too much."

"I think I love you," said Boone.

"What?"

"As far as I'm concerned, that sounds perfect. Let's face it—after the honeymoon period is over, you don't really want to see each other all the time, do you? After ten days of you being away, I'd really look forward to seeing you. Then we'd spend time together but I'd be more than happy to get rid of you on the fourth day and get on with my own stuff. You must have felt that too."

"Well, I guess . . . I've never thought about it that way before, but maybe you're right."

Elif lived in Worcester, which meant that if he wanted to go home with her that night, Boone would have to ride through at least one Hell's Angel stronghold. With tensions high and the Outlaws on their guard for retaliatory attacks, Boone decided to do the sensible thing and got a prospect to drive them home in the club van.

During the journey, Elif kept bringing up the subject of her ex-boyfriend. He had a temper, she explained. He was pretty crazy and had turned into something of a stalker. Boone wasn't interested. "Listen," he said, "I'm not going to tell you anything about my exes and you don't need to tell me anything about yours. It's not relevant and it's none of my business. I'm sure the guy's got his issues but at the end of the day there are two sides to every story so let's just leave it at that."

Within a couple of weeks the relationship was going strong, although as Elif had predicted she spent most of her time away from home so the couple only spent a few days together at a time. It suited Boone down to the ground. A few days of intense passion followed by a chance to get on with the rest of his life with no hassle. They were good times—the best of times.

The honeymoon period came to an abrupt end one morning at Elif's house, when Boone was woken by a noise from outside. Concerned that someone might be attempting to steal his motorcycle, he got up and peered out of the window to see what was going on.

"It's probably just my ex," yawned Elif. "He comes around every now and then. He doesn't have a key. He won't do anything. You probably know him anyway. He's a biker too. They call him the Terminator."

Boone was suddenly jerked wide awake, "The Terminator? You mean Jed from Ashfield?"

"That's right."

"From Ashfield Hell's Angels?"

"Yes."

"For fuck's sake! Why didn't you tell me?"

"I've been trying to tell you. You kept shutting me up."

"But you didn't tell me he was a Hell's Angel! Is he likely to turn up here?"

"Well, he comes around every now and then. He's trying to get me back but I just want to be rid of him."

Boone realized he could easily die in this situation. Not only was he in the middle of enemy territory, he was with a woman who had been intimately involved with one of the most notorious fighters in the whole of the Hell's Angels. And the Angel was still sweet enough on this girl to turn up every now and then to check her out. Boone had no weapons, nothing to protect himself with. The Angel would have far better knowledge of the area than he did. He would also be able to call in reinforcements far quicker than Boone could summon backup. Boone didn't want to be a coward, but this was about common sense and self-preservation. There was no need to put himself in a situation that he couldn't escape from, just for the sake of a woman. He had to get out of there.

"Where are you going?"

"Home."

"It's two a.m. Is it because of him?"

"No. Of course not. That is . . . well, not technically, no. It's not because he's your boyfriend, it's because he's a fucking

Hell's Angel. If anything happens between me and him, the whole fucking club has to get involved. And I don't want people getting shot and stabbed just because I'm going out with you."

In his heart, Boone knew he should have ended things then and there but he was totally hooked on the amazing sex and the fact that Elif was away so often, giving him complete freedom to get on with his life just the way he wanted it, which was a real bonus, so he stuck with it, but going forward would meet her only within Outlaws territory.

A few more weeks into the relationship, Elif mentioned that her best friend Susan who lived in New Zealand was going to be coming to England for a few days and wanted to see some of the sights. Would Boone, she wondered, be able to act as tour guide and perhaps even put her friend up for a few days? As soon as he saw a picture of Susan, Boone agreed. And from the get-go he was happy to have her staying at his house. She was good company and seemed at ease with his lifestyle. He had no reason not to trust her. Then, three days after she arrived, Susan dropped her bombshell.

"Elif told me not to say anything to you, but I feel I have to tell you. My boyfriend is the president of the Hell's Angels chapter in New South Wales."

"Fucking hell. I thought there was something about you. The way you seemed at ease with the whole biker thing."

"He's coming over for the Bulldog Bash and I thought I'd come early and do a bit of sightseeing. It's not a problem is it? You'd really like him you know. He's just like you. I'm sure you've got loads in common."

"I don't want to hear this."

"I mean it. He does so much to protect the club but he just ends up with a reputation for being vicious, I get the feeling you're like that too, aren't you?"

Boone knew exactly what she meant, but he still didn't want to hear it. Instead, he had to try to work out if the Angels were possibly using Susan to try to get information about the Outlaws.

Internal security was becoming a major concern to the club in the aftermath of Taco's trial, during which details had emerged about various undercover police operations against bikers. Although the UK police were unlikely to have sufficient resources to be able to place an officer in a club for a year or two with no guarantee of uncovering any criminal activity at the end of it, it would not be beyond the scope of other biker clubs to launch an operation of their own. All of the lifestyle elements that made it difficult for undercover officers to fully engage with the biker lifestyle—drinking and driving, massive drug taking, sexual shenanigans and violence—would not pose any difficulty for a biker attempting to infiltrate a rival club.

There were also growing concerns within the club about just how much the old ladies knew about what was going on. Officially, members were not supposed to say anything about club business but in reality, most bikers would talk about—or even brag about—whatever they had going on.

One of the regular international updates at a church meeting earlier that year had been something of a cautionary tale about such indiscretions. David Wolf, a member of the Wisconsin/Stateline chapter, had told his wife about murdering a member of a rival gang a few years earlier. When his club president suspected this to be the case, Wolf denied it. His wife later struck a deal with the authorities, not only providing a grand jury with evidence of the killing but also phoning Wolf's president to inform him that he had been deceived. Wolf was later sentenced to twenty-seven years but made it clear that his biggest concern was that he had been caught lying to his club president, not that he would be spending the rest of his life behind bars.

Boone began to wonder how much he had told Elif, how much she had told Susan and how much the two women had told each other. He wasn't too worried about the Hell's Angels knowing his home address because he figured they already had access to that information. He had lived there for such a long time that the details had been recorded countless times on court and electoral records. For as long as he could remember he had had defenses in place. If the Angels or anyone else came calling, they would be unlikely to leave alive.

With an untraceable firearm on hand, he would use it and then immediately call the police, claiming that someone had tried to shoot him and there had been an accident, that he had managed to grab his attacker's weapon and use it in self-defense. Boone had made sure that his plans were widely known within Angel circles. But he still always looked both ways to make sure the coast was clear when he left his front door. And the legacy of the time he spent in Canada was that he always checked underneath his car before starting the engine.

Although he didn't known Susan that well, Boone reckoned he was a good enough judge of character to see that she genuinely didn't mean him any harm. He weighed his options. He hadn't taken her to the clubhouse, where it would have been assumed that she was there to spy, scoping out the security systems and the number of Outlaws who were there. But if the rest of the Outlaws were to find out he had been harboring the partner of a senior Hell's Angel, there would be all sorts of implications. He would be accused of fraternizing with the enemy and, in the absence of any evidence to the contrary, would be liable to have his patches pulled or even be kicked out of the club completely.

Susan herself would suffer the most serious penalties. She would be kidnapped and tortured until she told the Outlaws everything she knew. The fact that her own boyfriend, a senior Angel, was coming to the UK later that week would inevitably go against her. She would be used as bait to draw him into a trap where he would be severely beaten, possibly killed. She would be repeatedly raped by certain members of the club who had a predilection for that sort of thing.

Boone couldn't stomach any of that happening. Not once had Susan asked questions about the club or shown any interest in obtaining information that could prove detrimental to members. The only person who was truly at risk was Boone himself. He was happy with that, or at least as happy as he could be. He decided to confide in Caz.

"Has she asked any questions about the club?"

"No, nothing like that at all."

"Well, if she is up to anything, it might be too late to stop it. At the end of the day, it's your life that's on the line. You'll be the first one who gets it if this is a setup. So you'd better keep seeing her and keep an eye out for trouble."

"I don't think there will be any. I'm happy. I trust her."

"Okay. Here's what we're going to do. You're going to take some time away from the club. I'll tell everyone that you're on a mission or something. You don't come in for any reason, not even the mandatory stuff. Whatever happens, you stay the fuck away from the club. And whatever you do, don't let anyone see you with her."

For Boone, it felt like a massive weight had been lifted. Susan had a long list of places that she wanted to visit— Canterbury Cathedral, Stonehenge, Warwick Castle—and Boone was more than happy to travel around with the girls and show them the sights. He had always liked the idea of having two women on his arm.

"It must be great having all this on your doorstep," said Susan.

"You'd think so, but I never do any of this stuff."

Once Susan had left the country, he ended things with Elif and thanked his lucky stars that neither his relationship with her nor his friendship with Susan had been to the detriment of the club. However, for the first time since joining the Pagans almost twenty years earlier, Boone found himself questioning his commitment to the MC world and its values. Nearing forty, he had lived long enough, and made enough of his own mistakes, to realize that each club had its share of idiots, troublemakers, egos and cowards. Then there were the intelligent ones and the tacticians, and they didn't all join the same club. Not to mention that at one point, the Pagans had considered becoming Angels themselves. If the women couldn't tell the two sides apart, perhaps the differences were not as great as they imagined them to be.

Although it was unsettling to think about, Boone was starting to see that, in many ways, the actual patch was immaterial to the person and that perhaps it wasn't really worth dying for after all.

21

ABSOLUTE POWER

The years that followed the 2001 shooting at the Bulldog Bash saw the British contingent of the AOA grow in influence. With more manpower than any other country in Europe, and two lucrative festivals—the Rock and Blues and the Ink and Iron—bolstering the amount of funds that could be sent back to the mother chapter, the club had become a force to be reckoned with.

Dink was spending increasing amounts of time and money traveling the world, meeting other national presidents and coordinating activities between the various chapters. His hard work was soon rewarded with his appointment as the first-ever European president of the AOA, a title that confirmed his status as the most powerful Outlaw outside of America. Around this time, he was spending up to twenty thousand pounds per year on foreign travel, visiting Philadelphia, Chicago, Florida, Germany and Mexico all within the space of a few months.

Part of the reason for the appointment was that international president James "Frank" Wheeler had gone the way of his predecessor, Taco Bowman, and was awaiting trial on charges of racketeering, drug trafficking and attempted murder. As has been the case with Taco, dozens of Outlaws cut deals on their own charges by agreeing to give evidence against the president. It was a turn of events that rocked many club members on both sides of the Atlantic to the core: the whole notion of true brotherhood seemed to be in danger of being lost altogether.

In Wheeler's absence, a caretaker president had been appointed but rather than having that person assume responsibility for the worldwide operations of the AOA, Dink had been given responsibility for the European end of things.

Boone liked Dink a lot. The pair had first met years earlier when Dink was still president of the Henchmen and had agreed to go back to a Midland Outlaws clubhouse for an after-party drink after all the other members of his club had gone. Dink had agreed to go solo even though he suspected it was a trap and that the twenty-odd Outlaws were about to administer a severe beating. When this turned out not to be the case, Dink confessed what had been on his mind. "Why the fuck did you come back if you thought it was a trap?" asked Boone. Dink smiled. "Well, I didn't want you guys thinking I was soft, did I?" Ever since that day, Boone had held Dink in high regard.

Thanks to Dink's leadership and political skills, the UK was now the leading force in the AOA outside the United States, even eclipsing those chapters in France that had been established almost a decade earlier. For Boone and the other rank-and-file members of the Outlaws, this elevated status came at a hefty price. The pressure to bring more and more money into the club—through legitimate or illegitimate means—was growing. A new line of designer biker merchandise, branded SYLO, was launched and brought in some much-needed cash—proving popular with associates of the Hell's Angels, until they realized the letters stood for "support your local Outlaws." Behind the scenes, Dink and other senior members of the club were continuing to coordinate the distribution of drugs between chapters. As before, individual members were tasked with selling small amounts and returning the profits to the club.

The Outlaws were not the only club waging a high-profile war against the Angels. The Mongols had been doing so virtually since the club had started back in the seventies, but now it was time for them to take center stage.

The Mongols had a long-held reputation for being one of the more violent MCs around—in virtue of the fact that anyone joining the club would immediately have to take on the baggage of an ongoing war with the Hell's Angels that had left dozens dead on both sides. As their fight song attests, the Mongols have never shied away from a good scrap:

> We are Mongol raiders, we're raiders of the night
> We're dirty sons of bitches, we'd rather fuck and fight
> Hidy, hidy, Christ Almighty, who the fuck are we?
> Shit, fuck, cunt, suck, Mongols MC!

Despite both the Angels and the Mongols being regulars among the sixty thousand or so attendees at the annual River Run, the event had been more or less trouble free for twenty years. All that changed just after 2 a.m. on April 27 when eighty Angels squared off against forty Mongols on the casino floor of Harrah's.

Caught on the casino's security cameras, the vicious fight

that followed left one Mongol and two Angels dead, a dozen more bikers seriously injured and several innocent bystanders also in need of hospital treatment. Six guns and fifty knives would later be recovered from the crime scene and a third Angel was shot to death later that same day as he made his way back from Laughlin. Although six Angels and the same number of Mongols would later be convicted of their part in the riot, at least thirty-five bikers had the charges against them dismissed.

The incident brought the Mongols and their protracted war with the Angels to the attention of the public at large and the Outlaws in particular, resulting in an invitation for the club to attend the Daytona Beach event the following year.

Dozens of Mongols from California and beyond accepted the invite and were duly photographed—classic back-to-the-camera style—alongside Outlaws from all over the world. The pictures were quickly posted on the web in an effort to further antagonize the Angels and make it clear to the rest of the MC world exactly where the Outlaws stood in relation to the conflict between the clubs.

Following a series of trials in which a host of former Outlaws including several presidents of smaller chapters gave evidence, Frank Wheeler was found guilty in December 2004 of racketeering and conspiracy charges. Despite mitigation that Wheeler had often intervened in disputes and acted as a peacemaker between the Outlaws and some of their rivals, he was sentenced to life imprisonment for running a drug distribution ring and conspiring to murder other gang members. It also emerged that part of the reason Taco had managed to stay out of sight from the authorities for so long was that Wheeler had been helping to hide him.

The conviction was a foregone conclusion. As well as having several Outlaws testifying against the president, the authorities had also managed to convince a number of informants to record their conversations with Wheeler, providing firsthand evidence of his involvement in a wide variety of crimes. Despite his looking like everyone's favorite grandfather, these tapes proved that, when necessary, Wheeler could be every bit as vicious and uncompromising as someone like Taco.

On one tape, Wheeler could be heard complaining about the fact that several club members had failed to rip off a group of Mexican drug dealers who were working within their territory. "Where are my fucking robbers at?" bellowed Wheeler. "Where are my goddamn gangster Outlaws?" He was sentenced to sixteen and a half years.

Wheeler's trial was followed almost immediately by a series of trials resulting from the arrest of more than fifty-five Outlaws in Ontario—more than 60 percent of the city's members—including Rainier, who would eventually be convicted of multiple counts of murder. All over the world law enforcement were pouring more and more resources into tackling all the major motorcycle gangs. If the Outlaws were to survive, they were going to need a whole new approach.

Wheeler's replacement was Jack "Milwaukee Jack" Rosga, a nonsmoker, occasional drinker and owner of a successful trucking company that he had run for more than three decades and that provided him with legitimate a salary of at least one hundred thousand dollars per year. With no criminal record to speak of—one minor conviction in the 1970s and an arrest for violating a restraining order taken out by his wife in 1996—Rosga was a major departure from the usual Outlaws leaders and soon decided to run things in a different way too.

Rather than appointing himself international president as his predecessors had done, Rosga would simply be national president of the Outlaws while others—most notably Britain's Dink—would take charge of various areas outside of the United States.

Only a few weeks after his appointment, Rosga's reign seemed in danger of being over. In September 2006, police raided the Milwaukee clubhouse after Rosga and two other men were spotted on the roof with what appeared to be a hunting rifle. No arrests were made and Rosga and others would later sue the police, claiming they had merely been on the roof checking for leaks, though the suit was ultimately dropped.

Rosga was determined to ensure the Outlaws continued their rapid growth—ideally at the expense of the Hell's Angels and their allies—and helped to negotiate an alliance with the club's one-time rivals: the Pagan's. It was a shrewd move. The previous year the Pagan's had been suspected of murdering the vice president of the Angels chapter in Philadelphia as he drove his truck along the freeway. The entire chapter closed down shortly afterward as a result.

Under Rosga's supervision, Outlaws and Pagan's joined forces to prevent the Angels from opening a chapter in Virginia by forcing a support club to close. The alliance with the Pagan's had other benefits too: the club had access to new drug supplies and markets that could be of benefit to both sides.

In late 2006, the Outlaws became the first major international biker gang to open a chapter in Japan—with the granting of a full charter to a club in Okinawa City. Motorcycle gangs had been a huge part of Japanese culture for over half a century, threatening the obedient status quo of the nation since the end of World War II. Legend has it that the early gangs were formed by fearless kamikaze pilots not "blessed" with the opportunity to die for their emperor, and desperate for new kicks. They were joined by thousands of antisocial young punks who customized their motorcycles, removing the mufflers to maximize the ear-splitting revs, earning them the nickname *kaminari-zoku* (thunder tribes).

When trouble came, it arrived by the truckload, but in-

stead of fighting one another, these gangs and their supporters joined forces against what they saw as a common enemy:
the police. In Toyoma in 1972, a motorcycle gang led three
thousand rioters in a vicious battle with the police during
which several cars were torched and many stores looted.
Four years later, in Kobe, an even larger riot took place when
police attempted to stop an illicit race meeting. A crowd of
ten thousand went on the rampage, destroying patrol cars
and taxis and stoning and setting fire to several police stations. A crowd pushed a police truck into a cameraman and
killed him and the incident gave birth to a new name for the
biker gangs: *bosozoku* (violent running tribes).

In the same way that Western motorcycle gangs rebel
against authority, so the *bosozoku* took great pleasure in
turning traditional Japanese values like *wabisabi* (elegant
simplicity) on its head. They would paint their bikes a variety
of garish colors and fit them with oversized windshields and
banana-seat backs that reached up as much as ten feet high.

The *bosozoku* acted as a recruiting ground for the Yakuza
(the Japanese Mafia), but anti-*boso* legislation ensured that
they never became a serious threat. By the early aughts, the
police were detaining more than one hundred thousand each
year on traffic violations. Then a law was passed that allowed
police to prosecute the crowds of spectators who turned out
to see the gangs ride. The *bosozoku* fell apart, and in their
place Japan saw the creation of smaller, more discreet clubs
riding modified Harley-Davidsons and aping the style of
American gangs.

It was one such club that approached the Outlaws with the
idea of obtaining a charter and becoming Outlaws Japan MC.
And after a period of several months prospecting, representatives from Canada, Germany and the AOA's mother chapter
in Chicago made their way to Okinawa for the joining-forces
party, along with members from Canada and Germany, but
the main contingent of the dozen attendees came from

England and Wales. And the patches themselves were handed over by Dink, now promoted by Rosga to the role of European and Asian president of the Outlaws.

It was, by all accounts, an eventful trip. "They're not like us," Dink told Boone soon after he returned. "Pretty fucking weird as it goes. I'm not sure they completely understand what they're getting into. But they're part of the club now so if you ever fancy a trip to Japan, you know you'll be looked after."

Boone couldn't get too excited by the club's overseas expansion or the new opportunities to travel that came with it. Back home in the Midlands, a power struggle inside the Warwickshire chapter was getting close to the breaking point.

The main source of the trouble was one of the newer members, Simon Turner, whom Boone had first become acquainted with in the late nineties when Turner was operating a stolen motorcycle ring. Able to supply virtually any model to order, Turner was a skilled motorcycle thief. He was also fascinated by the whole MC scene and desperately wanted to be a part of it. He repeatedly asked Boone to sponsor him as a prospect.

Boone had his reservations; Turner had a vicious temper and had been sentenced to a ten-year term for pouring gas over a man and threatening to set him on fire in order to secure a drug debt. That sort of behavior was fair enough, but in Turner's case the debt hadn't even been his—he was collecting it on behalf of a friend—and he'd never even met the man before so had not even attempted to collect any of the money before launching the attack. He would later claim that he was only trying to scare the man and was desperate for his share of the cash in order to buy Christmas presents for his kids, but Boone could only see a man who had precious little self-control—or common sense.

There was, however, pressure to keep growing the club and boost the numbers by bringing in newcomers. There was also the consideration that anyone the club missed or passed over might be tempted to join the Angels instead so, even if they never made it past prospect, it was important to at least give them a chance.

Turner's insistence eventually broke Boone's resolve. He knew he had to put the good of the club first. He may not have had much time for Turner personally, but no one in the club would ever claim that every member of the Outlaws was their best friend. The club was big enough for people to pick and choose their friends so it didn't really matter as you could easily avoid those you had less of a connection with. Though Caz shared a few of Boone's reservations, Dozer and Link both seemed to like Turner well enough, and the feeling that Caz had was not strong enough for him to decide to blackball him, so Turner was in.

The new recruit worked hard and had no problem showing the dedication required to win his full patch. Clearly ambitious, it seemed that his one aim in life was to get into the club as quickly as possible. Once this goal had been achieved, his true craving for violence came to the fore. During regular fights and bar fights, Turner would be the one everyone else had to watch, and pull off, lest he ended up killing someone when nothing more than a solid beating was called for. And while others looked upon the occasional patrols that involved hunting members of the enemy as a necessary evil and a grim duty, Turner looked forward to them with little short of psychotic relish.

By the end of 2006, Turner was becoming increasingly frustrated with the direction his chapter was taking, particularly when it came to the war with the Angels. Although bound by the laws and constitution of the AOA, each chapter of the Outlaws operates independently and is responsible for the conduct of its own members. Turner wanted to be far more proactive about carrying out attacks on the enemy—and with a large chapter like Warwickshire behind him, he was eager to give the other side a beating they would never forget.

Consumed with a frantic desire to acquire more power, he did everything he could to gather the support needed for an attempt to oust Caz and become president of the chapter himself. During church meetings, he was belligerent, voting against the majority just for the hell of it. If he failed to get an agreement to attend a certain venue for a run, he would take a few of his closest supporters and head there anyway, claiming there had been a misunderstanding or that he had been forced to divert because of a breakdown.

There were many in the chapter who wanted to curtail Turner's power. It wasn't so much that people were scared of him, it was more that he was an unpredictable character and it made sense to be wary around him. On the other hand, some of Boone's closest comrades made it clear that they liked Turner, they shared his obsession with guns and his appetite for fighting, and they would follow him to the end of the earth. One of his biggest fans was Dean "Trotter" Taylor, whom Boone had bonded with when they shared a cell in prison in the mideighties.

Boone hated the way things were shaping up, and it was becoming hard for him to disguise his hostility. "I found that piece of crap [Turner] on life's scrap heap," he confided to a friend. "And now I realize I should have left him there."

The only way to deal with Turner was to get rid of him and Caz had a solution. Warwickshire was a big area, he explained during a national meeting for the Outlaws MC, which both he and Turner attended. That was a problem the Pagans had encountered when they had been operating on their own. The best thing to do, he suggested, was to split the chapter in two. North Warwickshire would be led by Caz; the South Warwickshire chapter would be run by Turner. Anyone who wanted to move over to the new chapter was welcome to do so.

On its inaugural day, the South Warwickshire chapter had six full members and two prospects. So far as Turner was concerned, the time of reckoning had arrived. Along with Sean Creighton, his sergeant at arms, and Trotter, his loyal follower, he started to go out on mini raiding parties, attacking local bikers whether they were affiliated to MCs or not, ensuring that everyone on the scene knew his area belonged to the Outlaws and no one else.

Ultimately, however, his anger was directed at the Angels. Although they had come across numerous opportunities, the club had never taken revenge for the attack on Switch, the Warwickshire Outlaw who had been shot twice in the back while riding home after a church meeting. There was also the issue of the Bulldog Bash, the festival that had been started all those years earlier by the Wolf Outlaws and then had been hijacked by the Angels and turned into a massive cash cow. It took place on ground that the Outlaws regarded as theirs—but now that the club had split, it would be taking place in territory that belonged exclusively to the South Warwickshire chapter. Turner saw this as a personal insult, a commentary on his ability to control the area belonging to his club.

The other members of the chapter were cut from a similar cloth to Turner himself. Creighton was obsessed with firearms far beyond the degree that his role demanded and shared Turner's desire to take the fight to the Angels whenever possible. Dane Garside, a truck driver and father of seven, had wanted to be in an MC since the age of thirteen and, as soon as he had been old enough, had the word *warrior* tattooed on the back of his head. As he had been a member of the Satan's Slaves prior to joining the Outlaws, that club's patch had also been tattooed on his head and remained, despite attempts to cover it. Dane's younger brother, Karl, was also prospecting for the club, having been attracted by what he had seen of the biker lifestyle.

Feeding into Turner's frustrations was his knowledge that, internationally at least, the Outlaws were making good on the old motto, ADIOS. He had read about the assassination of Hell's Angel Roger "Bear" Mariani, shot dead on the I-95 earlier that year. When the cuttings landed on his desk, Turner and his sergeant at arms Sean Creighton immediately drew parallels between that case and the shooting of the French Canadian Angel on the M40 in 2001. No one had been arrested in either incident. The perpetrators, it seemed, had gotten away scot-free.

A few months earlier, in June 2006, Christopher Legere, sergeant at arms of the New Hampshire chapter of the Outlaws, was arrested for the murder of a man who had been wearing a T-shirt supporting the enemy. Once again, details of the case were circulated to Outlaws chapters around the world. The reports told how John Denoncourt tried to enter the Three Cousins Lounge, an Outlaws' hangout, while wearing a Hell's Angels T-shirt he bought as a souvenir the previous Father's Day. At least two people tried to dissuade him from going into the bar, saying the shirt would cause problems, but Denoncourt said he didn't care. Legere was seen to go over to the main windows and start pacing, becoming increasing irate, until he finally stormed out. Moments later he returned. The same people who had tried to talk Denoncourt into removing his shirt or turning it inside out now tried to restrain Legere, but the Outlaw pulled out a semi-automatic handgun and fired at least three shots in the direction of Denoncourt. One bullet ripped through his heart, killing him as he tried to run away.

The bar had been packed but most people insisted they had been in the toilet at the time of the shooting or that they had not seen anything. Legere's girlfriend, who worked behind the bar, told the court she simply could not remember what had happened on the night in question. Little wonder people were reluctant to speak—the chief prosecution witnesses was himself murdered shortly after the death of Denoncourt.

So far as Turner and the rest of the South Warwickshire chapter was concerned, the Outlaws seemed to have the Angels on the run. Turner was eager to do his bit to keep the momentum going—and to take things to the next level. At this point, however, the Outlaws suffered a series of humiliating setbacks.

Across America, the Outlaws had been feeling so strong and so confident that they decided to attend the 2006 Sturgis Motorcycle Rally in South Dakota. One of the largest biker gatherings in the United States, Sturgis has been going since 1938 and attracts over half a million participants each year. Some Hell's Angels own property in the area and the club always makes a strong showing at the festival, selling thousands of dollars worth of merchandise and scouting out potential recruits.

The Outlaws have traditionally stayed away. They made an appearance in 1990 and the visit ended in violence when one of their members was shot by a Sons of Silence gang member. Sixteen years later, a statement was placed on the club's Web site: "Law enforcement agencies have been informed of the Outlaws MC intention to visit Sturgis this year. We are not going there to make any type of statement or display of power. We are simply going there to enjoy the Sturgis venue, see the historical sites and spend time with our brothers."

Around 300 Outlaws, representing a total of 191 chapters, decided to attend. Rather than staying in the heart of the festival, they based themselves in a rented campsite in the Black Hills, some 75 miles from Sturgis itself. Fewer than 100 Angels were believed to be at the festival at the same time.

Yet during the Outlaws visit to Custer State Park, two

Hell's Angels in a white pickup truck ambushed them. The exact details of what happened remain unclear (none of the bikers involved made any kind of statement) but what is beyond doubt is that one of the Angels took aim at the Outlaws with a handgun, shooting and wounding five. One of those targeted returned fire, but by then the truck was speeding away.

No Outlaws were killed in the incident, but Turner felt sickened that members of his club had been attacked in this way. Jim Vlahakis, the State Division criminal investigation director, told the press that he planned to meet with the two gangs to "try to head off any potential problems," and added that eventual retaliation was likely. "It may not happen here. It could happen a month from now somewhere else," he said. Turner added a quote of his own: "It could even happen on the other side of the Atlantic."

More bad news came in June 2007. Outlaw Frank Vital was shot dead in the parking lot of the Crazy Horse Saloon in Forest Park, Georgia—killed by a member of the Renegades MC, a support club for the Hell's Angels.

Soon all Turner could think about was revenge. He wanted to send a message out into the world: that wherever they were, no Hell's Angel would ever be safe. He had the means and the motivation, and inspired by international events, he also had the method. So far as he was concerned, the sanction for carrying out a hit came from none other than national president Jack Rosga—the most senior Outlaw on the planet and a man to whom all the members of the British chapter paid a massive amount of respect whenever they met up with him.

Daytona Beach Bike Week was by now an annual pilgrimage for Outlaws all over the world and the UK chapters were no exception. Turner had been over at least once and got to know many key figures from the leading American chapters of the club. He appreciated their no-nonsense approach to the biker life and their attitude to taking care of business. And Rosga, in particular, was an inspirational figure in Turner's mind.

Despite making every effort to appear to be a legitimate businessman, Rosga was in fact directing campaigns of violence against enemies of the Outlaws across the country and beyond. In late June 2007, soon after the fatal shooting of Frank Vital, he gave members the "green light" to retaliate in any way they saw fit. He also demanded revenge on the Hell's Angels after two members were attacked in Florida. And it was at this point that he issued the edict that Outlaws should seek out and shoot members of the rival gang. So far as Turner and the other members of the South Warwickshire chapter were concerned, that ruling applied to them as well.

Turner decided that an attack from a moving car seemed to be the way to go. The car itself would be easy to identify but it would also be easy to get rid of. Hitting a moving target at speed would be difficult but, leaving nothing to chance, Creighton spent weeks practicing his marksmanship on a tailor's dummy that he kept at home.

Ideally Turner would have preferred the up-close-and-personal approach. During Wheeler's trial the court had heard about the murder of a Hell's Angel associate by an Outlaw during which the victim had been shot three times until the gun had jammed. The Outlaws then proceeded to beat the man with the butt of his gun and finally killed him by jamming a screwdriver into his neck.

A few of the more junior members of the chapter were reluctant to get involved but they were soon goaded into action. "Are you a fucking Hell's Angel lover?" asked Turner. "Do you want to be a fucking Hell's Angel or something? No? Then why aren't you coming with me to shoot one of the fuckers?"

Turner's word was law within the chapter and the others were terrified of him, not just because of his enormous potential to commit acts of violence but because of his power to dictate whether or not they all remained in the club. Dane Garside had already experienced just how strict Turner could be. After he failed to answer his phone quickly enough, Turner ripped off his patches and demoted him back to prospect for a few months.

When it came to the final plan, every member of the chapter had a specific role to play. Dane Garside would drive the main car, a green Rover 600. Creighton would be in the passenger seat with one handgun and Turner would be in the rear of the car with another. Creighton, the more accomplished marksman of the two, would aim at the actual target, Turner would shoot at the motorcycle itself with the intention of bringing it down. Even if the first shot missed, crashing a heavy Harley at eighty or ninety mph on a busy highway was almost certain to prove fatal and their mission would be accomplished by default.

Numerous contingencies and backup strategies were in place so that in the event that their chosen Angel survived the initial burst of gunfire, Dean "Trotter" Taylor was a little farther behind in a white Range Rover along with probationers Karl Garside and Ian Cameron, while a final member, club treasurer Malcolm Bull, was patrolling the area in a Renault Laguna, acting as a link between their two vehicles. Whatever happened, at the end of the day, at least one Angel had to be dead.

On August 9, 2007, the first day of the Bulldog Bash, the team began carrying out reconnaissance of the network of roads around the festival, performing dry runs of the planned execution. The hit itself was planned for Sunday and the seven men gathered that morning at five a.m. waiting for a suitable victim.

It had to be a full-patch Angel—there would be little kudos

in taking out a prospect or a hangaround—and he had to be
traveling in a small group. If there were too many of them, the
killers risked being pursued by the remaining bikers and
being caught. If there were only two or three in the group,
they would all stop to assist their fallen brother. With any
luck, the bikers might even crash into one another and take
out a couple more Angels.

A 2:10 P.M., the team in the green Rover was waiting in
a pull-off area on the A46 when they spotted the perfect
target—a three-motorcycle convoy. The full-patch Angel was
at the front followed by a prospect and then what appeared
to be a hangaround. Garside slammed his foot down on the
gas pedal, pulling onto the highway without warning and
causing several other vehicles to swerve in order to avoid an
accident. He followed the convoy for the next thirty miles,
gaining on them every second. It was time for the South Warwickshire chapter of the Outlaws to make their mark in the
war against the Angels.

22

MOVING TARGET

August 12, 2007, Warwickshire, England

By the time he saw the gun it was already too late.
Hell's Angel hangaround Pawel Lec was halfway
home, riding his Harley south down the M40 highway after
an exhausting weekend at the Bulldog Bash, when he spotted
a dark green car coming up fast from behind and pulled into
the middle lane to let it pass.

Lec was bringing up the rear of a three-motorcycle convoy and as he approached junction 12, near Leamington Spa, the car, a Rover 620 sedan, raced past him and then suddenly slowed down to match its speed with that of the man at the front of the group, Gerry Tobin.

Lec could only watch in horror as a gun appeared out of the passenger side window and fired two shots in quick succession. "The car drove off and it looked like nothing had happened to Gerry," Lec would say later. "Then after a very short time—two or three seconds—I noticed that Gerry let go of the handles of his cycle and fell underneath the wheels of my cycle."

The first bullet had smashed through the metal mudguard at the back of Tobin's Harley-Davidson FXTB Night Train and skirted through the tread of his rear wheel; the second skimmed the base of the biker's helmet and lodged in his skull. Somehow, in the course of his fall, both of Tobin's heavy biker boots came off. He ended up face down on the tarmac close to the center divider while his bike traveled on alone down the highway for a further one hundred feet before skidding off onto the grass shoulder to the left of the road.

Traffic on the highway came to a sudden halt as drivers did their best to avoid what many assumed was simply a horrific motorcycle accident. Only those who had seen the gun or heard the shots knew better. A middle-aged woman driving a BMW pulled up beside the fallen biker, removed a first-aid kit from her trunk and went to assist Lec, who was frantically trying to administer CPR. The woman found no pulse and realized there was nothing that could be done.

The first call to the emergency services was made at 2:23 P.M. and an air ambulance arrived on the scene just six minutes later. By this time, Lec, remembering who he would ultimately have to answer to, had made a series of calls to other club members and they too were on their way to the scene. Moments before the freeway was shut down in both directions by police to aid a fingertip search for evidence, a heavy-set Angel traveling in the opposite direction parked his Harley on the shoulder and walked across four lanes of traffic and the center divider to reach Tobin's body.

Ignoring a storm of protest from the paramedics and members of the public who had gathered around, the Angel then proceeded to rip away Tobin's back patches before returning to his motorcycle and racing off.

For Detective Superintendent Ken Lawrence, the police officer placed in charge of the investigation, the case would be like nothing else he had ever encountered in his career.

He had never dealt with the Hell's Angels before and soon found out the hard way that they do not cooperate with police, regardless of whether they are the victims or perpetrators of a crime. Much to his surprise, the club immediately refused to assist in any way whatsoever, even going so far as to refuse to provide anyone to identify the body or even confirmation that one of their members had been killed.

As Tobin was carrying a wallet, identification was not a huge issue but, with a key early line of inquiry being to establish whether Tobin was the victim of a random attack or whether he had been targeted specifically as a result of something he had done in his personal or professional life, police needed to talk to people who knew him. Again, the request was denied, as was any access to Tobin's girlfriend, Rebecca Smith.

"They do not talk to us, as witnesses and victims, they do not talk to us so sometimes we do not know what is really going on," Lawrence lamented. "We are having great difficulty talking to his partner. They guard her very closely and won't allow us to speak with her. We have no power to change that right now."

It wasn't as though the Angels didn't have plenty to say: John "Bilbo" Britt, a member of the biker club for more than thirty years and chief organizer of the Bulldog Bash, was happy to speak to the press. "I knew the guy and you couldn't wish to meet a better person. We're used to deaths, as bikers. People die in accidents but we don't expect someone to get shot. This is murder, plain and simple, and we have got no idea why this has happened.... This year was a massive event and it went off virtually trouble free. We had an amazing weekend and then this happened and it has totally shaken everybody. It's a massive loss to the biker community as a whole."

Once the road had been sealed off in both directions, trapping around four hundred vehicles, experts from the Forensic Science Service were rushed in to examine Tobin's wounds in situ, confirming that he had been shot from a moving vehicle. Lawrence's task suddenly became even more daunting: his crime scene was four lanes wide and more than a mile long.

Volunteers from the Red Cross brought food, water and foil blankets for the stranded motorists while dozens of police officers carried out a meticulous fingertip search of the highway and checked the tires of each and every car to ensure none of them had a spent cartridge caught in the tread. It was a time-intensive tactic that eventually paid off when a spent cartridge case from a self-loading pistol was discovered. It was the first clue to the identity of the killers. It would not be the last.

The minute the national officers of the Outlaws heard that a Hell's Angel had been shot dead on the M40, they knew the South Warwickshire chapter was responsible. An emergency meeting was called and all chapter presidents were told to drop whatever they were doing and get themselves to Birmingham as quickly as possible. The alert level was immediately raised to the biker equivalent of DEFCON 1 with an expectation of immediate retaliation.

Turner had been sidelined from the rest of the club in the

expectation that he wouldn't be able to cause much trouble. The revelations about what the chapter had been up to hit the rest of the club like a tsunami.

"A few friends of the club from Coventry have been getting in touch," Caz told the rest of his chapter after returning from the national officers meeting. "Those fucking idiots have been smoking crystal meth and abusing people left, right and center. They've even been taking potshots at police cars. They've completely lost the plot. They should have been finished off before any of this happened. As of right now, we're all targets. Every single one of us."

The enemy had their own sources of information too. At least two Angel hit squads were seen in the Coventry area in the days after Tobin's death, hunting for Turner and his cohorts. In the Outlaws camp, standing orders were introduced, forbidding any member from staying in the same place for more than forty minutes without moving on. Members had to call in every two hours to let their local sergeant at arms know exactly where they were. Additional guards were posted at all clubhouses and increased security protocols were implemented. Only full members and prospects were allowed entry. CCTV cameras were scrutinized before anyone came in or left.

It didn't matter if you wore your patches or not. Within a mile of the clubhouse, anyone on a customized chopper could be linked to the Outlaws and taken out. Members developed rituals to avoid being shot. Boone would jump on his motorcycle and head off in one direction as quickly as possible and then break, turn and head back the other way. He would take every possible shortcut, cut through traffic and generally drive like a lunatic. Once he was a mile away he would feel safe enough to drive normally but he was acutely aware of the target zone.

Members who felt their home addresses were too well known moved their families to safe houses as quickly as they could. Others chose to arm themselves. Plainclothes spotters were placed half a mile from the clubhouses, looking out for potential revenge attacks. No one expected the Angels to come by motorcycle (too obvious and risky); instead the watchers were looking out for cars and vans. Club members were told to travel in pairs. Those considered to be remotely high risk would be provided with a security escort, even on their way to and from work. All the stops were pulled out to keep people as safe as possible.

For Boone and his fellow Outlaws there was little sympathy over the death of the Angel himself. The hardship was the realization that their lives had been turned upside down and that they did not have a say in this change of fortune. Going out for a ride and flying their patches, even in the heart of their own territory, was unthinkable. They were all targets for execution and, at least in the early days, their wives and children were just as much at risk as they were.

There was a certain degree of guilt among those who had turned a blind eye to everything that the South Warwickshire chapter was doing. Although every individual chapter of the Outlaws had the authority to carry out attacks on members of the Hell's Angels, the idea was to ensure such incidents were kept as discreet as possible. Beating an Angel to within an inch of his life and taking his patches resulted in massive humiliation for the enemy but rarely, if ever, generated any kind of police response. Even if the authorities found out, the bikers would never talk and an investigation would immediately stall.

There had been times when Boone had been part of a group of Outlaws that had gone out with the specific intention of murdering members of the Angels, in revenge for the shooting of Switch for example, but any hunting expeditions had always followed strict protocols to ensure nothing could be pinned on any individual member of the club. What the South

Warwickshire chapter had done was so ill conceived it amounted to a massive tactical error, and a PR disaster.

It seemed that Turner and his gang could not have chosen a worse random victim. They had not only killed a Hell's Angel. According to those who knew him outside of the biker fraternity, Tobin was the closest thing to a real angel you could hope to find. Born in England, brought up in northern Alberta, Canada, in his youth Tobin had been a born-again Christian, who "used to have Bible talks at work in the mornings and prayer meetings in the afternoon," according to former colleague Tim Pogue.

He had lived in southeast London and worked as a mechanic in a Harley-Davidson dealership since 1999. His comrades knew him as "Gentlemen Gerry." Police described him as "hardworking, friendly, but private." He had no criminal record in England or Canada. And when his girlfriend Rebecca Smith appeared to the press, tearfully standing beside Marcus Berriman, president of the London chapter of the Hell's Angels, she won the sympathy of a nation.

A statement read out on her behalf said: "Gerry was a thinking man, always ready and able to offer guidance and support to others, a true inspiration to many people, a charming personality whose quick-witted humor always kept everyone smiling. He was a rare breed of man with the heart of a lion and a soul filled with compassion and selflessness. Gerry was both a man of his word and a defender of his principles.

"The nature of his untimely death due to a callous and cowardly act of violence from which it was impossible to defend himself, only accentuates further the pain and suffering that we are all experiencing due to this terrible loss." More than three thousand Hell's Angels from around the world attended his funeral.

Yet despite the palpable fear and dissent in the Outlaws

camp, there was no question about what the official line would be once the perpetrators were fully identified: the club would back them every inch of the way, no matter what. *Your brother isn't always right, but he is always your brother.*

Although he had no choice but to toe the party line—and understood why the club as a whole had to do so—Boone didn't feel as though the killers of Tobin were his brothers at all. All their actions had done was to make each and every Outlaw a target for some form of retribution.

It was as if someone was slowly but surely sucking all the fun out of being an outlaw biker. Weekend runs usually ran from Saturday morning to Sunday evening but if people could get time off, a few of the guys would often head off on Friday night or even Friday morning to make more of a break of it. Now, with security such a major concern, such independence was banned. The club had to travel together and anyone who headed off on his own faced being fined.

When runs did take place, everyone wanted to be in the security cars rather than on their motorcycles. At times the number of cars would threaten to exceed the number of cycles; that was how ridiculous it was getting. For those who were on their cycles, no one wanted to be at the back of the group—though that honor usually went to the prospects, otherwise known as human shields. Similarly, no one wanted to be the last person to leave the clubhouse after a night of partying and anyone who did leave without checking the CCTV was again likely to be fined.

More and more of Boone's life was being controlled by rules and regulations that had been introduced almost wholly as a result of Tobin's murder. Time and again he found himself wanting to rebel—"I'm a fucking Outlaw for fuck's sake"— but knew he had to rein himself in or risk being seen as a troublemaker, or even a traitor.

• • •

Detective Superintendent Lawrence was expecting a long and difficult investigation, the type that stretches on for months and months with little progress and repeatedly runs into brick wall after brick wall. With even the victim's friends unwilling to lift a finger to help, there seemed to be little hope of things turning out any other way. He could not have been more wrong.

While the actual execution of Gerry Tobin had been carried out with a high degree of slick professionalism, the preplanning and the coverup were both utterly shoddy. The investigating team knew the vehicle they were looking for was a green Rover 600 series, so when a burned-out model was found in a Coventry side street the day after the killing, alarm bells sounded. Although the fire had destroyed all the paint and rendered the interior forensically useless, the serial number on the engine block allowed detectives to trace the registered owner. The details were false but when detectives looked to see who had owned the car before that, it turned out to be someone described as "a biker type" going by the name Sean Creighton. For all the care and planning that had been put into the murder, the main vehicle was one with a clear link to the gang.

After that, the clues came thick and fast. Creighton and another man—later identified as Dane Garside—had been caught on CCTV at a nearby gas station wrapped in hats and warm clothes despite it being a hot summer's day, filling up the green Rover just hours before the murder. The clothes were an attempt to disguise themselves but, in fact, they just made themselves stand out from the crowd.

Over the days that followed, an undercover surveillance team followed and filmed Creighton as he met up with the rest of the South Warwickshire chapter of the Outlaws at a bar where they sat outside and bought no drinks but took extensive notes during an intensive debriefing session. The other members of the chapter were quickly identified and the two other vehicles that had been used on the day of the murder were also found on surveillance footage, putting the entire club in the frame.

A raid on the clubhouse in Coventry turned up two shotguns in a bag with Simon Turner's fingerprints on them. More guns were found at Creighton's home address. Police also found the dummy used for shooting practice. Evidence from cell phone towers showed that Turner's handset was in the exact vicinity at the time Tobin was shot. Within ten days of Tobin's death, the entire chapter had been rounded up and was being questioned about his murder.

Turner, Creighton and four of the others stuck to the rules through the forty hours of interrogation that followed, responding to every question, no matter how innocuous, with a curt "no comment" or total silence. Only Malcolm Bull, the club's bespectacled treasurer, let anything slip.

Bull explained that he was involved in gathering intelligence about Hell's Angels in and around the vicinity of the Bulldog Bash. He insisted that this was an entirely innocent activity and that he knew nothing about any shooting. Although Bull hadn't given away much at all, he had still broken Rule 14, and would ultimately have to face the consequences.

Despite their lack of statements, the evidence against all seven members of the club proved to be overwhelming and the entire chapter was charged with Tobin's murder. Solving the case had taken just thirteen days.

23

CALL TO ACTION

January 2008

Five months later, with the seven members of the South Warwickshire chapter jailed and awaiting trial, it was business as usual for the ever-expanding AOA. A handful of Outlaws, including Dozer and Tank, flew to the southeast coast of Spain in order to help celebrate the launch of the newly formed Costa Blanca chapter. After a week of hard partying, the bikers arrived at Alicante Airport, only to find a similar number of patched-up Hell's Angels getting ready to board the same return flight home.

It was nothing more than a bizarre coincidence, but neither the Angels nor the Outlaws were willing to dismiss the idea that they had somehow been set up. Had cooler heads prevailed, the whole thing might have passed off without incident but neither side trusted the other to keep the peace. Knowing they would be subjected to stringent security checks, none of the bikers had any weapons on them, so, in an effort to gain an upper hand on UK soil, a series of frantic phone calls were made with both clubs calling for reinforcements to meet the flight with as many weapons as they could get their hands on. Both gangs knew the score by now—nobody had forgotten the airport attacks in Denmark in which bikers on both sides of the conflict had been killed. This was about as serious as biker wars could get.

Boone had thought about traveling to Spain with the others but had decided to wait until the new chapter was more established and take a trip out there then. He was at work when Dozer called him, a distinct note of panic in his voice.

"You got to get your ass to Birmingham Airport as fast as you can," Dozer told him, going on to explain what had happened and that he and Tank were unable to do anything, as they had been booked on a later return flight and had been unable to change it.

Some Outlaws—particularly those with good friends on the first incoming flight—were already on their way to the scene in order to defend their brothers. *It's one in, all in.* Dozer's words were spinning around in Boone's head but it was a phrase of his own making that was foremost in his mind: this is going to be a disaster.

"How far away are you?" asked Dozer.

"Shit man. I'm in south London," Boone lied. "I don't know if I'll be able to get there in time."

A part of Boone still believed in the club, still believed in the values of the brotherhood, but this was just plain crazy. The Outlaws were already under heavy scrutiny following the murder of Tobin and a series of other incidents around the world. This was the last thing they needed. More than anything, there was the sheer folly of the situation. This wasn't an ambush with a carefully planned getaway, just a mass confrontation at an airport. An airport! With hundreds of CCTV cameras, armed police, metal detectors and a one-way road system that would make any kind of quick getaway all but impossible.

To make matters worse, there had been no time to formulate any kind of plan and, with the club members unable to be contacted while they were up in the air, there was no time to put one together. People were rushing to the scene with no thought of what would actually happen once they got there. It would be the worst kind of disaster and Boone wanted no part of it.

It was exactly the kind of situation he feared most—not because of the potential for violence but simply because people would be acting without thinking things through. They were all fully grown men, yet they were acting with all the finesse of a bunch of unruly teenagers. And so far as Boone could see, they were all going to pay a heavy price.

By the time the flight landed in Birmingham, more than thirty bikers from across the West Midlands and beyond had gathered at the airport to meet the twenty or so Angels and Outlaws who came through arrivals. Some of those present had expected to at least wait until they got out of the main building but the fight broke out almost as soon as the reinforcements were spotted, taking place in a passageway joining the two terminals, close to where the passengers emerge after clearing customs. Those fresh off the plane met up with fellow gang members, grabbed their weapons and charged. Knives and meat cleavers as well as iron bars, knuckle dusters, hammers and even a tire iron were all put to savage use as terrified families ran for cover. Witnesses even reported one man wielding a samurai sword.

The airport is patrolled by armed police, but the officers on duty saw the carnage and decided it simply wasn't safe for them to intervene. Several officers actually ran for cover, fearful that they might be accosted by the mob and have their weapons taken away.

Remarkably, only one of the bikers was critically injured in the clash. Boone felt grateful that at least the South Warwickshire boys were in jail over the Tobin murder. Had they been free, no doubt they would have been first on the scene and the carnage would have been far worse.

Twelve bikers were eventually brought to court. The average age of the seven Outlaws in the holding pen was forty-seven, the eldest being fifty-one and the youngest forty-four. (At forty-one years old, Boone still found himself one of the younger members of the club.) By contrast, the Angels had spent the months before the battle recruiting heavily—the average age of their defendants was forty, with the youngest just twenty-eight.

The new Angels were not necessarily bikers at heart, but they had enough of an interest to allow them to be fast-tracked into the club. Many were thought to be actively involved in drugs and gun dealing, all part of an effort by the Angels to establish themselves further in the UK market and to boost their fighting strength in the aftermath of the murder of Gerry Tobin. Boone's appetite for violence and destruction wasn't what it used to be, and yet it was obvious that the war was going to continue and that there would be more clashes in the future—clashes in which the Outlaws were likely to find themselves up against men who were considerably younger and fitter.

Inevitably, recriminations bounced around the club. Those Outlaws who had failed to make it to Birmingham on time were questioned about just how hard they had tried. So far as Boone was concerned, the only real winners from the situation had been the police and it was crazy for the gang to keep losing members to prison, but he couldn't say anything. But Outlaw rules state that a call to action must be answered; fines were issued and a couple of members were busted back to prospect for failing to respond in time. Boone escaped punishment but could feel several club members seemed to be unsure about exactly how hard he had tried.

In the months that followed, partly as a result of the airport fight, the Outlaws came under even more intense scrutiny. In March 2008, Outlaw David Melles was arrested in Gloucestershire after police found an armory of illegal guns at his home. The fifty-two-year-old grandfather had stashed a sawed-off and pump-action shotgun, a Derringer pistol, hollow-point bullets and other ammunition at his house near Stroud. He was sentenced to twelve years in prison.

In May 2008, the Derbyshire Constabulary received intelligence that the Hell's Angels were planning a retaliatory attack against the Outlaws at the Rock and Blues Show that year. The twenty-fifth anniversary show was set to have a great lineup, but the police's objections were sufficient to force the organizers to retract their application for a premises license.

The club was stunned—the Rock and Blues was a major money earner for the Outlaws. Without it, they would have to find other ways of swelling the coffers—and so far as the senior officers were concerned, this meant stepping up their involvement in the drug trade, even if it meant going head to head with other gangs in the trade.

The trial of the seven men accused of the murder of Gerry Tobin was scheduled to begin on October 3, 2008. The day before the jury was sworn in, Sean Creighton dramatically changed his plea, claiming that he alone had murdered Gerry Tobin. It soon became clear that this was a tactical move aimed at giving the rest of the chapter the chance of getting off scot-free. Creighton also claimed that, rather than being sergeant at arms, he was in fact president of the chapter and the only one with the authority to arrange and order such a murder.

Turner took full advantage of his comrade's confession and told the court that he had been working at an industrial unit on the day of the killing but had handed over his phone to Creighton, neatly explaining why the police had traced his mobile signal along the same route the killers took. Turner added that he had been suspended from the chapter after arguing with other members at a motorcycle repair unit in Coventry, just a few hours before Tobin was shot.

He was, however, unable to explain how plastic bags containing two shotguns were found at his workplace, with his fingerprints on them. When Raggatt asked if the fingerprints were an unhappy coincidence, he replied: "My whole life seems to be an unhappy coincidence."

Turner also told the court that codefendant Malcolm Bull had insulted his fellow Outlaws by making statements to the police and breaking Rule 14. "Everything about Mr. Bull is disreputable to me," Turner told the court. "[He] has turned on everything that we are—he has brought us to this junction in our life."

With Creighton prepared to take the rap, the rest of the Outlaws claimed total ignorance of the shooting, saying that they thought they were just carrying out a surveillance operation aimed at the Thames Valley Coalition, a loose group of bikers that included various Angel support clubs. There had been a minor fracas a few days before the Bulldog Bash between members of the Coalition and the Outlaws so it seemed to be a plausible explanation.

Both Turner and Dane Garside claimed to have thought the surveillance idea to be a silly one, but, as loyal chapter members, said they had no choice but to follow orders. Giving evidence, Garside refused to identify those involved on the day apart from Creighton. "I was in bits," he told the court of his reaction to the shooting. "I didn't expect anything like that to happen. I thought: he's [Creighton's] going to start shouting verbal [yelling abuse]. Then all I heard was bang! Bang! I screamed, 'What the hell is going on?' I was told not to look around. As I looked around, I could still see the gentleman [Tobin] riding the bike. Sean Creighton said, 'You just fucking drive this car.'"

The jury found all seven men guilty and life sentences with minimum prison terms totaling 191 years were handed out, the longest being for Turner and Taylor, who will each have to serve a minimum of 30 years behind bars before they become eligible for parole.

When Creighton was sentenced, the judge ordered that he

be taken down to the cells. Prison guards began leading him away but he suddenly broke free, rushed up to Malcolm Bull and hissed: "Know this, you fucker: I'll see you again."

In December 2008, less than a month after their convictions, Karl Garside and Ian Cameron, prospects at the time of the murder, were voted in as fully patched members of the Outlaws. They had kept their mouths shut during the court proceedings and this was their ultimate reward. *Your brother isn't always right, but he is always your brother!*

Although both would be spending the next twenty-five years in prison, they would at least know that their families would be well provided for and that they could always count on the club to provide whatever support they needed.

Dane Garside—who was felt to have said far too much during his testimony—was stripped of his membership, as was Malcolm Bull, who is serving out his time in a prison separate from the other members of the chapter for his own safety.

24

PUBLIC RELATIONS

March 2009

As the new riding season approached, Boone and the other Outlaws were eager to reestablish the image of bikers as charitable, lovable rogues, if only to lessen some of the law enforcement attention that was now being directed their way as a result of the events of the previous two years.

Several police forces seemed to have developed major hard-ons for Britain's bikers and—having finally realized just what they were capable of—were determined to take out as many of their members as possible.

After a few months without incident, the Outlaws were hoping that things would start to get back to normal. Then a story broke on the other side of the world and all the progress they had made up until that point seemed to come undone. As soon as Boone saw the headlines, it felt like déjà vu all over again. Shortly before midday on March 22, 2009, Mahmoud "Mick" Hawi, national president of the Comanchero MC, boarded Qantas flight QF430 from Melbourne to Sydney and realized that the man sitting a few rows in front of him was none other than his mortal enemy, Derek Wainohou, president of the Sydney Hell's Angels.

The two men took their seats and, in what was fast becoming a tradition of the global biker wars, began frantically began sending out a stream of text messages until the flight was ready for takeoff and they had to switch off their phones.

By the time the plane arrived at Gate 5, reinforcements for both sides had arrived with some heavy-duty weaponry. The rival factions entered arrivals via two glass doors, perhaps eighty meters apart. And then there was a charge to the center of the vast hall. Wainohou shoulder-charged Hawi. One of the Comancheros responded by punching Wainohou in the face, knocking him to the ground, and then everyone started fighting.

The fight erupted inside the security barrier, then moved past it "like one big rolling ball of mayhem" toward the terminal's doors. Angel associate Anthony Zervas pulled out a pair of scissors with no handles and lunged toward Hawi, aiming for his eyes. Hawi raised his hand just in time and the blade sank into his forearm.

Zervas then took a hard shot to the face and crumpled to the floor. Hawi picked up one of the metal security stanchions, grasping it between both hands like a golf club, and then swung it with great force as if he were doing a chip shot with Zervas's head. Witnesses reported hearing a loud "crunching" sound and watched as a pool of dark red began to spread out from under the victim's body.

The fighters broke up and fled through the terminal's main doors. The whole thing had lasted less than thirty seconds but that was long enough for Zervas. He died from multiple fractures to the base of the skull and was also found to have three stab wounds to the chest and abdomen.

Boone followed what was happening in Australia with a sense of impending doom. Although the Sydney battle wasn't directly connected to the Outlaws, the international media had picked up on the story, and the aftermath was being felt by back-patch gangs around the world, with talk of an outright flying ban being imposed on bikers. Added to which, the fight between the Australian bikers could not have occurred at a worse time.

One month later, in April 2009, the Hell's Angels and the Outlaws found themselves back in the media spotlight as the trial for the Birmingham Airport riot began. The jury heard how up to thirty bikers had clashed in the terminal and watched CCTV footage of some of the fighting. The security cameras clearly showed terrified travelers wheeling their suitcases just meters from where the fighting took place. Others were seen trying to find a place of safety while the battle raged around them.

A small number of Outlaws attended the trial to show support for their brothers. Unlike the Tobin murder case, in which up to one hundred bikers in full colors had paraded around the courthouse and taken turns going inside to listen to the proceedings, the group wore no colors and maintained a low profile.

A massive police operation was in place to prevent further trouble from breaking out and the last thing anyone wanted was another very public confrontation with the authorities. The Outlaws had only just lost the lucrative Rock and Blues Show. The last thing they wanted was to lose the Ink and Iron Show—another big money earner for the club.

After six weeks of evidence at Birmingham Crown Court and six more days of jury deliberation, three men were cleared and the jury failed to reach a verdict on one of the others. The remaining eight men were handed six-year terms. As he handed out the sentences, Judge Patrick Thomas QC said it gave him "no pleasure at all" to impose the prison sentences on "men who, in many ways, are honorable, decent, hard-working family men." But, he added, "your conduct gives me no choice. You are all family men, and the effects of your actions on your families will be very substantial."

In the summer of 2009, a few weeks after the airport riot sentences had been handed down, and with the recent Tobin murder convictions still seared into the public consciousness, Dink decided to do his part for club PR. As he was European and Asian president of the Outlaws, and thus a key player in one of the world's biggest and most notorious biker gangs, *Sky News* was eager to secure an exclusive interview with him at the annual Ink and Iron Festival in Birmingham, ahead of the Bulldog Bash.

Speaking to Midlands' correspondent Darren Little, Dink was eager to brush off allegations that his motorcycle club was involved in anything criminal, pointing out that they were simply an easy target for the police.

Dink did, however, admit that, despite being convicted of murder, the men remained full-patch members of the Outlaws, that both they and their families were being supported financially. In his view, this was only fair. "If you have a friend who has done wrong but has been punished, would you just cast him aside?"

Warwickshire police assistant chief constable Bill Holland remained unconvinced. "If law enforcement does tolerate something like the murder of Gerry Tobin," he said, "if it's seen as an isolated event, you run the risk of doing the same as happened in Australia and in other parts of the world where this has been allowed to continue and escalate."

Warning the public about the dangers posed by the biker gangs was no longer enough, argued Holland. With the Bull-dog Bash generating cash profits of up to one million pounds over its four-day run, the police were extremely concerned about just what the Hell's Angels were up to with that kind of money.

Stratford-upon-Avon District Council's licensing commit-tee had granted the event a new ten-year license in 2008 but Holland asked the panel to review this (yet again) in the light of "heightened" tensions between the Hell's Angels and the Outlaws. In his statement to the committee, Holland said: "I am satisfied that the Bulldog Bash Ltd is made up of 'full-patch' members of the Hell's Angels and their close associ-ates, and that the Hell's Angels are involved in serious and organized crime. There has previously been serious, includ-ing fatal, violence connected to the event and this poses a serious risk."

The previous year, Warwickshire detectives had spent 1.4 million pounds mounting a massive operation to police the festival. Sniffer dogs and metal detectors were employed to disrupt any planned illegal activity, and hundreds of officers set up stop-and-search stations along the route. Having failed to get the license revoked, Holland insisted on carrying out a similar operation, "with the idea of protecting people from harm for the duration of the event."

Bulldog Bash festival organizer John "Bilbo" Britt claimed the force was wasting its money. "They have tried three times to stop this show and have failed each time. Certain people in the police think us bikers are in some kind of war but we are not. It is discrimination, because we are in a fight with the police to stop them ruining part of our lifestyle. We are not just going to sit back and let them do that. If the police have the evidence that we are involved in organized crime, take us to court. We've been doing it for twenty-three years and never had any trouble in the festival. Under our leathers we're just lovely big, cuddly teddy bears."

During the Bash, the Angels stepped up their own PR campaign with their latest weapon in the media war—a brand new press officer. "Echo" first appeared in the national press criticizing the overly heavy-handed police operation. "If we are organized criminals, why do we ride around quite openly displaying patches saying who we are? We get together to ride our motorcycles, visit our brothers in Britain and overseas and have a party. Just because some of our members have crossed the line doesn't make every member a criminal nor the club a criminal organization."

He also appeared in a video on the Web site of a local newspaper, decked out in full Angel regalia and again criticizing the police. "It's a completely over-the-top reaction," he said. "We accept that the police have a responsibility for law and order, public safety, etc. But we police the event and there's never any trouble on the site. . . . This is a family event that's gone on for twenty years without any problem."

Echo was supremely articulate and seemed a natural on camera, even eclipsing the likes of the late Maz Harris. Little wonder—his real name was Steve Jones and his day job was working as a BBC journalist, reporting for both television and radio. When his distinctive face and voice were recognized by colleagues, the BBC launched an inquiry into his (undeclared) extracurricular activities. It transpired that Jones had previously received a warning from his bosses for presenting an item in a short-sleeve shirt, showing off his tattoos. Once they were satisfied that Jones was in fact Echo, the BBC dismissed him on the spot.

• • •

While the police struggled to substantially link the Hell's Angels with any kind of organized criminality, the Outlaws proved to be a far easier target. In November 2009, just a few months after he had appeared on *Sky News*, Dink and six other members of the club were caught red-handed with around forty thousand pounds worth of amphetamines.

North Wales police had received a tip that drug exchanges were taking place between members of the North Wales Outlaws and representatives of the West Wales chapter. A surveillance operation was set up and when two members visited the Outlaws clubhouse in Colwyn Bay, the vehicle was later stopped in a seemingly random check and two kilos of amphetamine were recovered. Unaware that they had been compromised, the gang continued to move drugs around the country under the watchful eye of the police team. Two months later, a van was stopped on the same highway and a similar quantity of amphetamine was found hidden in the lining of the roof. Cell phones were seized and showed a pattern of regular calls between Dink and other senior Outlaws around the time of each delivery. A raid on the Colwyn Bay clubhouse also unearthed a quantity of cocaine.

Sentencing Dink to six years, the judge said: "The Outlaws are a perfectly lawful organization but you used your role as the European president to further your own criminal activities. You brought the organization into disrepute by the wholesale and commercial supply of drugs."

Everywhere Boone looked, Outlaws were getting involved in ever-more serious crimes and going to prison for longer and longer terms. The time he had spent inside as a result of the battle at the George Street clubhouse had been more than enough and he had no desire to spend any more time behind bars.

He was, of course, risking his freedom every day as a result of his activities within the drug business but, even though the club received a portion of this income as a result of an earlier investment, this was very much his own choice. What Boone didn't care for was the idea of finding himself behind bars as a result of someone else's lack of planning or foresight—like the incident at Birmingham Airport.

For Boone, the arrest and incarceration of the club's national president was the final nail in the coffin. By now he had a new girlfriend, Sally. Although she rode a motorcycle herself and loved being around bikers, she was not part of the MC scene and despised it with a vengeance. At first, Boone had ignored her complaints. He had heard the same thing from other women in the past. They all tried to make a stand, but in the end they all came around, especially when they built up solid friendships with the old ladies of his club associates.

But Sally stood firm. And finally, it seemed that Boone had caught up with her way of thinking. He had considered leaving in the days after Gerry Tobin had been shot and had become thoroughly disillusioned after the fallout from the Birmingham Airport incident. He loved the club, the partying, the fights and the brotherly love. What he didn't like was the paranoid skulking around in the dark, the constant hounding by police, the trying not to get shot, and the feeling that he would end up in prison. Plus, if he wanted to move on with his life, Sally had made it clear that she wouldn't even entertain the idea of starting a family with a practicing Outlaw.

Boone knew the Outlaws would never let him go voluntarily. He had been there too long, knew too much and was too useful to them. If he was going to get out, Boone would have to make them want to get rid of him. In the end, the simplest route seemed to be to breach one of the key rules—no fighting with other members. Following a meeting in the Birmingham clubhouse one night in April 2009, Boone made his move.

Although he had tried to keep his feelings to himself as much as possible, several of his close friends in the club knew what had been going through his mind. When he tried to deliberately pick a fight with one of them for no reason, the friend simply shook his head and walked away. "I know what you're trying to do," he said, "and I'm not prepared to help you out."

The next person Boone tried felt the same way and he was soon feeling increasingly frustrated. Drastic action was called for, so he came up with the most extreme solution he could think of. As head of security for the run to Birmingham, he was under orders to be armed at all times. He now took out the heavy silver revolver from the small of his back and pointed it directly at the head of one of the vice presidents.

The whole clubhouse fell silent. The VP's head fell forward and he exhaled slowly. Disappointment and shock was etched all over his face. "What are you doing, man?" he asked softly.

"I need out. I can't take it anymore."

"But not like this, not this way."

"It's the only thing I can think of."

Boone had barely finished his sentence when the inevitable happened. Virtually every biker in the building pounced on him. He was quickly disarmed and knocked to the floor where punches and kicks rained down on him. As he tried to cover his face he was spun over onto his back. By now a few of the Outlaws had picked up makeshift weapons—pool cues, chair legs—and he could feel them impacting on his body.

Then there were hands on his jacket, tearing at his top and bottom rockers, then at his center logo, ripping the patches right off his back. Had he been a newer, less popular member, he probably would have been killed or, at the very least, left severely injured. But almost as quickly as it started, the beating stopped and Boone found himself being propelled through the reinforced door of the clubhouse.

He was now an outsider in every sense of the word. He knew that within days, possibly within hours, members of the club would turn up at his house to ensure that everything connected to the Outlaws was removed or destroyed. He knew that he would be given just seven days to have his club tattoos covered up or removed. He knew nothing in his life would ever be the same again.

For the first few weeks, he felt as though he had lost a limb. The club had been such a huge part of his life for so many years; he hadn't registered just how much time it had taken up. But once the initial shock subsided, he could see that he had done the right thing. A massive source of stress and worry suddenly evaporated. Boone still felt incredibly loyal to the Outlaws and his brothers in the MC, but it was as if his feelings belonged to another era, back when the club was truly about nothing more than biking and fighting.

His MC had grown into a monster—big and corporate, with something indefinable having been lost along the way. As a Pagan, Boone had not only felt part of an elite group, he had also found himself to be essential to everything that happened. Now, even though the UK was one of the most powerful chapters in the world, they were part of the AOA and could only be seen as a small cog in a much larger wheel. Although the change had been inevitable, it hadn't been what he'd signed up for. Now that was all behind him and he was free to live the life he wanted to live. And he planned to make the most of it.

PART FIVE

LEGACY

25

THE NEXT GENERATION

When a reporter from *Texas Monthly* secured an invite to a Bandido funeral, he eagerly eavesdropped on a conversation among some of the more senior bikers, thinking he might hear some interesting anecdotes about the club. "Jesus, my fucking cholesterol," one of them said, "fucking off the fucking charts!" And then there was the reporter at a recent Sturgis festival who overheard a group of Hell's Angels complaining about the fact that the T-shirt vendors did not offer a senior discount. The truth is as plain as the liver spots on their faces: the hard-core element of most biker gangs is fast becoming filled with old men.

Despite this trend, within a year of Boone's leaving, the Outlaws had grown to more than twice its original size. A massive push aimed at expanding the club and bringing in newer, younger members had been incredibly successful. In part, this was a reaction to the incident at Birmingham Airport where the Outlaws had found themselves going toe-to-toe with a far younger, more physically able crowd. No one wanted to risk that happening again.

Europe is the continent with the highest increase in new biker gang chapters anywhere in the world. During the last five years, the Bandidos, the Hell's Angels and the Outlaws have opened more than 120 chapters, which makes the total number of chapters in Europe more than 425. The number of chapters for these three large groups in the United States and Canada is around 300.

The fastest growth among biker gangs in the United States

involves mostly smaller clubs, many of which already have alliances with the big four. The FBI's 2011 National Gang Threat Assessment names the Mongols, the Pagan's, the Vagos and the Wheels of Soul (an ostensibly multiracial club founded in Philadelphia but with a definite bias toward black members in the same way that the majority of senior Mongols are of Latino descent) as being of most concern.

Outside of the United States, all three of the major international biker gangs have expanded rapidly, in Sweden in particular. In the preceding five years the Hell's Angels have started up five new chapters in the Scandinavian country. The Outlaws have also established a base there and the Bandidos have increased the number of their own chapters to a total of nine.

And the more the gangs expand, the greater the potential for conflict. In June 2010, the Outlaws planned to open a new chapter in Ehrendingen, Switzerland. Hundreds of guests were invited from all over Europe. While the preparations were still going on for the Swiss bikers, their old ladies and children, up to two hundred people with motorcycles and cars appeared in the club grounds and launched a massive unprovoked attack with baseball bats, steel pipes, clubs, knives and firearms, firing several shots and destroying dozens of cars and motorcycles. Local media infuriated the Outlaws by stating the attack had taken place because they had failed to seek advance permission to establish a chapter from the local Hell's Angels.

There is the potential for serious trouble in Ireland too, where tensions have never been higher. Many years have passed on the Emerald Isle since Boone and his fellow Pagans fought in the Battle of Kilmeaden. The Alliance that had been formed in the aftermath of that conflict, with the sole aim of preventing the major MCs from gaining a foothold in Ireland, is looking increasingly fragile. The Outlaws set up shop in the Republic in 2001 and the Hell's Angels followed suit in 2007 with a chapter in Belfast and every intention of spreading south.

Both the Angels and the Outlaws are building up their Irish chapters, cherry-picking the best members from existing, independent clubs and making them offers they can't refuse in order to get them to switch sides. And with both of these gangs expanding in Ireland, it is very possible that the feud between them will ignite there too.

Sporadic trouble has also broken out among the existing Irish gangs (which goes to show that the presence of the big international MCs isn't always necessary for violence to ensue). In August 2010, a meticulously planned attack on thirty-two-year-old biker Gary Lee was put into motion in County Wicklow. The three guard dogs—two rottweilers and a Staffordshire bull terrier—which had been purchased by the target only a few weeks earlier, as an extra layer of protection, were quickly rendered useless by slabs of heavily drugged meat.

Once the coast was clear, the assault team silently smashed their way into the isolated cottage at Rathduffmore, near Knockananna on the Carlow-Wicklow border of Ireland. The sole occupant, hunting enthusiast Lee, had his wrists bound with cable ties and was then beaten about the head and face with the butt of a pistol. His attackers demanded to know where he kept his legally owned firearms—two shotguns and a rifle. When Lee refused to talk, they shot him in the arm by way of encouragement. This proved highly persuasive and Lee soon gave up the location of his gun safe.

But this was no simple robbery. As well as access to his guns, the men also wanted Lee's MC colors. A former member of the Devil's Disciples, he had recently joined a new club, the Celtic Demons, and was proudly wearing a three-piece patch with a bottom rocker that read "Ireland" in spite of the fact that several other clubs in the area had warned the Demons not to do so.

These days, MCs have extensive connections throughout the world through which they can access confidential personal data—including addresses and phone numbers. One man left Ireland because he feared he would be attacked by members of a hostile MC. Within a week or two, they rang him at home in the United States to say: "You don't think we don't know where you are, do you?"

The gangs that make up the Alliance—the Devil's Disciples, the Freewheelers, the Road Tramps, the Vikings and the Chosen Few—have been recruiting heavily, bringing in fresh manpower, their own, younger generation of bikers ready to fend off attack. Most observers believe it highly unlikely that the Alliance can win the turf war, or stem the growth of the big syndicates, given these gangs' international clout, but the fact that they are prepared to try shows that they are demanding to be taken seriously.

Another potential biker feud is simmering in mainland Europe, where eighty particularly brutal members of the Bandidos in Berlin, all from an ethnic Turkish background, left the club together in early 2010 and joined forces with the Hell's Angels. The group is now known as the Hell's Angels Nomads Turkiye.

The move came just months after the Angels and the Bandidos signed a peace agreement to end more than three years of bloody fighting between the clubs that saw deaths on both sides. The fallout (including potential retribution by the Bandidos) would be bad enough, but what makes the situation particularly troubling is that a far greater enemy of the Hell's Angels has arrived on the scene—the Mongols MC.

Having started out in California, the Mongols now have chapters in Italy and Germany, and strong alliances with other gangs lined up against the Angels. The German contingent of the Mongols is based in Bremen and is a motorcycle gang by name only. Founded in October 2010, the chapter is composed of a local crime syndicate of Kurdish immigrants called the Miri clan. They dress in T-shirts and jackets decorated with Mongol colors, but when founding president Mustafa B. went out for a spin on a red Honda Fireblade (capable of 180 mph) with a license only two weeks old, he lost control, crashed into a tree and died on the spot. Mustafa was the only member of the club to have a motorcycle license and his demise is unlikely to inspire others to follow in his footsteps. Instead, when the gang move around the city, they travel by car.

The association with the American club is important as it provides an infrastructure and trading channels to assist the group in profits from the drug trade and other criminal activity. Most of the members of the Bremen Mongols chapter also have extensive police records. Ibrahim M., the man investigators believe succeeded Mustafa B. as the head of the club, has been associated with no fewer than 147 crimes, ranging from grievous bodily harm to illegal possession of a weapon.

In Sydney, Australia, intelligence officials are increasingly concerned by the links between Lebanese crime cells and bikers, with Lebanese membership growing in the previously white-only Sydney Hell's Angels and the Comancheros. In 1997, the president of the Parramatta Nomads (a Sydney MC) handed over control of his gang to nightclub owner and alleged underworld figure Hassan "Sam" Ibrahim. Not only was Ibrahim from a Middle Eastern background, he had never even been a biker. Despite this, he instantly became president of the club, bypassing the usual hangaround and prospect stage. The Parramatta Nomads went on to become one of the most notorious criminal gangs of the nineties until a fallout among the leadership led to a split in 2007 and the formation of a new club, Notorious MC.

Led by former Nomad Allan Sarkis, the members of Notorious are mostly from a Middle Eastern background and although the club is structured like a traditional outlaw motorcycle gang, only a tiny proportion ride motorcycles. Its members are sometimes called "Nike bikies," for wearing expensive sneakers, fashionable T-shirts, being clean shaven and listening to R&B, Hip-Hop and Rap—a far cry from the traditional biker uniform of dirty jackets, leather boots and beards. The gang has been linked to a significant number of bombings, shootings and murders as part of ongoing feuds with the Hell's Angels, the Bandidos and the Comanchero.

In the United States, the war between the Outlaws and the Angels continues to be fought on multiple fronts, despite both clubs attracting more and more attention from law enforcement officials. In September 2009, two Florida Outlaws were attacked by a group of Angels while filling up at a gas station in New Haven, Connecticut. Both Outlaws had their patches taken during the assault and were left needing hospital treatment. As soon as Rosga found out what had happened, he began to plot an act of vengeance, pressing for it to take place as soon as possible. "Jack is all over this thing," one biker told an Outlaw named Gringo, who had only just received his full patch but was seen as a rising star in the organization.

A few days later, Rosga met Gringo in person. When Gringo complained about Hell's Angels taking liberties on his territory, Rosga told him: "The best way to stop that is to put a cap in 'em." He also confessed that he fully expected to go to prison one day because of his actions on behalf of the club.

The job of avenging the attack on the Florida Outlaws was assigned to Michael "Madman" Pedini and Thomas "Tomcat" Mayne, who spent several days planning the hit before shooting sixty-three-year-old Gary Watson as he sat in a pickup truck in the driveway of a Hell's Angel clubhouse in Maine. Watson survived despite suffering multiple gunshot wounds but both Madman and Tomcat received SS patches in recognition of the work they had done.

While some, like Boone, would never consider wearing the patch because of its potential implications for law enforcement officials, Tomcat had no such qualms. "If the police ever come to arrest me," he told Gringo, "I'll become the most famous member of the Outlaws in the world because I won't go down without a fight."

When federal agents went to arrest Thomas "Tomcat" Mayne in June 2010, he kept to his word. Video footage released later shows a handful of federal agents approaching the remote house at the end of a woodland path with an ancient Lincoln in the driveway. As the agents took up their positions, gunfire erupted from the window directly opposite the camera, which was positioned in a vehicle farther up the drive. The agents returned fire and took cover before one used a bullhorn to ask Mayne to put down his weapons and leave the building with his hands in the air. But Mayne was already dead, hit by seven of the twenty rounds fired by agents in the first brief exchange of fire. He was found with a .45 revolver in his hand and had fired all six shots before dying. One of Mayne's bullets hit an agent square in the chest, but the impact was absorbed by the man's bulletproof vest.

The same indictment that led to Mayne's death also named twenty-six other current and former members of the Outlaws in a list headed by none other than Milwaukee Jack Rosga himself. It transpired that the Outlaw named Gringo, the man in whom Rosga had confided on numerous occasions, was actually an ATF agent named Jeffrey Grabman.

In an undercover stint that lasted two years, Grabman ultimately became president of his own Outlaws chapter, with members made up of other law enforcement officers, and witnessed numerous acts of violence against Hell's Angels, other bikers and members of the Outlaws themselves. Caught up in one of many bar fights, Grabman was hit in the face with a broken bottle, creating a wound that required fourteen stitches to close.

The main government witness against Rosga in the subsequent trial, Grabman helped ensure that Rosga was found guilty of virtually all of the charges against him, ultimately receiving a sentence of twenty years in April 2011.

Despite numerous predictions that the MC lifestyle no longer appeals and that the entire subculture is on the verge of dying out, biker gangs are actually enjoying a massive resurgence all over the world. Repeated successful law enforcement actions seem to do nothing to deter potential recruits and the total number of MC members is currently at an all-time high.

They even have their own hit television show, courtesy of FX's *Sons of Anarchy*. While MCs around the world continue to deny large-scale involvement in organized crime, the birth of clubs like the Bremen Mongols and Notorious is further proof that those who are involved can clearly see the benefits that discipline, codes of conduct and brotherhood bring to those who wish to make profits from illegitimate means.

Whatever the future holds for the biker movement, one thing is for sure: the new generation promises to be even more ruthless than those of the past.

EPILOGUE: LL&R

Two years after leaving the club, Boone took Sally to Amsterdam for a belated birthday celebration. At twenty-four weeks pregnant she was reluctant to fly anywhere, so the pair chose a destination that could be easily reached by train. It would be their last chance for a child-free break and they were both determined to enjoy themselves.

After three days, Sally was thoroughly exhausted by the endless rounds of shopping and sightseeing and opted to have an early night. Boone watched a little television but still had energy to spare and eventually decided to head back out and get a few more drinks at a quiet Thai-run canal-side bar that had become one of his favorite spots in the city. He was just about to call it a night when three men walked in, two of them wearing black leather vests bearing the unmistakable red and white colors of the Hell's Angels. As they moved around to search for seats, Boone could see that one man was a prospect, the other a full member, and that both were from Sweden.

The full-patch Angel approached the bar close to where Boone was sitting. When he was an arm's length away, he suddenly stumbled and reached out to steady himself, his hand brushing firmly against the back of Boone's shoulder.

"Sorry," the Angel said.

Boone ignored him.

"I tripped on the bar rail."

Boone looked down, then slowly turned to face the Angel. He had recognized the ploy immediately. It was almost identical to the move that one of the Road Rats had performed on him when he had fled to London after Rabbi had been shot.

"There is no bar rail."

The Angel smiled. He was full of swagger and confidence. "You're right. Actually, I was checking to see if you had patches under your jacket. I think you're a club member."

Boone shook his head. "No, I'm not."

"Well you look like a club member." The Angel reached over and gently lifted the sleeve of Boone's jacket. "And you've got tattoos like a club member. Why are you lying to me?"

Boone finished the last of his beer in one long swig. It was clear the Angel wasn't going to let it go. He had to give him something. "Well I used to be a member of the Pagans, but that was a long, long time ago."

The Angel stiffened visibly all too aware that, in America, the ongoing war between the Pagans and the HA had flared up again. Boone saw the man's reaction and moved quickly to defuse the tension. "Not the American Pagan's, the English Pagans."

"English Pagans? Never heard of them."

Deeply offended, Boone fought a losing battle to stay calm.

"Well, it was a long time ago," he said through gritted teeth. "And since then, the club has changed its name. They're now called the Outlaws."

"Outlaws!"

Again the Angel stiffened. Tall and slim with a mop of neatly styled blond hair, he was in his midtwenties and his patches were new so Boone figured he had only recently become a full member and didn't have much experience. He had clearly gotten used to people being so intimidated by the patch that they would bend to his will. Boone decided to go the other way.

"Fuck it. Tell you what, let's you and me go outside right now and get this over with."

"What are you talking about?"

"I'm one of the original members of the Outlaws in the UK and now we're AOA. It seems you have a problem with that so why don't you and I step outside and dance?"

Seeing the aggressive change in Boone's body language, the prospect had rushed over and was now hovering directly behind his fellow Angel, ready to join the fight at a moment's notice. The other man remained sitting in the corner, watching with detached interest. Yet despite the odds being in his favor, the Angel was clearly alarmed by Boone's willingness to take him on. Perhaps he had assumed the man at the bar was a member of a more minor MC. Either way, his initial bravado suddenly and rapidly deserted him.

"Well hang on a minute. Let's not be hasty. You're not club anymore, right?"

"No, I'm not club anymore."

"Well, in that case, there's no problem."

"Whatever. I'm just leaving anyway."

"Where are you staying?"

"What's it to you? I thought you said there was no problem."

"With me, no, but the members of the local chapter might want to talk to you, find out why you're here." The prospect took a step closer, making it clear that Boone wasn't going anywhere without telling them what they wanted to hear.

"Okay. Sure. I'm at the Grand Krasnapolsky."

"You might be bullshitting me. We're going to need to know which room you're in. We're going to need to see you put the key in the door."

It was nearly two in the morning when Boone, the two Angels and the third man crossed over the narrow canal bridges, through the edge of the red-light district toward Dam Square. Along the way Boone had been planning his escape strategy, thinking through the layout of his hotel room. Although he had not seen the Angel make any phone calls to bring in reinforcements, he was convinced that once they confirmed where he was, it was only a matter of time before the whole fucking Amsterdam chapter of the Hell's Angels was on his doorstep.

He had to seize the initiative. He knew that, so long as he got them inside the room at the right angle, he could barge the full member right out of the window and onto the street, three floors below. Then it would just be him and the prospect. The third man was small, skinny and didn't seem to have much fight in him so Boone wrote him out of the equation altogether.

In the hotel corridor, the two Angels waited on either side of the door as Boone opened it and then hustled him inside, following close behind. *Shit.* Now he was the one with his back to the window. He needed to come up with a new plan. And fast. The commotion startled Sally, who had been sound asleep in bed, and she immediately assumed her boyfriend had brought back yet another load of biker friends for a late-night drinking session, as he had done so many times before. It was the last straw.

"Fuck this for a laugh," she screamed, sitting up in the half-light. "I'm fucking off out of here. I'm going home. I'm not going to let you party in the room until all hours for another night!"

Boone was usually calm in the face of storm but this was a serious situation and he felt the pressure. "Shut the fuck up, bitch," he retorted. "This is a Hell's Angel here. I could be in big fucking trouble."

Sally was stunned by his outburst and immediately started apologizing, but it turned out that the Angel was even more shocked by what Boone had said.

"You can't talk to women like that," he gasped, then turned to Sally and began to apologize for the intrusion. Whatever he had planned, he clearly wasn't going to do it with Sally around so after apologizing some more he suggested they all leave the room and go to the foyer to get a drink.

With surveillance cameras in every corner Boone did his best to ensure they were captured on film wherever they went. Convinced that he was going to be ambushed at any moment, he was determined to take at least one of them with him. Although he was in mortal danger, he still felt loyal to the biker code. Calling the police or asking the staff to help was a nonoption. The most he was willing to do was ensure that his killers were caught on camera. If they got convicted of his murder because of that, no one could say it was anything to do with him.

The group found an area in the atrium with some patio chairs, sat down and ordered more drinks. Boone turned to the man who had been accompanying the Angels who up until that point had said almost nothing.

"What are you then? A prospect? A hangaround or what?"

"No, I am just a friend of the club."

"A what?"

"A friend of the club."

"Sounds like you're not very much of anything at all then."

The man's lip began to curl with anger. "I'll tell you exactly what I am," his chest started to swell, "I am the biggest cocaine dealer in all of Sweden."

Boone could only hope the cameras had been wired for sound and were picking up every word. "Did you say cocaine?"

"Yes, the biggest cocaine dealer in all of Sweden; isn't that right, Joergen?"

The full-patch Angel nodded enthusiastically. "Yes, the biggest of them all."

"Well then," said Boone, leaning in close so he could whisper, "you'd better get some out."

The more coke they snorted the more confident they all became. Thanks to his time in Canada and 1,001 biker parties ever since, it took a serious amount of cocaine for Boone to lose focus. The others were coping less well, especially the prospect. After an hour or so his eyes were rolling all over the place and he looked like he was about to pass out.

Somehow the subject turned to other clubs in Scandinavia

and Boone explained that he had regularly spent time in the company of Bandidos.

"Ah yes, we fought a war with them," said the Angel. "It was a difficult time. We had to kill many of them."

The topic kept coming up and increasingly, Boone got the impression that the Angel was claiming that he had been involved in the biker war himself.

"How old are you?" asked Boone.

"Twenty-six," came the reply.

"For fuck's sake, you must have been, what, eleven when that war broke out? You weren't part of it at all."

"No but I remember it."

"You were still at school."

"Well I heard about it. It was very high profile."

"Bullshit! I'll tell you something. I was there. I was part of that war. I got shot at in Denmark. And you guys were a bunch of fucking cowards! You murdered a friend of mine. Joe was my pal. You cornered him and put your guns inside his bullet-proof jacket and emptied both clips. That's how heroic you guys were."

"I don't know anything about that."

"But it was your guys that did it!"

"I didn't know them. I don't know who was responsible."

"Whatever."

Boone was becoming increasingly belligerent. He wasn't trying to belittle the Angel, but he had decided to take control of the situation. It was clear that he was the elder and more experienced MC member in the group and he wanted to ensure that no one there forgot it. Also, it got to him that the Angel had never heard of the Warwickshire Pagans, a club that had been such a huge part of Boone's life and that he still felt enormous loyalty toward.

It took a little more time, a few more drinks and a lot more coke for the mood to mellow out once again and in the end, the drinkers departed on relatively friendly terms.

"We'll come and see you tomorrow and then you can visit the clubhouse and talk to us about all of this, about your time in the Outlaws," said the Angel.

"Yeah, no problem," said Boone. "But it was all a very long time ago."

"We'll come anyway. You can tell us about other chapters and what things are like in England."

"Okay. But I don't see those guys anymore, so I don't know much about it at all."

The second they were out of sight, Boone rushed back to his room. "Sal, get your shit together—we're getting the fuck out of here. We're off!" They checked out and got a room in a hotel on the other side of the square with a good view of the entrance of the Krasnapolsky, had a few more stiff drinks while Boone explained what had happened and then promptly passed out.

When Boone woke the following morning, he looked out at the square and saw that it was full of Angels. There were about twenty of them, hanging about in groups of two or three, all fully patched up, and it was pretty obvious that they were looking for him. He knew he had done the right thing: there was no doubt in his mind that he would not have gotten out of Amsterdam alive if they had managed to track him down.

Had they gotten hold of him, the Angels would have undoubtedly subjected Boone to a vicious torture session as they did their best to extract as much information as possible about rival gangs and planned operations. The fact that Boone was genuinely out of the club made little difference— he would still have been considered a valuable source of inside intelligence.

What saved Boone was the fact that the Angel he met was Swedish and unfamiliar with the level of hostility between his own club and the Outlaws, having mostly been at war with the Bandidos. He would have been severely reprimanded the following morning when he told members of the local chapter exactly what had happened. Proper procedure would have been to call in right away and get reinforcements over to the bar to check things out. He would have been given a reprieve when he explained that he not only knew which hotel the Outlaw was staying in but had even gone so far as to note and confirm the number of his room, but that would have lasted only as long as it took for the rest of the Angels to realize that Boone had already moved out.

As Boone watched them searching for him, he knew that coming out of the club when he did had been for the best. At the same time he knew that the legacy of the time he had spent in the Pagans and the Outlaws and the AOA was never going to leave him. No matter what he said, no matter what he wore or where he went, he was always going to be a one percenter. And that meant he was always going to be a target.

It took a while to come to terms with this but when he did, Boone realized that strangely, he wouldn't have had it any other way.

GLOSSARY

13—a common patch or tattoo among outlaw bikers. It refers to "M," the thirteenth letter of the alphabet, and symbolizes that the wearer smokes or deals marijuana or methamphetamine. It is also said to represent twelve jurors and one judge, suggesting the wearers are responsible for their own justice.

81—a metonym for the Hell's Angels. H is the eighth letter of the alphabet and A is the first letter of the alphabet, thus 81 = HA.

666—a patch worn by the Hell's Angels that stands for Filthy Few Forever (F being the sixth letter of the alphabet), as well as symbolizing the mark of the beast and the fact that the biker wearing it is hell bound.

ADIOS—one of several slogans used by the Outlaws MC at the start of their war with the Hell's Angels. It stands for Angels Die in Outlaw States. No longer used formally in order to protect club members from RICO prosecutions.

AOA—American Outlaws Association, the governing body of the Outlaws.

Ape hangers—high-rise handlebars common on customized motorcycles.

Back pack—a full set of colors tattooed on the back. Seen as the ultimate mark of commitment to a club.

Bad standing—a member who leaves in bad standing is considered an enemy of the club.

Big Four—the collective term for the largest MCs in the world. In order of size, they are the Hell's Angels, the Bandidos, the Outlaws and the Pagans.

Big House Crew—imprisoned Hell's Angels.

Big Red Machine—a nickname for the Hell's Angels. Derived from the fact that the club name is printed in red on a white background.

Bikie—the name used for an outlaw MC member in Australia.

Bosozoku—Japanese biker gangs. Literally translates as "violent running tribe."

Bulldog Bash—the largest biker festival in Europe. Hosted by the Hell's Angels, it takes place in Warwickshire each summer.

Cage—car.

Central funds—monies collected from MC members and used to support the overall goals of the club.

Chapter—regional division of a larger club. New chapters require a charter from the mother chapter. Each chapter operates as a self-contained unit but is overseen by the overall leaders of the club.

Charlie—the affectionate name for the Outlaws back patch, inspired by the design worn by the Black Rebels Motorcycle Gang in the iconic biker movie *The Wild One*, and featuring a skull and crossed pistons.

Chopper—a customized motorcycle, usually with extended front forks and raised handlebars among other modifications.

Church—the name given to the weekly mandatory meeting of all chapter members. Missing church without good reason will result in a fine.

Citizens—non-club members.

Cleaning house—an outlaw biker metaphor for killing members of one's own club.

Clubhouse—the headquarters of a chapter. Many are heavily fortified and fitted with CCTV cameras. The center of activities for most club members.

Colors—see "Patches."

Crash truck—a van that follows club runs and picks up broken-down motorcycles. May also be used to carry booze, weapons and other supplies.

Cut—see "Patches."

Daytona Beach Bike Week—a major biker festival and rally held in Florida each March that attracts up to half a million visitors. The location has traditionally been a stronghold for the Outlaws MC.

Death's Head—the name of the logo of the Hell's Angels. Taken from the insignia of the 85th Fighter Squadron of the U.S. Air Force.

Filthy Few—a patch supposedly awarded to Hell's Angels who have killed or attempted to kill on behalf of the club. This is denied by Sonny Barger, who insists the patch is merely awarded to those who are first to arrive at a party and last to leave.

Fly colors—to ride on a motorcycle wearing one's patches.

FTW—Fuck the World, a common tattoo among outlaw bikers.

GBNF—gone but not forgotten; commonly used in memorials to bikers who have passed away.

Good standing—a member who leaves in good standing is allowed to maintain some level of contact with members, though they are no longer privy to club business.

HA—Hell's Angels.

HAMC—Hell's Angels Motorcycle Club.

Hangaround—a potential prospect who is allowed to hang around the clubhouse so that club members can get to know him.

Harley-Davidson—the motorcycle of choice for OMGs, although the legendary Sonny Barger is quoted as saying, "Harleys are junk, technology-wise. If I was not a Hell's Angel I would probably be riding an ST1100, a BMW or a Triumph."

Hells Angels/Hell's Angels—I have included the apostrophe in Hell's Angels throughout this book. The seamstress who sewed the first-ever, back patch for the club forgot to leave space for the apostrophe, and it has been officially omitted ever since. But in his autobiography, *Hell's Angel* (2000), Sonny Barger states: "The apostrophe is used in the name of the club and the corporation, but not on the patch"—hence its appearance here.

Hog—a Harley-Davidson motorcycle.

Ink—tattoo.

Ink and Iron—a major custom bike and tattoo show, which takes place in Birmingham each year and is organized by the UK chapter of the Outlaws MC.

Jugs—cylinders.

Knucklehead—a Harley-Davidson engine produced during the Second World War.

LL&R—Love, Loyalty & Respect/Live Long & Ride, a common sign-off on outlaw biker Internet forums.

Lounge Lizards—imprisoned members of the Outlaws MC. Some former inmates have the initials "LL" tattooed on their bodies.

Mama—a woman who is sexually available to all members of a club.

MC—Motorcycle club. Outlaw bikers wear these initials on a square cloth patch on the right side of their colors.

Mother chapter—the chapter responsible for issuing and approving new charters. Usually the original founding chapter of the club.

Nike Bikies—term used to describe a new generation of Australian motorcycle gangs whose members wear designer jeans and sneakers instead of traditional biker boots.

OFFO—Outlaws Forever, Forever Outlaws, a common tattoo. Variations of this are used by virtually every outlaw club in the world, substituting the letters to fit their own club name.

Old lady—the wife or steady girlfriend of an MC member.

OMG—Outlaw motorcycle gang. The official FBI designation for members of the Big Four. Used to designate all one-percenter clubs, not just the Outlaws MC.

One percenter (sometimes 1%)—a diamond-shaped patch worn by members of outlaw motorcycle clubs. It originates from a statement made by the American Motorcycle Association that 99 percent of the country's bikers were law-abiding individuals.

Pasta rockets—derogatory term for Italian sports motorcycles.

Patches (also known as "colors" or "cut")—the collective name given to the insignias and logos worn on a leather or denim vest by all outlaw bikers, denoting the name of their club and its location. Patches are considered absolutely sacred. Losing a set in the wrong circumstances can get you kicked out of the club.

Patch holder—a full member of an MC. Members must be male, should usually be at least twenty-one years old and own a motorcycle over 750 cc.

President—the head of a chapter. The president is usually required to attend regular national meetings with other chapter presidents.

Property patch/property belt—an item of clothing worn by an old lady to show that she belongs to either an individual club member or the club as a whole. Although considered demeaning, some women are happy to wear them as it prevents them being approached by bikers who want to know if they are available.

Prospect—probationary members of an MC. They are required to carry out menial tasks for the club, often for a year or more, to prove their worthiness. They require a 100 percent vote to be awarded their full patches.

Puppet club (also known as "support club")—a smaller MC, overseen by the major clubs, it acts on behalf of the larger club and is used as a source of potential recruits. The official Outlaws' puppet club is known as the Black Pistons. The Hell's Angels have designated numerous small MCs as support clubs.

Red and White—a nickname for the Hell's Angels. The club's official colors are red letters on a white background.

Rice burner—derogatory term used by outlaw bikers for any Japanese motorcycle. Also known as "Jap crap."

RICO—the Racketeering Influenced and Corrupt Organizations Act. A federal statute passed by the U.S. Congress in 1970 to deal with organized racketeering activity. RICO law is specifically directed at individuals or organizations involved in systematic, long-term illegal activities. It increases criminal penalties and allows civil claims to be pursued against individuals, businesses or groups for actions taken as part of a criminal organization.

Riding season—in those parts of the world where the weather does not allow year-round biking, club members are required to have their motorcycles in full working order during the riding season or risk expulsion. In the UK, the season runs from April 1 to September 30.

Rock and Blues—a large motorcycle festival organized by the Outlaws MC in the UK each summer. The Outlaws equivalent of the Bulldog Bash.

Rocker—a curved cloth strip worn as part of the patches. The top rocker contains the club's name; the bottom rocker contains the location of the chapter. Together with the central logo, the two rockers comprise the three-piece patch of a full member of an outlaw motorcycle club.

Run—a club outing for members and associates, often lasting an entire weekend and usually involving a long ride in tight formation. Some runs are mandatory and will often involve other chapters or clubs, creating convoys of more than one hundred motorcycles.

Secretary—the title of the elected chapter officer who is responsible for general administration. He will keep minutes of all church meetings and send them to the mother chapter on a regular basis.

Sergeant at arms—the officer responsible for club discipline and issuing weapons. An elected position, only the sergeant at arms is allowed to strike members of the club.

SS—awarded to Outlaws who have killed or attempted to kill on behalf of the club (and equivalent to the Hell's Angels' Filthy Few), the patch features two lightning bolts on the inner arm, a reference to the insignia of the Nazi Schutzstaffel.

Sturgis Motorcycle Rally—a major biker event that takes place in Sturgis, South Dakota, during the first full week of August.

Support club—see "Puppet club."

Treasurer—the elected officer responsible for club finances within a chapter.

Vice president—the elected officer of a chapter who deputizes for the president in his absence.

War fund—a money drive among club members that takes place during times of conflict. The funds raised are used to purchase weapons.

War wagon—a vehicle used to transport the club's arsenal during an outing when trouble is expected from rival clubs.

World Run—an annual rally that all club members are required to attend. The location changes each year.

INDEX

Loners MC, 221
Lost Tribe MC, 238
Lounge Lizards, 55, 186
LSD, 50–51, 52
Luttman, Paul, 44–45
Lynn, Mike, 202–3, 246
Lyon, Danny, 115

Mackay, Queensland, 229
Mafia, xiv, 245
Maiale, Christopher "Slasher," 191
Mariani, Roger "Bear," xxv, 272
marijuana. *See* cannabis
Markopoulos, Athanase "Tom
    Thumb," 138
Matilda's Bar, 114
"Maximum John" (John Wood,
    Jr.), 157–58
Mayne, Thomas "Tomcat," 310–11
McCombie, Colin 'Animal,' 58
McCook Outlaws, 114
McCoy, Tony "Dog," 226
McLean, Donald, 138, 140
McLean, James "Moose," 190–91
media, 244. *See also* public
    relations
Megson, John, 57–58
Megson, Shaun, 57–58
Melbourne Outlaws MC, 227–28
Melles, David, 290
Men in Gear (MIG), 86–89
methamphetamine, 15, 77
Middle Eastern MCs, 309–10
Midland Outlaws MC
    and AOA criminality, 246
    and AOA patch over, 247–49
    and Bandidos patch overs,
        164–65, 204
    Canada trip, 143–46, 146–49,
        149–51, 151–53
    and Daytona Beach Bike Week,
        173, 184–89, 191–92, 194–96,
        196–200, 200–203
    feud with Hell's Angels, 113–21
    formation of, 103–9, 109–13
    and the Great Nordic Biker

War, 204, 206–7, 208–13,
    214–15
and the Paul Ricard Circuit
    rally, 159–63
and road accidents, 123–25
and sexual exploitation, 166,
    169
military training, 119, 207, 220–
    21, 236–37
Mills, Gary, 51
Milperra Bikie Massacre, 158, 195,
    219–27
Miri clan, 309
Molotov cocktails, 27
Mongols MC
    European expansion, 308–9,
        312
    and international crime, xv
    international expansion, 306
    patches of, xxii
    and prospect hazing, 75
    and recruitment, 7
    war with Hell's Angels, 263–64
Morbids MC, 161–62, 206–8
motor cycle clubs (MCCs), xxi,
    xxii–xxiii, 59
Motorcycle Action Group (MAG),
    249
motorcycle clubs (MCs), xxi, xxii–
    xxiii
motorcycle theft, 72–74, 268
mottos of MCs, vii, 118, 156, 272
murders
    and Bandidos, 157
    conviction of Bowman, 246
    and "Filthy Few" patches, 137,
        142
    and initiation of Hell's Angels,
        116–17
    and Outlaws/Hell's Angels
        feud, 116–18, 139–40
    and Pagan/Ratae feud, 12, 56
    and prostitution, 178–79
    of Tessaro, 85–86
    of Tobin, xxvi, 278–80, 283,
        285, 290–91, 300